Garage and Workshop Gear Guide

Garage and Workshop Gear Guide

Tom Benford

MOTORBOOKS

Dedication

This book is dedicated to my daughter, who is also a writer, Adina Marie Judith Benford.
I look forward to reading her books someday soon.

On the cover: A well-organized workbench, complete with a comfortable stool and rubber floor mat, is an essential part of keeping your tools and ongoing projects in order. *Courtesy: Griot's Garage, Inc.*

On the back cover: Garage cabinets are a great way to store all the gear you'll need to make your garage a gearhead's haven. *Courtesy: Coleman Renegade/O'Sullivan*

About the author:
Tom Benford is a longtime automotive author, writer, and editor, whose articles have appeared in *The New York Times*, *The Wall Street Journal*, and *USA Today*. An avid automotive enthusiast with a penchant for Corvettes, Benford often contributes to *Corvette Fever*, *Corvette Enthusiast*, *Car Collector*, and *Cars & Parts*.

His prior Motorbooks titles include *The Street Rod*, *Corvette Performance Projects 1968-1982*, and *Corvette: Five Decades of Sports Car Speed*. He lives with his wife Liz and their German Shepherd, Major, in Brick, New Jersey, where his own garage and tool collection underwent an overhaul during the making of this book. You can visit his website at www.tombenford.com and email him at tbenford@comcast.net.

CONTENTS

ACKNOWLEDGMENTS

No book, regardless of its size or subject matter, is ever the product of a single individual; the help and support of many others is essential to the success of the finished tome. With that thought in mind, I'd like to take this opportunity to thank these great folks for all their efforts on my behalf during this project:

Liz Benford, my wife and soul mate for all her support and encouragement
John Sloane, The Eastwood Company
Michael Trueba, Auto Chic
Timothy Hines, Genuine Parts Company / NAPA
Jayson Keever, Genuine Parts Company / NAPA
Valerie Stump, Loctite/Henkel, Inc.
Christina Smith, Dell Computers
Eric Montague, Stanley Tools
Ray Van Hilst, Ryobi
Chad MacDonald, BernzOmatic
Craig Kass, Arrow Group Industries
John Hauter, Dremel
Jim Hegadorn, Fuji Photofilm U.S.A.
Denise McCarthy, Brother International
Betsy Shaw, Skil Tools
Ray Farrar, Winner International/Juice Batteries
Lisa Foss, Pactiv Corp./Hefty
Sandy Berk, Solder-It, Inc.
Julie Metting, Dell Computers
John Heinz, RaceRamps/Brute Industries

Robert Kielhorn, Lenmar
Ken Keuter, Craftsman
Matt Thomas, BoltDepot.com
Jordan Cazault, BoltDepot.com
Don Russell, GxT Inc.
Ken Laga, Storehorse/Crawford/The Lehigh Group, Inc.
Chuck Freeman, Panther Vision, Inc.
Tony Weir, Powermate Corporation
Nicole Toledo, Powermate Corporation
Steve Golich, Rust-Oleum Corporation
Russ Vossen, Microflex Corporation
Phil Renfrow, Microflex Corporation
Gary Melliere, Irwin Industrial Tools
Melissa Gambrill, Irwin Industrial Tools
Andrea Halpin, American Saw & Mfg. Co. / Lenox
Paul Fitzmaurice, Husky Tools
Chris Feather, Aearo / AO Safety
Jennifer Imrie, GoJo Industries
Gary Case, Genuine Hot Rod Hardware, Inc.
Shannon Blake, O'Sullivan Industries, Inc.
Craig Short, O'Sullivan Industries, Inc.
Stefan Ehlers, Monti Tools, Inc.
Tony Weber, SuperLifts, Inc.
Bob Jackvony, T&L Industries Co.
Jennifer Rifold, Mechanixwear
Lee Klancher, MBI Publishing Company

Please accept my sincere thanks, one and all!

PREFACE

Believe it or not, no tool book could ever encompass every item that gearheads might want in their garage. Why? Well, let me explain. First, as technology forges on, bright minds come up with better, more innovative, and more efficient tools. The scope of garage gear is continually expanding, so it's virtually impossible to include things that are being developed right now but haven't come to market. Second, if the book included every garage tool or accessory in existence, it would be more like a multivolume encyclopedia—perhaps a little more information than most car nuts really want to know.

So I've taken the approach of having some "jump-off" points. Here's what I mean: Hammers—at first blush, you're probably thinking, "Hammers, yeah, there are claw hammers, ball pein hammers, sledge hammers. What's the big deal with hammers?" But did you know there are more than 75 different hammers for doing automotive bodywork? So this book features a good assortment of those, yet leaves out many that are similar in appearance and application.

In other words, there's no need to "beat you to death" with hammers. Don't feel shortchanged, though. I promise there's more than enough hammer coverage included to make you a happy camper. The same holds true for other tools as well. *Garage and Workshop Gear Guide* covers the tools and gear that will be used 99.9 percent of the time for the projects and tasks you're most likely to undertake.

None of this is to say that you won't find some arcane items covered, which is intentional. Sometimes you'll need a special tool or piece of equipment for an unusual project, and you may not know exactly what that tool may be. That's why you'll find some off-the-wall pieces listed in this book. Here's an example: Let's say you have a slight leak in your car's radiator, so you take it out of the car and solder the repair yourself. While you're at it, you decide to straighten some of the bent fins and give it a coat of paint before replacing it. How are you going to straighten the fins?

Most folks opt to use a thin-blade screwdriver or a butter knife secreted from the kitchen drawer. Either of these implements will do the job, but it will be tedious and boring. Or, you could spring about $5 for a radiator fin rake (there's a photo of one above) and do the job professionally and quickly. Most folks don't own a radiator fin rake—or even know they exist, for that matter. This tool is also great for straightening the cooling fins of your household window-mounted air conditioner.

See, you've already learned about a unique tool and its uses in the beginning of the book! There's a lot of good stuff in here like that, if I do say so myself.

I like tools and garage gear. In fact, I'll go even further and admit that I never met a tool I didn't like. I love trolling the aisles of the local NAPA store or the Craftsman section of the neighborhood Sears store. It's my thing. But to be honest, tools can be a somewhat dry subject, so I've injected humor into this book to lighten things up. The goal of *Garage and Workshop Gear Guide* is to provide valuable information lubricated by some levity. I hope you enjoy this handbook now and for many years to come.

— Tom Benford

CHAPTER 1
BETTER SAFE THAN SORRY

Before you dig in and become the biggest garage gearhead around, you have to think about the most important factor when working with tools—safety.

Of course, the best source of safety in your garage isn't something you can buy or stack on your shelves—it's prevention. There's no substitute for being careful. In fact, the two biggest factors involved in accidents and injuries in the garage are carelessness and distractions.

Carelessness can rear its ugly head in many ways—not picking up that air hose that's lying on the garage floor, leaving a tool or piece of equipment where it can be tripped over, or piling stuff up rather than stowing it properly. All of these hazards can easily be avoided by taking the time to be careful rather than careless.

Carelessness is a first-person hazard. By that I mean that if you left the hose on the floor or created the hazard, you are the one responsible. But you don't get off that lightly. If someone else created the hazard and you don't do anything to correct and eliminate it, you're still to blame.

Distractions, on the other hand, can have shared causes. For example, you may be involved with working on something and the cell phone rings, which you answer and still continue to work. Now that's a distraction. Similarly, you can be immersed and focused on what you're doing when the kids come running in chasing the dog and that pulls your attention away from the task at hand. Sometimes the distraction was caused even before you entered the garage. Perhaps you had an argument with your spouse, and it's still on your mind while you're working. That's a distraction, too, because it's keeping you from totally focusing on what you're doing. And lack of focus leads to accidents.

Now I don't want to come off sounding holier than thou because I've had more than my fair share of cuts, scrapes, bruises, blackened fingernails, and burns as a result of working on various vehicles in my garage. Minor injuries are inevitable anytime you're working with tools and on materials that are harder than your own flesh and bone. The thing here is to minimize their occurrence as much as possible. Injuries don't need any help or encouragement. They'll happen anyway.

That being said, there are certain things you should have in your garage to deal with unfortunate events if and when they occur.

A Little Neatness Goes a Long Way

Many of us consider the garage to be our space. We don't want our spouse in there moving things around, and we might place restrictions on the kids, too. But even if it's your retreat, being neat and keeping things in their place will make for a safer environment for a couple of reasons.

That air hose across a walking lane I already mentioned—well, having tools scattered around is the same sort of hazard. You can trip or slip on them, or fall onto them. There's also the frustration factor, when you're trying to finish a job before nightfall—or midnight—and you can't find the tool you need. Anger is another distraction that can lead to injury, or at least to work that is not up to your usual standards. Tools left inside an engine bay or by other moving parts can get thrown out forcefully and injure a person or the vehicle.

You can avoid all of these problems by taking a few minutes at the end of the day to gather up all the tools you used, wipe them off as appropriate, and place them back where they belong. That takes them out of harm's way and lets you return to the job with everything clean and where you can find it to help the work go smoothly. If you're working on a part with safety implications, such as a wheel or steering member, tighten the bolts to spec before you walk away for the day. This will prevent you from forgetting about it if you can't return to the project soon. Also, before you run a project, double check the bolts on things you've worked on to be sure everything is secure.

Finally, if you spill something, clean it up right away. You don't want anyone to slip and get hurt, drop a breakable part, or slam something into the side of the vehicle you've spent months restoring. Some liquids, like anti-freeze, are hazardous not only because they're slippery, but also because they're poisonous. A clean floor is also a lot more pleasant to scoot around on or lie on when you need to work down there.

Where There's Smoke

Every garage must have at least one good, fully charged fire extinguisher. Fire can be absolutely devastating, and it can spread faster than you can imagine. This is especially true in the garage, where chemicals and accelerants will spread flames even more quickly.

Having a fire extinguisher that's inaccessible is almost the same as not having one at all. An extinguisher should be

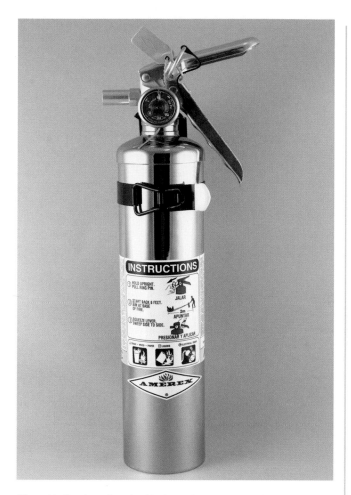

This good-looking chrome fire extinguisher is rated for class A, B, and C fires, and it has a handy quick-release mounting bracket that makes it an ideal candidate for garage fire protection. Courtesy: Genuine Hot Rod Hardware

mounted on a quick-release bracket so it can be reached quickly. Also make sure that you don't have any obstructions blocking your access to it.

When you get your extinguishers, make sure you spend a few minutes to familiarize yourself not only with their operation but also how to detach them from their mounting brackets. By all means, practice retrieving so that you can grab your extinguisher in an instant without fumbling. Another very important safety step is to make sure the extinguisher is fully charged and in proper working order. The extinguisher should be inspected and, if necessary, recharged on a yearly basis.

Fire extinguishers have different ratings according to the types of fires they can successfully put out. Here are the classes:
- **Class A:** trash, wood, paper
- **Class B:** liquids
- **Class C:** electrical equipment

Since all of these materials are typically found in the garage and a fire can involve some or all of them, the ideal fire extinguisher to have in your garage is a general-purpose unit that can handle all three classes. It's also never a bad idea to have more than one fire extinguisher in your garage workshop. Place them in different locations, such as opposite corners, so that if fire blocks your access to one of them you can get to the other. When you use the extinguisher, spray at the base of the flames; that's its source and the point you need to deprive of oxygen.

One last piece of advice: do not skimp when purchasing a fire extinguisher. Your very life could depend on it, as well as that of your family. And that's not to mention how you would instantly become the most unpopular person on earth with your co-habitants if you burn the house down.

Is There a Doctor in the House?

Probably not, but you should at least have a well-stocked first-aid kit in your garage. At the very minimum, the kit should have adhesive bandages in a couple of sizes big enough to accommodate cuts and scrapes, some antibiotic ointment, sterile gauze pads, and adhesive tape. It's even better if you have some additional items like ibuprofen, acetaminophen,

First-aid kits come in a variety of sizes and price ranges. Even an inexpensive, minimal first-aid kit is better than nothing, and no garage should be without one. Courtesy: Johnson & Johnson

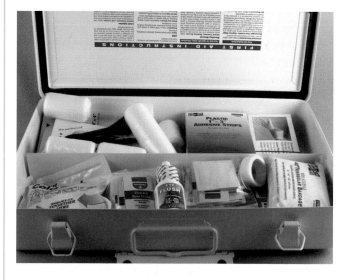

I recommend going with a commercial/industrial kit like this one if you can. It only costs a few dollars more than the consumer first-aid kits, and it provides additional supplies as well as a handy case that can be hung on the wall of your garage for fast access. Courtesy: AO Safety

HOLD YOUR FIRE

Having a means to put out a fire is essential. But your fire extinguisher is one piece of equipment you buy with the hope of not using it. Garages are natural collection points for many things that can start or feed a flame. Taking proper care with those items is the best way to keep your garage safe and standing.

Don't store gasoline in an attached garage. Keep it in a shed, barn, or other separate building. Gas fumes spread and ignite easily and are the cause of many a garage reduced to cinders. Gasoline should only be stored in a container made for that purpose and in a well-ventilated area. Never use gas as a cleaning agent. It's dangerous, poisonous, and there are other products made for that purpose that do a better job.

In addition to gas, many paints, cleaners, solvents, and other products can ignite if exposed to a heat source. Flammable and poisonous products should be stored in the containers in which they came. You won't have any mystery liquids lying around that way, and the container will provide important safety information. Keep these containers closed snugly and store hazardous chemicals in a metal cabinet, and according to manufacturer's directions. If children come into your garage, it's safest to keep the cabinet locked.

When it's time to dispose of a flammable liquid, follow the manufacturer's recommendations, as well as the hazardous substance laws in your area. Many substances that are flammable are also poisonous and cannot simply be dumped out back or down the drain. You'll want to protect your family and neighbors from poisoned groundwater for the same reason you take precautions against fire. Some flammable and poisonous substances can be recycled, either at a municipal facility or a commercial garage. Make a quick phone call or check the Internet to learn where you can take items for disposal.

Any heat or spark source, be it a heater, water heater, dryer, welder, generator, metal grinder, etc., should be kept in a well-ventilated area and removed from all flammable substances. Remember that fire fuel needn't be liquid or gas. Sawdust is near explosive when exposed to a flame, and newspapers also burn readily and tend to collect in garages. Sweep up and pick up these combustibles before generating a flame or sparks.

Car batteries also start an unfortunate number of fires. If you don't need the battery in the car you're working on, take it out and put caps over the terminals so a piece of metal can't short across them. You may want to run a trickle charger on it to keep it alive during the course of your project, but do this in a place and manner recommended by the manufacturer.

Likewise, oily rags can be receptive to combustion. They should be stored in a metal rag can with a snug lid. This will deprive them of oxygen should something in there ignite, and it will protect them from other combustion sources. Some substances, like linseed oil and other "drying oils," can combust on their own if left in a pile of rags. Rags containing oils with this property should be soaked in water or left to dry in a safe, open-air location. Any time you buy a new product, check the label to learn what hazards it presents and how to deal with them.

In any garage, there is a risk of fire from electricity. If you have any doubts about your garage wiring's integrity or its ability to serve your power needs, consult a qualified electrician. Even a sound, newer electrical system may fall short of your needs in terms of number of outlets or lights. Better to rectify that properly before you get deep into an elaborate project, rather than overload existing outlets or clutter up your work space with extension cords.

One final step you can take to stay fire safe was recommended in an article in *Grassroots Motorsports* magazine: the "15-minute rule." If you spend your last 15 minutes in the shop cleaning up and admiring your work, you give any errant spark time to flare up or die before lights out.

aspirin (or some other analgesic for relieving pain), eye wash, and a cold pack to reduce swelling. Tweezers and scissors, burn cream, and sterile disposable gloves are also good items to have in the first-aid kit, too. You'll usually find these latter items in the more complete kits intended for industrial and corporate use. These kits are also usually equipped with provisions for hanging them on the wall. Putting them next to your fire extinguisher is the best option.

Protective Gear

To help prevent getting cuts and scrapes, and to keep you from looking like a complete grease monkey, you can clothe yourself in all kinds of protective gear.

Mechanic's gloves come in a variety of styles, and they're great for providing cushioning for your hands as well as protection when "wrenching" around. No one who turns wrenches is unfamiliar with the phenomenon of having one slip off and bash your knuckles into some nearby surface or edge a lot harder than your hand. Mechanic's gloves offer a lot of tactile response (in plain English, you can still feel what you're touching) while still protecting your hands. They come in most handy when you're doing heavy work, whether that be using wrenches, ratchets, sockets, air tools, or hammers. Some even have built-in lights to illuminate whatever you're working on. A pair of these gloves will set you back some bucks, but they should last a long time.

If you're working on electrical projects, wiring, or installing gauges, you may want to wear a lighter glove, where you'll really be able to feel what you're doing. If you're allergic to latex gloves, nitrile gloves are a good substitute when doing

Protective mechanic's gloves from MechanixWear come in a variety of styles and colors, so there's something for every "wrench" out there. Courtesy: MechanixWear

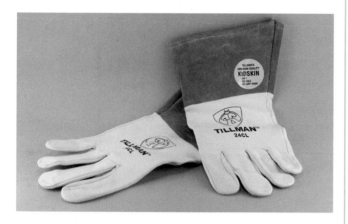

These Tillman welding gloves are made of kidskin and they offer a lot of protection while welding, yet they still provide plenty of flexibility and dexterity. I use them for lots of other jobs besides welding, too. Courtesy: The Eastwood Company

this kind of work. Sold in boxes of 100, nitrile gloves are inexpensive and disposable, so when you're done using them, you toss them into the trash and use a fresh pair next time. You can also get a wall dispenser to hold the box of gloves for easy access.

When using a MIG welder or MAPP torch, I prefer to wear leather welder's gloves. My trusty old Tillman's are made of kidskin so they offer a lot of tactile response, while the leather provides good protection from heat and errant sparks. Welder's gloves also are great for other tasks, even outside of the garage, that require a lot of dexterity—such as gardening.

Putting Your Best Foot Forward

Wearing protective footwear is also a good idea when you're out working in the garage. If I'm going to be in the garage all day, I like to wear high-top mechanic's boots because they give lots of ankle support. They're also nice and warm for when the garage is a bit on the chilly side.

Ankle-high mechanic's shoes, which can best be described as super sneakers, are also a good choice. With leather uppers and cushioned interiors, they're extremely comfortable and, with their sure-footed rubber soles, you get plenty of non-slip traction, even on slippery surfaces.

I also have a pair of team-issue pit shoes that have a spill-proof tongue under the laces, which prevents liquids from entering the interior of the shoe. These are great anytime you're working around liquids. They're terrific for washing the car, too.

Lift That Bar, Tote That Bale

Just be sure you're wearing a support belt when you do it. In addition to preventing back strain, these belts are also excellent hernia protection since they keep your lower abdomen (and the organs inside it) compressed, so you're less likely to tear muscle or tissue while wearing one.

If you've been to your local home improvement center recently, you've probably noticed that all the employees are wearing belts. Why? Because they work hard, and by wearing these belts fewer employees are injured on the job. See why they're a good idea?

Get yourself one, and use it anytime you have heavy lifting to do. Your back will thank you for it.

High-top pit-crew boots like these from MechanixWear offer your ankles extra support while protecting your feet from liquid splashes, thanks to a sealed tongue under the laces. Courtesy: MechanixWear

The Eyes Have It

Protecting your eyes from injury is one of the most important things you can do when you're working in the garage. Just think about it for a minute . . . you won't be doing any more work in your garage if you can't see what you're doing, right? So, if for no other reason (and there are millions of them), protect your eyes so you can continue to play in the garage.

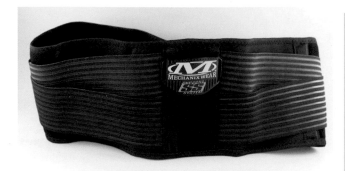

A support belt is something you should have in your garage and use anytime you have to lift anything heavy. Remember what I said about prevention? This is an excellent piece of preventative gear. Courtesy: MechanixWear

Eye protection comes in many forms, some of it quite stylish (if you want to make a garage fashion statement, that is). You have your choice of full-face safety shields that have an adjustable head-band, safety glasses, goggles, and even magnifier glasses. There are a lot of options; find what's right for you and the task at hand.

Welding, be it gas or electric arc, requires very special eye protection. If you're doing gas welding, you'll need welding goggles that are equipped with a No. 5 lens. For comfort, select goggles that have air vents and an adjustable head strap. If you wear glasses, be sure to get goggles big enough to fit over them. One more important note: gas welding goggles should *never* be used for any form of electric arc welding!

If you're going to be MIG, TIG, or open arc welding (or plasma cutting, for that matter), you'll need a self-darkening welding helmet to protect your eyes sufficiently. These helmets can be battery- or solar-powered, and they go from full visibility to welding-dark in less than a 250,000th of a second. I prefer the solar-powered helmets myself, since I don't have to worry about keeping a fresh battery on hand. Prior to using it,

A full-face shield is a good thing to wear when mixing paints, using aerosol adhesives, or working with other materials that may splash or spatter during use. Courtesy: AO Safety

An assortment of protective eyewear in numerous styles and colors is offered by AO Safety to protect your baby blues (or browns, hazels, blacks, greens, or whatever). Courtesy: AO Safety

I just let it sit outside in the sun for a little while and it stores a charge that lasts for months. As with the eyewear glasses and goggles, you can make a fashion statement with these helmets if you wish. I'm a big fan of the flame motif, myself.

Eye protection is important not only with obvious dangers, like a welder, but equally so on very simple tasks where you might be less inclined to reach for your goggles. How many times have you scooted under the car to check something without safety goggles? One touch to the floor pan, exhaust system, brake lines, or virtually anything else can dislodge a little piece of rust and odds are, for the best sight lines, you've got your eyes directly below your hands. So that's where that rust sliver is going to fall. Metal slivers, whether they come from falling rust or are kicked up by a drill, grinder,

Goggles with a No. 5 lens, air vents, and an adjustable head strap are what you'll want to wear any time you do any gas welding. These are not to be used for any type of electric arc welding, however. Courtesy: Bernzomatic

An auto-dimming welding helmet like this cool flamed-model is just what you need to protect your eyes from the harmful electric arcs produced by MIGs, TIGs, plasma cutters, and arc welders. For more information on the importance of protecting your eyes and the eyes of anyone, including pets, who may be exposed to arc light, read Chapter 14.
Courtesy: The Eastwood Company

Ventilation is equally critical if you do any painting in your garage. For that job, consult a paint professional.

Solvents, cleaners, lubricants, and airborne dust can also harm your lungs. Leave a window or the garage door open when you use chemicals and sprays, and use an appropriate face mask and dust-collection system with tools. While you can get disposable dust masks for only a few cents apiece to keep dust from entering your nasal passages, these won't offer any protection from noxious odors or very fine air-borne

A good quality respirator with replaceable filters is just what you need to breathe a little easier, especially when working around stuff with noxious vapors in your garage.
Courtesy: AO Safety

sander, metal lathe, or anything else, can do serious and even permanent damage. Don't mess around with your vision. Wear eye protection for even the little tasks that might dislodge something eye-bound.

One last note on eye protection: take care of it. If your goggles are all dirty or scratched up, you won't wear them because you can't see well through them. Store your goggles in a place where they won't get stepped on or hit against sharp tools. Wash the grease off them with non-abrasive dish soap and dry them with a soft towel. If you keep them in a resealable plastic bag, they'll always be clean when you need them.

Breathe Easy

Good ventilation does more than help prevent fires. It can also prolong your health and life. Any work space you use should be well ventilated to avoid collection of poisonous fumes from exhaust, paint, cleaners, solvents, and other chemicals. Carbon monoxide is lethal and will collect quickly in an enclosed space; that's why you should never run an engine in a closed garage. Pull the car out instead. Carbon monoxide can even collect when the garage door is open, particularly if the tailpipe is pointed in. A carbon monoxide detector is cheap insurance.

A heavy canvas blasting hood like this will protect both your eyes and head from media while doing sand or media blasting. Courtesy: The Eastwood Company

You can shut out the noise using a pair of Worktunes hearing protectors from AO Safety. These hearing protectors feature a built-in AM/FM radio so you can work without skipping a beat.

Courtesy: AO Safety

particulates the way a respirator will. When purchasing a respirator, be sure to get one that has replaceable filter elements, since they offer the best and most flexible protection. Be sure to get filter elements that are rated to protect against the kinds of vapors you'll be using the respirator with.

Keep in mind that fumes that can make you sick can also be flammable. Good ventilation prevents harmful accumulation of dangerous gases.

If you're going to be doing abrasive blasting, you'll want to get a blasting hood that affords both eye protection and head/face protection at the same time. Blast media is nasty stuff that really stings if you get hit with it, and it can injure your eyes seriously. A decent pair of protective gloves goes hand-in-hand with the blasting hood, too.

Do You Hear What I Hear?

While I love the speed and efficiency of my air tools, I really hate the sound of my air compressor. Ditto that for the sound of my John Deere lawn tractor, chain saw, circular saw, leaf blower, and several other pieces of gear I have around the house and frequently use. So what do I use to drown out this dreadful din? A pair of quality hearing protectors. If the sound of silence (or at least greatly-muffled noise) isn't your cup of tea, though, you may want to get a set of hearing protectors with a built-in AM/FM stereo radio to help you tap your foot in time with the music while you go about your noisy chores.

On the other side of the coin, you can get an inexpensive pair of foam rubber ear plugs for a couple of bucks that will

cut down on the noise substantially, too. It's entirely your choice here.

On Your Knees

If you have to spend any length of time working on your knees, then by all means you'll want to invest in a pair of knee protectors. These padded pads have Velcro fasteners that keep them attached while still letting your knees have free movement. They really take the burden off your knee caps.

You can use them for lots of other things outside the garage, too, like roofing, gardening, and other low-level chores that require you to be on all fours. Appropriate hand protection is the perfect complement for these knee protectors, too.

Hold It Right There

Every year a few enthusiasts fall victim to insecure methods for supporting their project—a jack slips, a jack stand fails, or a vehicle rolls and comes off its ramp or tips a support. Our minds tend to focus on the task at hand; once the vehicle is up, we forget about what's holding it up. For that reason, supporting the vehicle safely is an essential starting point.

Jack stands and a sturdy floor jack are important safety items. Bumper jacks and scissor jacks that come with the vehicle are for changing flat tires, but they are inadequate to support a vehicle for serious work. A good hydraulic floor jack is a safe way to raise the vehicle. Once elevated, the car should be supported, level, on jack stands. These should be placed far enough apart to provide a stable base and should make good contact with a solid component, like an axle or frame crossmember.

Ramps are a sturdy means to support one end of the vehicle, but they can slide out as you try to run up on them.

The old knees get particularly tender when you have to spend any amount of time on them, especially on hard or rough surfaces. A pair of knee protectors will come to your aid nicely for these occasions. Courtesy: MechanixWear

Have a friend, standing at a safe distance, help guide you onto the ramps so that the tires are centered in the "dip" at the top of each ramp. Ramps pose another hazard, requiring you to keep in mind how the car is supported. If the drive wheels are on ramps and the car is in gear, it will lurch if someone engages the starter. You could leave yourself a note taped to the steering wheel or with the key: "start in neutral."

Your vehicle's owner's manual should have jacking instructions, as may the jack and jack stands. Secure jacking points for modern vehicles with unibody construction may be less obvious than with older, separate-chassis cars and trucks.

Some people raise engines or vehicles with overhead pulleys—an old school approach. If you plan on hooking a pulley to a crossmember in your garage or barn, make sure it's up to the task. If you have any doubts, talk to a licensed builder or structural engineer. The crossmember is designed to hold up the roof and might help support the walls, including some extra forces from snow and wind. Odds are, though, the builders did not factor in the weight of an engine or the front end of your vehicle. Given gravity's ability to wreck the motor and any digits or limbs in the way, you're better safe than sorry. Engine hoists can be rented cheaply, or there's a good chance one of your hobbyist friends has one you can borrow—ask him to give you a hand, too!

For more on jack stands, ramps, and even lifts, read Chapter 9.

ARC LIGHT WARNING

I've already mentioned how the intense light generated by the electric arcs in MIG, TIG, or arc welding and plasma cutting can seriously injure your eyes in a couple of seconds, and I reiterate the dangers in the chapter on welding later on in this book. But this is such a serious subject that I feel compelled to say a bit more about it.

While you'll be using an eye shield or self-darkening helmet while welding, the chance of a relative, neighbor, friend, or pet entering the garage unannounced may subject them to serious eye injury from the arc light. It's a good idea to mount a red light over any doors that permit access to the garage with a sign warning that when the light is on, welding is in progress and no one should enter without eye protection. Anytime you're going to be welding, flip the switch for the light on and leave it on until you're finished.

At first, this precaution may seem to be a bit overly dramatic, but believe me, it isn't. Working safely and responsibly in your garage workshop means protecting yourself and others from any chances for harm or injury.

CHAPTER 2
SETTING UP YOUR
SANCTUARY (er, GARAGE)

A garage, in its purest sense, is a home for your vehicle(s). However, if you're like most folks, your garage plays host to a multitude of things—recreational or utilitarian—that have nothing to do with your vehicle. Therein lies your first problem: if you have the lawn mower, garden tractor, wheel barrow, bicycles, and other such clutter taking up valuable garage floor real estate, there's bound to be less usable space for your tools, gear, and favorite rides.

If this sort of situation rings true, you're in good company. While writing this book I, too, faced the same problem, and to an extreme degree. My attached two-car garage was loaded literally from the floor to the ceiling with all kinds of stuff that had nothing to do with my vehicles. In addition to extra folding chairs, surplus furniture, snow shovels, several gallons of partially used paint (in a variety of colors), extra ceramic floor tile, bricks, PVC tubing, and ladders, there was a plethora of other stuff.

True, a lot of it was actually useless junk that was going to be tossed, but the rest still had a legitimate use. Where could I store it? The garage was no longer an option. No siree. I had a four-post lift on its way and a load of cabinets for gear storage waiting to be assembled, so this other stuff had to find a new home.

If you have the space on your property, the easiest and, in the long run, least expensive way to gain more usable garage space is to relocate these non-vehicular items to a storage shed. You can build one yourself if you have some basic carpentry tools and a moderate amount of skill, or you can purchase one, either assembled or unassembled, from the local home improvement center. Whether you build or buy, this is definitely a less expensive way to gain more garage space than adding an extension onto your garage or paying monthly rent at a storage facility.

This is the option I chose. After some comparison shopping, I settled on a model from Arrow Storage Buildings, the Vinyl Sheridan, model VS1014, a spacious 10x14-foot unit. In addition to the 129 square feet of storage space it had, the maintenance-free vinyl-over-steel finish and the 15-year warranty really appealed to me.

Of course, you can also choose to add on to your garage if you want a more permanent storage solution. A three-car garage is no longer a luxury in many communities; it's a must-have. If you really want a fresh start, you may decide to build a whole new garage—not an inexpensive option, but one you may want to consider if you want to add some fancy features like a transverse beam electric hoist.

Measuring Up

OK, so now that you've found a place to store all of this non-vehicular stuff, it's time to take stock of what you really want

This is an actual before shot of my garage. With all this stuff cramming up the space, it's a wonder I was able to pull my Corvette in without scratching it up. Getting in and out the driver's door, however, was quite a feat. I just couldn't go on like this any longer. I wanted—no, I needed—a functional garage that I could work in, and this definitely wasn't it. Liz Benford

This is the VS1014 Vinyl Sheridan 10x14-foot storage building from Arrow Group Industries. I picked it because its steel panels are hot-dipped galvanized and the vinyl coating is five times thicker than other standard storage buildings. With 129 square feet of floor space, that adds up to 852 cubic feet of storage space. Add a 15-year warranty and a 55.5-inch-wide by 60-inch-tall door opening and you have a winner that will store a lot of stuff, for sure. Courtesy: Arrow Group Industries

Powered by a 9-volt battery, this neat EMPT006 Sonic Measure with laser dimension finder measures distances up to 50 feet and can calculate square and cubic interior measurements. It also does double-duty as a metal/wood stud finder. The stud finder feature is particularly useful when hanging storage cabinets or racks and hooks on the garage walls. Courtesy: Ryobi

in your main garage workshop area. First, take some measurements of your space and do a basic floor plan. By using graph paper while creating this plan, you'll keep everything in proportionate scale.

For measuring, you can, of course, use a tried and trusted tool: a traditional tape measure. If you want to be more high-tech, though, you can find your dimensions by using a sonic measure with laser/dimension calculator built in.

You can also use a yard stick or a folding ruler if you wish, but either of these measuring devices require more time and effort to get the dimensions you're after.

In my garage plan, I had six basic areas that needed specific attention: the floor, walls, lighting, power, temperature control, and storage. A floor plan grid would help me best plot the positions and placement of these elements.

I'm Floored

Flooring was the first area I addressed. My options included laying down some vinyl tile, lining the floor with removable interlocking floor tile, or coating the current cement floor with some epoxy.

The advantage of using vinyl tiles is that if you choose tiles designed for industrial or commercial use, they can hold up for

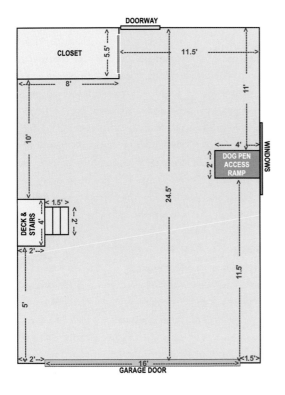

This is floor plan for my garage. The closet at the rear is going to stay, although another one just like it on the opposite side of the doorway (not shown on this drawing) will be dismantled and the space will be used to accommodate the SuperLift four-post lift. The 2x4-foot ramp provides access for our German Shepherd, Major, to go from the garage into his pen/dog run. The five-foot bank of double windows provides natural daylight and ventilation.

If you've got a large floor to cover, you can get creative with the design of your plastic interlocking tiles, making your garage even more unique. It's best, though, to lay out your plans on a piece of grid paper first before going through all the trouble of getting them lined up right on the floor. Courtesy: Mid America Motorworks

GETTING WIRED

When homes are built with attached garages, the electrical power in the garage is basic, utilitarian stuff: two or three double 120-volt AC outlets, an overhead light or two, and that's about it. For most folks, this bare minimum is enough to get by on, but for gearheads it's a different story.

By buying this book, you expect to be using your garage for a lot more than just sheltering the family transportation from the elements. Your garage will be the center of activity and a base of operations, both now and in the future, right? Right.

That's why you should give some serious thought to your electrical needs. What your garage has right now may be perfectly adequate for your current needs, but how is it going to handle things down the road? Suppose you decide that your current air compressor is too small and you want to add a more powerful unit with a bigger tank a couple of years from now. Perhaps you someday want to install a four-post electric lift, an electric engine hoist, or some other equipment that will need more electrical oomph. That's why some forward thinking now is in order.

The first thing to consider is the number and placement of electrical outlets in your garage. Ideally, you should have a couple of wall-mounted outlets placed about six feet apart on all three walls. It's OK to have exposed conduit tubing connecting these outlets. Burying the conduit inside the walls is more aesthetically pleasing, but it also costs more to conceal.

It's a good idea, though, to have the garage power on its own circuits, and even more desirable if you have a separate fuse or circuit breaker box (preferably right in the garage itself) for all of the garage circuitry. And given a choice of fuses or breakers, circuit breakers are definitely the way to go since they can be reset if tripped. You don't want to have to keep a variety of fuses on hand. And for heavy-amp circuits, you'll want to have ground-fault circuit breakers for added safety.

The best way to plan the power needs and capabilities of your garage workshop is to call in a licensed electrician or electrical contractor. Most reputable professionals will provide you with a no-cost/no-obligation consultation and price quote. Explain your needs, both current and anticipated. Be frank about your budget constraints and ask the electrician to work up a proposal that fits your needs and wallet.

Another thing you should consider is whether you'll want to have 220-volt AC service in your garage. If you have an electric clothes drier currently in the garage, chances are pretty good that you'll already have 220-volt power. If you don't, you may want to invest in it. That way if you ever add something that requires 220-volt power, such as an old electric oven for powder-coating automotive parts, you're all set. Remember it's cheaper to add all the electrical power you'll need now rather than having to set it up separately later.

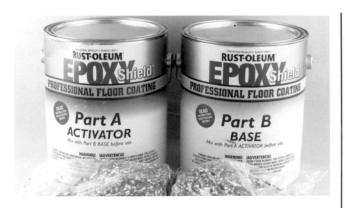

Rust-Oleum EpoxyShield Professional Floor Coating is a commercial-grade product intended for warehouses and other high-traffic floors. After checking out other products, I decided this was the way to go. You simply mix Part A together with Part B, and apply it with either a coarse roller or brush. The "confetti" in the plastic bags gets sprinkled on before the coating dries and it helps to give some traction to the floor surface. It's easy to apply, efficient, and durable—just the way I like it. Courtesy: Rust-Oleum

a long time. The disadvantage, though, is that installing these can take a lot of time and money, which won't make life easier when you're just itching to get working on your next vehicle project.

Interlocking floor tile is a really popular alternative. If you live in an area where you get a lot of rain or snow, these tiles work great. The moisture will just flow out from right underneath them out of your garage. You can also remove them, as needed, to really get all the dirt off your floor.

I elected, however, to go with the simplest and most inexpensive flooring option: epoxy. I added a layer of Rust-Oleum EpoxyShield Professional Floor Coating because I felt it was the most durable and cost-effective solution for my needs.

Each two-gallon kit covers about 200 square feet, so I needed three kits to cover the 459-square-foot floor in my garage. Extra coating went on the wooden expansion joints between the concrete slabs of the floor.

Let There Be Light

Adding lighting to your garage is a great way to make your project area easier to work in. Whether you're just adding a couple of fluorescent light boxes or fancy incandescent recessed lights, you won't regret being able to see better out there. You'll also want to keep some portable lights in your garage to illuminate those areas of your vehicle that are hard to see.

When adding lighting, don't forget to think about upping the number of electrical outlets (or electricity amps) in your garage. Make sure you know the building codes in your area before you go too far here, though. You may need a local building inspector to come out and check on your electrical upgrades, and they often prefer it if the work has been done by a professional electrician—not average Joe gearhead.

If you intend to use your garage workshop year 'round, you should give some thought to keeping it warm when the weather turns cold. Generally speaking, the cheapest way to heat your garage is to extend whatever heating system you're using to heat your home. For example, if your home heating system is gas/forced hot air or electric heat, it shouldn't be too big a problem to run and install ducting or baseboard heaters in your garage that are fed from the house furnace or heating circuits. This setup assumes that your existing furnace can handle the additional output. Check with a heating professional to make sure of this.

You can also opt for stand-alone heating solutions for the garage, such as a kerosene or propane heater, and either one of these can be stationary or portable. Some types can be mounted on the ceiling, while others are designed to mount between the studs in your garage wall. Since both kerosene and propane heaters use exposed flames to generate heat, they pose potential fire hazards as well as potential sources of carbon monoxide. Adequate ventilation is an absolute must whenever using these heaters, and a licensed, qualified heating contractor should be consulted not only for establishing the safest and most efficient heating solution, but also for a safe installation that adheres to local building codes.

Several other options are available to the seeker of a warm garage. Electric space heaters are worthy of consideration if you have a 500-square-foot or smaller space to heat and only need the warmth occasionally.

Using a natural gas furnace or space heater is another good option. The better-quality units come with completely sealed flame chambers that eliminate the safety concerns of having an open flame in your garage. This will require a natural gas line run out to your garage, and professional installation of the unit is highly recommended. And bear in mind that if you can find a good-quality used natural gas furnace designed for home use, they provide plenty of heat for even a large garage.

If you are using your garage on a more regular or a professional basis, in-floor heating is worth considering. The system needs to be done with a new floor, as flexible tubing needs to be laid down before the concrete floor is poured. Warm water is circulated in the tubes, warming the concrete and hence the garage. The warm floor is a joy to work on and economical to run. The drawback is that it takes anywhere from several hours to several days to warm up and cool down, and the system is complex and expensive to install.

If you opt for in-floor heating, bear in mind that you need to use a heater certified for in-floor heat use. If you use a regular water heater (which is what some contractors suggest), you may void your homeowners' insurance.

Also, you will have the option of using a tank-type water heater or one of the new tankless water heaters. The tankless heaters are the preferred choice for garage heat, as they are more compact and, in most cases, more efficient than the tank-type heaters.

Another option to consider is whether to use a natural gas or electric water heater. At this book's press time, natural gas prices were skyrocketing, making electric the more economical choice. Note that with an electric water heater, some have the option of running the heater on an off-peak meter. These plans offer a discounted rate for electrical power during low-use hours of the day. You could set up your in-floor heat to run only at night to take advantage of such a plan. Contact your local power company for details about these plans.

An important part of a more sophisticated heating system is a thermostat, which is used to regulate the temperature if you keep the garage warm for extended periods of time. The electronic thermostats are easy to program, and available for less than $15.

My choice for cool temperature control in the garage was a 16-inch Porta-Cool evaporative cooling unit from NAPA. It throws plenty of cold air and, since it's on casters, you can direct the cooling anywhere you want it. The fact that it uses less electrical juice than a conventional window-mount air conditioner is another big plus. Courtesy: NAPA

A simple fix is adding a ceiling-mounted retractable extension cord with three outlets in it. It will allow you additional mobility while you're working, yet deliver that all-important electrical power.

Baby It's Cold (or Hot) Outside

I'm not really what you'd call a cold-weather fan, so I rarely do any work in the garage when the temperature outside is less than 40 degrees. For that reason, I didn't bother installing any heating devices in the garage, although I did consider a propane heater (didn't like the fire or asphyxiation risks), and I decided against a kerosene heater for the same reasons.

Cooling, on the other hand, is a big deal to me, since I do most of my gearhead work in the spring, summer, and early fall when the temperatures on the New Jersey shore vary from mildly warm to downright hot and uncomfortable. I had

A BENCH TO WORK ON

If you fancy yourself the high priest of your garage, then surely a suitable workbench should be your altar.

You'll need a sturdy workbench for hundreds of tasks you'll undoubtedly be doing over the years, so you should really think about what you want in the planning stage. Fortunately, you have several options.

For starters, you can purchase a workbench kit at Sears, Lowe's, Home Depot, and other home improvement outlets. The kit will contain everything you'll need. You'll just have to bolt it all together.

If you don't mind putting in some extra elbow grease, you can purchase workbench plans (or get them off the internet) and build a workbench from scratch. If you're ambitious and want to save some money, it's a good way to go.

Or you can go the route I did—buy a heavy-duty worktop that sits on your storage cabinets and provides a great (yet inexpensive) work surface.

As with everything suggested in this book, this garage workshop is your place and the furnishings, gear, and items should make it work for you. The choice is always yours.

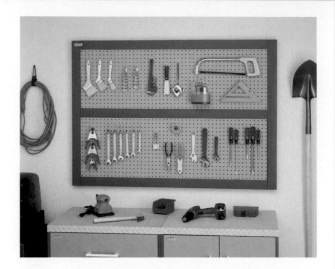

This 60-inch worktop from O'Sullivan's Renegade line of garage storage solutions measures 19.5 inches deep by 62.125 inches wide. It is 1-inch thick. It features a steel-tread plate rail on the front for extra durability, and it fits perfectly on top of two O'Sullivan Renegade cabinets. With a retail price of under $40, it's an excellent and affordable way to put a sturdy work surface (or two, for that matter) in your garage and make double use of those cabinet tops at the same time. Courtesy: O'Sullivan Renegade

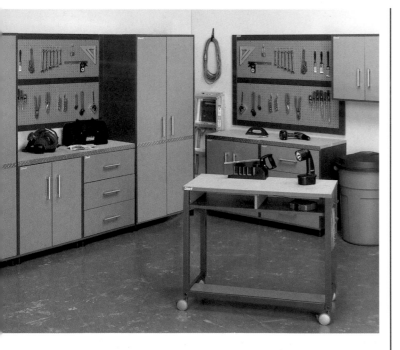

The Coleman Renegade line of garage storage solutions, made by O'Sullivan Furniture, provides an attractive, sturdy, and flexible way to stow your tools and gear. Contrast this photo with the before shot earlier in this chapter—quite a night-and-day difference, wouldn't you agree? Courtesy: Coleman Renegade/O'Sullivan

If you want all of your stuff in plain view, you might want to consider large chrome shelving units for your garage storage. Courtesy: Griot's Garage, Inc.

thought of installing a window-mounted air conditioner, but that would have significantly cut down the amount of ambient daylight entering the garage. Instead I opted for a Porta-Cool evaporative cooling unit from NAPA. The advantages of the Porta-Cool are several, not the least of which are that it uses a lot less electricity than a conventional air conditioner and that

The ceiling is a great place to store things you don't use often. With out-of-the-way metal shelving, you can pretty much hide these items from view. Of course, you probably want to label any storage containers you stash up here, so you actually remember what's in them.

Courtesy: Griot's Garage, Inc.

Crawford makes a wide variety of steel brackets that are absolutely great for hanging things from the walls and rafters of your garage. These are useful for removing clutter from the garage floor, and there's a bracket for just about any storage need you can think of.

Courtesy: Crawford/The Lehigh Group

it can be moved anywhere you want to direct the cool air stream, since it's on casters.

Now, with the floor coated, the walls painted, the lighting improved, and my garage properly cooled, it was time to move all of the "keeper" tools and gear back in the garage—with some help, of course, from some garage storage solutions.

Room for More

When it comes to finding a place to put all the gear you actually want to keep in your garage, storage cabinets are an easy solution. They come in a wide array of styles, sizes, and price ranges, so there really is something for everyone.

I really did my homework in selecting the cabinetry that would provide me the best value. After comparing prices on several brands from different manufacturers, I went with the Coleman line of garage storage solutions from O'Sullivan.

Sure, lots of glitzy cabinets are out there, but you have to ask yourself a very important question: do you want to spend your money on some very expensive cabinets and have little or nothing left over for new tools and gear, or do you want to go with solid, affordable cabinets and have plenty of dough left over for stuff to go in them? For me this was a no-brainer. The Coleman Renegade cabinets are made by O'Sullivan Furniture right here in the United States. They're solidly constructed and easy to assemble. They are available with doors or drawers and even a handy roll-about cart that can serve as a workbench. Best of all, they're very reasonably priced. What's not to love?

While the Renegade cabinets come with sturdy plastic feet, I opted to mount casters on mine so they would be easier to move when I wanted to clean the garage or—should the whim hit—do some rearranging as my needs may dictate.

Also, I made sure to consult my garage plan before I bought them, making sure I had enough space for them to fit where I wanted them on a more permanent basis.

Hangin' It Up

Once the cabinetry is squared away, it's time to start taking stock of other space that can be used for storage. In many cases, garages have room in their rafters for gear, and there's no reason to let perfectly good hanging space go unused.

With brackets, hangers, and ceiling-mounted racks, you can store away stuff that you don't use very much. From saw horses and drive-on ramps to a short step-ladder and athletic gear, all of this can be moved up and off your garage floor.

A Treasure Chest, Indeed

I genuinely treasure my tools, so what could be more fitting than to store them in a treasure chest? Well, a stackable tool chest. I've had the same 27-inch-wide Craftsman tool chest for more than a decade and it's full of all the features you want: ball-bearing drawer glides, heavy steel construction with powder-coat finish, ball-bearing casters with lockable wheels, nice deep drawers, and a keyed lock.

While a tool chest this size may seem to be overkill for your tool collection, especially if you're just starting out, your money won't be foolishly spent if you go for the big boy. You'll be absolutely amazed at how quickly it gets filled, and before long you'll be glad you went with the bigger chest. In fact, you may wish you had gone for an even larger one.

Some day you may have to upgrade, or get another tool chest of the same size or larger (which I did after my tool collection just didn't stop growing).

A quality stackable tool chest like this 27- inch-wide 11-drawer unit from Craftsman is a wise investment for keeping your tools safe and securely stored when you're not using them. The locking caster wheels make it easy to move about, and the top section has a removable tray for carrying whatever you need to the work area rather than moving the whole chest. Courtesy: Craftsman Tools

Magnetic trays like these give you readily accessible storage for frequently used items like utility knives, staplers, tape measures, and so forth. The magnets are rubber-coated, so they won't mar the surface of your tool chest, and they come in various sizes. The round parts tray at the bottom is also magnetic and very useful for containing nuts and bolts as you disassemble something during a project. Courtesy: The Eastwood Company

Since I needed more tool storage, and since I was happy with my Craftsman tool storage chest, I opted to go with another Craftsman chest—this time with a 52-inch-wide stackable unit.

Magnetic Attraction

For even just a little bit of extra space, you can add magnetic trays to the side of your tool chest. These steel, powder-coated trays have rubber-coated magnets affixed to their backs so they will attach without marring. The magnets are surprisingly strong, so you can really load up the trays without them sliding or becoming detached.

These trays are a great place to keep frequently used items such as utility knives and tape measures. The trays come in sets of four and the sizes are varied, so there's one that's the right size for just about any small item you'd like to store in them.

Magnetic parts trays are also a very handy item to have when you want to keep track of the nuts, bolts, and washers you're taking off an assembly while working on it. The

magnetic rubber donut on the underside of the tray not only attracts and holds any ferrous object placed in the tray, it also attaches the tray to the side of your tool chest when not in use, thereby solving yet another storage problem. Pretty neat, huh? These magnetic parts trays come in round and oblong shapes, so you might want to get a couple of each.

Being Content with the Contents

Now, with two stackable chests, you wind up with a load of drawers that can be filled with all kinds of tools. The trick here is

Jars, containers, bins, and brackets that all hook into pegboard are excellent ways of storing small items and clearing up workbench clutter. Courtesy: Crawford/The Lehigh Group

This steel trash can is both stylish and functional. Its steel construction is also fire-retardant.
Courtesy: Genuine Hot Rod Hardware

trying to remember what's in which drawer in each chest. That's where putting labels on the drawers comes into play. If you have a Brother P-touch label machine, you're in great shape. Just pick a label stock that will contrast against the drawer and print away.

Of course, you can also make your own labels with duct tape and an ink marker, use file-folder adhesive labels, or print them out on your computer and affix them with transparent cello tape. The thing here is to have some means of identifying what each drawer contains so that when you need a tool you'll know where to find it without playing musical drawers for a few minutes.

A while back I came upon rubberized magnetic "icon" labels that show various tools. These labels provide a graphic representation of what's in each drawer, and you can combine a few of them if your drawers contain a variety of a given genre of tools. For example, if your "pliers" drawer contains slip-joints, side cutters, and shears, you could use three icons to indicate that on the face of the drawer. While these icon labels are handy, unfortunately they don't cover all the bases (e.g., no torch icon or icon for safety glasses/equipment), so you'll probably have to use some form of ancillary labeling as well.

Square Pegs in Round Holes

If you have a pegboard in your garage, then you have additional storage options, especially for small items. There's a plethora of jars, bins, and containers that readily attach to pegboards for holding things like nuts, bolts, washers, cotter pins, and so forth. These plastic storage solutions are inexpensive and available at most home improvement centers.

There are also numerous hooks, brackets, and loop holders that will attach to a pegboard. These are great for holding screwdrivers, hack saws, pliers, wrenches, and other hand tools that you want to keep readily available and exposed at all times.

Stash Your Trash

It's an inevitable fact of life that you're going to generate and accumulate trash in your garage, so you'll need a container to hold it until you take it out. A steel trash can (or garbage can, if you prefer) is the best way to go, especially if you have oily rags or paper towels that may pose a fire risk. The plastic cans are a bit lighter but, alas, they're also flammable, so a sturdy steel trash can gives you that extra peace of mind.

Lining your trash receptacle with trash bags is also a good idea, unless you like cleaning the can every time you throw something messy in it. I like Hefty cinch-type trash bags myself, but I also use the Hefty lawn and leaf bags when I have a lot of trash to take out.

Chilling Out

At first blush, some folks would think of a refrigerator in the garage as an extravagance. Yet, for anyone who spends a considerable amount of time working in there, it is an absolute necessity. You simply can't beat the convenience of having a fridge nearby stocked with cold sodas, iced teas, or other soft drinks (no, I don't condone drinking brewskies while working in the garage—save the partying for when the work is done, thank you).

You don't have to go out and buy a new refrigerator for the garage, though. You can often pick one up at a garage sale. Better yet, move the fridge in your kitchen out to the garage and then be a hero by purchasing a new one for the house! The cold box doesn't have to stand out like a sore thumb, either. You can get a refrigerator dress-up kit that will make it look like a stacker tool chest—how cool is that?

Camouflage your garage refrigerator to look like a stacker tool chest with one of these cool, refrigerator dress-up kits. Who says functional can't look good? Courtesy: Genuine Hot Rod Hardware

THE CYBER GARAGE

Computers are very much a part of our daily lives, and a computer most certainly has a place in your garage. Why? There will be times when you need to surf the Net to look up information for projects you're working on or to locate parts. You'll also probably want to check out other information contained on CDs or DVDs, and you may even want to play CD or MP3 music on the PC while you're working.

Rather than going with a desktop PC, however, I recommend using a notebook out in the garage. A notebook has several inherent advantages over a desktop PC. It takes up much less space on the workbench; you don't need separate outlets for the PC and the monitor; it will run off a battery if you don't have the AC adapter plugged in; it's portable so you can move it wherever you need it; and it's fast, powerful, and very affordable. Need I say more?

Then there's the e-mail factor—my e-mail stream is quite steady for about 18 to 20 hours a day. I get lots of e-mail from all 50 states and a lot of stuff coming in from other countries, too, so my notebook is on 24/7 to keep me abreast of what's happening and also to keep me in touch with the folks who are contacting me. It's very convenient to have the ability to read and respond to e-mail in the garage so I don't have to go into the house for it. And using a wireless network is the way to go, since you don't have to deal with any wires or cables.

If you don't already have one, you may also want to consider getting a pocket PC that connects wirelessly to your home network. These are great for checking e-mail while you're indisposed and can't see a normal PC screen (like when you're under a car). They're also handy for jotting down notes (like part numbers) when you don't have a pencil and paper handy. I use a Dell Axim 50, which is synched to my Dell Inspiron 9300 notebook so I'm really wirelessly wired-in.

I have a Dell Inspiron 9300 notebook computer in my garage and I love it! Courtesy: Dell Computers

A Pocket PC like this Dell Axim is the perfect companion for your notebook computer in your garage. It enables you to check email wirelessly and do other useful tasks, even when you're not near your notebook. Courtesy: Dell Computers

Keep those CDs and DVDs safe in your garage with a sturdy and good-looking case like this one. Courtesy: Genuine Hot Rod Hardware

This excellent DVD will teach and show you all you need to know about rebuilding a V-8 engine. Instruction like this is an absolute must if you've never done this sort of thing before, and it's a highly recommended aid even if you have. Courtesy: The Eastwood Company

You will surely find that having a printer available will make your life much easier when you want a hard copy of something you found on the Internet—perhaps a schematic, an exploded view of an assembly, or whatever. While a black-and-white printer will do, the cost of color inkjet printers has come down so much that you may as well have the benefits of color printing while you're at it.

If you're still not convinced that you should have a computer in your garage, consider the abundance of software that's available. I mean, there's a CD-ROM or DVD available for just almost anything you could think of—from rebuilding a small-block Chevy engine to doing wild custom paint effects on your favorite ride and just about everything in between. There are tutorial discs on how to MIG weld, how to form metal, how to pinstripe and paint flames, and technical articles on hundreds of maintenance and repair topics. When it comes to knowledge, the world is your oyster—but you'll need a computer to access it!

This is also a good time to mention that you should take proper precautions to avoid scratching your CDs or DVDs while using them in the garage, since they are fairly delicate. For this reason, you should always put them back in their jewel cases or, better yet, have a storage case that will keep your favorite and most-used discs safe and sound when they're not in the PC.

CHAPTER 3
WHOEVER HAS THE MOST TOOLS WINS

Long before you even have your own home or garage, you can start building your basic gearhead tool kit. Whether you're just planning to change your oil or replace your battery, it's not a bad idea to start getting your own tools to do the job.

But where do you start? Well even the most novice of gearheads should start by assembling the following in their first tool kit:

- A set of combination wrenches
- A 1/4-inch drive and 3/8-inch drive shallow and deep socket set
- A pair of 3-ton jack stands
- A 6-ton bottle jack with pump handles in front of it
- A 6-pack of disposable dust masks
- A small first-aid kit
- A retractable utility knife
- A pair of leather work gloves
- A pair of AO Safety glasses
- A 2-pound ball pein hammer
- A 5-pound dead-blow hammer
- An aluminum-frame hack saw
- Assorted Philips and flat-blade screwdrivers
- A pair of side cutters and a pair of lineman's pliers
- A pair of cushioned-grip vice-grip pliers
- A fire extinguisher
- A pair of slip-joint pliers
- A large pair of water pump pliers

Domestic- vs. Foreign-Made Tools

A half-century ago, you'd be very hard pressed to find a tool in your local hardware store, building center, or automotive supply house that wasn't made right here in the good old U.S.A. Not that foreign tools didn't exist, mind you—they

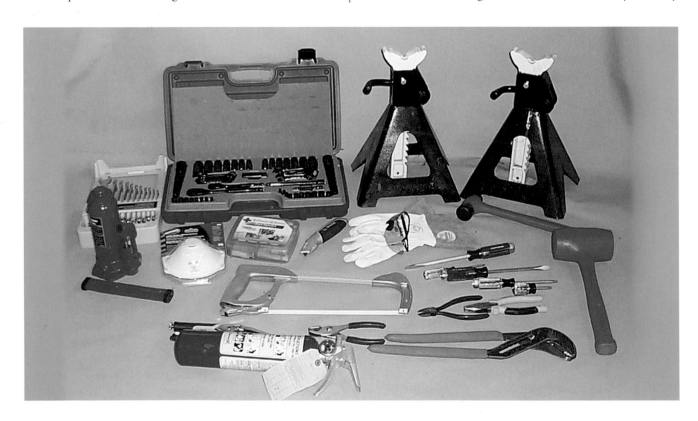

Every gearhead needs to start somewhere with his or her tool collection. This is a sampling of the basics that you should first stock your toolbox with before moving on to more specialized and elaborate gear. Author's Collection

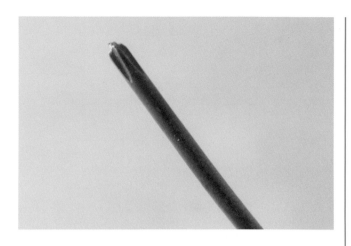

This Philips screwdriver is now a useless piece of metal, since its tip is badly worn and it will only damage any screw head it is used on. Quality screwdrivers have hardened tips that won't wear out the way this imported, non-hardened one did. Author's Collection

just weren't readily available. If you needed a set of Whitworth wrenches to work on your Austin-Healey or MG, or metric tools for your Volkswagen or Alfa, you'd have to special-order them. They weren't everyday off-the-shelf items. A lot has changed since then, however.

In today's global economy, tools of various manufacture from every corner of the earth are available. While variety is the spice of life, having this much variety when it comes to tools is not necessarily a good thing. Often the uninitiated buyer may very well be spending hard-earned dollars on what, in the long run, could prove to be junk.

It's very tempting to shop for price and to snatch up a bargain when the opportunity presents itself. It's also easy

to get caught up in a "low price frenzy." For example, let's say you want to purchase a hydraulic floor jack for lifting your car, so you go to the automotive section of your favorite department store. You find a two-ton jack on sale for only $49.95. Right next to it is another two-ton jack that has a price tag of $149.95. Both jacks are two-ton units, but there's a $100 difference in price. Why? What are the differences? The $49.95 unit was made in China, while the $149.95 unit was made in the United States. The Chinese-made jack has a one-year warranty, while the American-made jack has a lifetime warranty (a bit more on this later).

A little common sense should tell you there has to be a reason (or reasons) that one is only expected to be good for a year while the other jack is backed for life. Which one would you feel more comfortable using? Spending the extra $100 is probably worth the money for some added insurance that your vehicle won't come crashing down unexpectedly. Don't misinterpret this advice as "Chinese bashing"—it's not. It is a realistic example of the varied quality and pricing of tools. You'll encounter these discrepancies along the way when equipping your garage for your next big project.

The same rule can apply to jack stands. There's got to be some significant differences between a pair of stands that sell for $19.95 as opposed to the $49.95 pair. With items like this, it is crucially important to go with the better quality product since you will, in all likelihood, be underneath the vehicle while it's being supported by jack stands. Paying $30 more is a real bargain if it will prevent my car from crashing down on me!

Another example of bargain screwdrivers purchased at the neighborhood dollar store. The blades on these imported tools were made of inferior steel and not hardened properly (if at all), resulting in the chipping and rounding of the blades. Buying cheap tools like these is really false economy, since they won't last and will have to be replaced, probably sooner than later. Author's Collection

The jaws of this open-end wrench made in India aren't quite 9/16 of an inch apart, making them useless for tightening or loosening this 9/16-inch nut. Again, buy cheap and you get what you pay for. Author's Collection

There's an old adage about tools: buy cheap and you'll buy often; buy the best and you'll only buy once. That, my friends, is the gospel truth!

Don't get me wrong, though. Some foreign-made tools are absolutely exquisite in their manufacture, balance, and precision. German-made tools, in particular, are absolutely first-rate. I've also used some outstanding tools of Italian and French manufacture, as well as some British tools that can't be faulted in any way. The tools I have a problem with, for the most part, are the low-grade, low-priced tools from the Pacific Rim and the Far East. The two main problems with these tools are they don't fit or work correctly, and the metal they're made from is substandard.

A good example of this—and a true story, by the way—is a "hardened steel" impact socket set I purchased at a flea market about a decade ago for $15 (while I was still a naïve tool bargain hunter). The $15 price tag was about $65 less than what a hardened steel 1/2-inch-drive impact socket set was selling for at the local NAPA store. I later found out why this Taiwan-made impact socket set was such a "bargain." I tried to bust a badly rusted nut off the rear suspension of a Corvette and the socket literally disintegrated! No kidding, it shattered and cracked in three places. Sure, with its flat black finish, it looked like hardened steel but, in reality, it wasn't. Luckily, I didn't get injured, but I did do two things in short

order. First, I tossed the bogus hardened impact driver set into the scrap barrel. Second, I went right to the NAPA store and bought what I should have purchased in the first place—a decent, (real) hardened steel, guaranteed-for-life impact socket set. Fifteen bucks down the drain, but a good lesson learned, and learned well (almost the hard way, in fact).

An imported set of wrenches that doesn't fit your bolts precisely will round off the heads, slip while you're tightening the bolts, and may result in some skinned knuckles. You don't need this in your life, and that's the voice of experience speaking. Garage work should be fun, and being injured—even slightly— is not fun. And to add insult to injury, these cheapo tools break!

It's hard to believe that tools, like Gucci purses and Rolex watches, are being counterfeited these days as well. If you go to the local flea markets, you're highly likely to find Snapit-On socket sets (as opposed to Snap-On, the real thing) along with the dozen-packs of copper-top alkaline batteries. As if the low-ball price wasn't enough of a giveaway that these items are fakes, the misspellings and bad grammar used on the packages are a true indicator. Sometimes the faux pas are so bad they are comical. For example, Sears Roebuck makes and sells Craftsman tools. There is no such thing as a Sears wrench— at least not legitimately—available for sale anywhere. Yet I was able to purchase a Sears wrench at a flea market a few years

This combination wrench was made in Taiwan. The imprint on the shaft says it is made of Chrome Vanadium steel, yet one of the jaws on the open-end side snapped off under fairly light pressure. Do you think someone was being dishonest with the labeling? Could be! Author's Collection

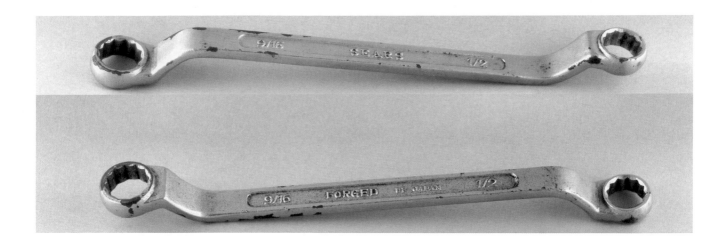

If you buy a wrench at Sears, it will say "Craftsman" on it—not Sears! This Japanese-made wrench should say "forgery" rather than "forged" on it. Even the chrome plating is inferior and is chipping off. Author's Collection

back! So when buying tools of any kind, the watchword is caveat emptor—let the buyer beware.

OK, now back to the warranty stuff. Remember that foreign-made floor jack I talked about earlier? Imagine this scenario: you bought the jack and now, about six months later, it gradually loses elevation due to a leaking hydraulic cylinder. It's guaranteed by the manufacturer for one year, so you take it back to the department store where you bought it and the automotive department clerk informs you that returns and exchanges are only honored for 60 days by the store. So, unless you ship this jack back to the distribution warehouse (on the opposite coast from where you're located) for a replacement, there's nothing else that can be done. Due to the heavy weight of the jack, the shipping is going to cost almost as much as the total cost of the jack. Plus, now you're going to have to get a box to pack it in and then bring it to the shipper. Are we having fun yet?

The American-made jack, on the other hand, has an 1-800-number you can call to find the nearest dealer authorized to honor the warranty, get a free replacement part, or get the defective jack repaired or replaced at no charge. Armed with this knowledge, the choice between purchasing the foreign jack or the domestic jack should now be a no-brainer.

Import-ant Exceptions

Without going into the complicated economics of manufacturing tools and equipment, it has become fairly common for American companies to have their products manufactured overseas where the cost of labor and materials is considerably less than in this country. It's entirely probable, for example, to purchase a brand-name tool—let's say a 3/8-inch air ratchet—that carries a nationally known American name on

it, yet has a sticker that says it was made in Taiwan or some other foreign locale. Does that automatically mean it's a piece of crap? No. This tool was made to the American company's specifications for materials that meet the specs and tolerances demanded. So, in effect, you're getting American quality that's manufactured overseas.

The important thing to remember is that if you can't get a tool that was made in America, it's safe to go with a brand-name American tool. You'll get a quality implement, regardless of where it's manufactured, and the American company that sells it will stand behind it, too.

Why Some Brands Are More Expensive

All tools are not created equal. Some tools cost more to make than others due to various factors, and this is true of the same

This is the bargain hardened impact socket that shattered in three places when I used it with my pneumatic impact wrench to loosen a stubborn suspension bolt. When I purchased a set of truly hardened impact sockets from NAPA and used them for the same job, the bolt gave up, not the sockets. That's the way it should be. Author's Collection

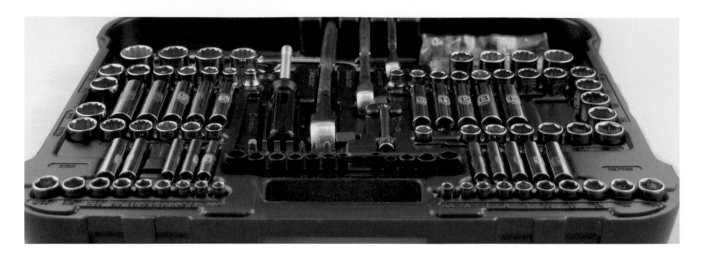

By purchasing a combination socket set like this one, you'll get both shallow and deep sockets, so you'll have at least two of each size. Not only will this save you some money over individual purchases, but you will be well equipped for just about every job that requires sockets. Courtesy: Craftsman Tools

tool from different manufacturers. Part of the reason behind that (and the ultimate price difference to you) is that there are different levels of tools: professional tools, "prosumer" tools, and consumer tools. The difference between the three segments is the amount of finesse, finish, and quality built into each one.

For example, a professional ratchet is sculpted to fit the hand precisely for optimal grip and balance. The steel used to make it is of the very best quality available; more often than not, the ratchet is triple chrome-plated for a finish that will last a lifetime without rusting. It is also inspected multiple times for quality assurance before being offered for sale.

A "prosumer" ratchet is comfortable to hold, looks good, and does its job reliably. It's made of good materials and has a nice finish. The average Joe won't find any fault with this grade of tool, and it represents a good investment that, with reasonable care, should last a lifetime.

On the other hand, a consumer ratchet typically is something you see on the counter of a convenience store or at the car wash checkout register. It's usually an imported item that's priced for the impulse buyer (under $10). It will do nicely to tighten up the loose nut or bolt and will even serve you well for some small projects, but it isn't something you'd want to spend hours using. It doesn't have the heft, balance, leverage, or comfort of a professional or even a prosumer-grade tool; nor does it have the longevity of either of these. Sooner or later it will most certainly fail, thus making it a disposable tool.

Bear in mind that the professional-grade tools are frequently not available in stores. Nationally recognized, professional brands such as Snap-On and Matco, to name but two, are sold directly to mechanics and garages from vendor trucks that make their rounds every week. Such personalized service adds to the price of the tools, but the convenience of having the tool salesman come to the mechanic is worth it to many professionals.

The Snap-On or Matco truck won't be making stops to your home, though, unless you make the local sales rep aware that you exist and that you're interested in making purchases. If your pockets are deep enough and you want to have the very best tools that money can buy, then, by all means, go with one of these excellent professional brands. Often these professional tool suppliers make financing the tools (time payments) available for new customers.

Craftsman is probably the best-known name when it comes to prosumer tools, yet many professional mechanics (including NASCAR pit crews) use Craftsman tools, blurring the line between "prosumer" and professional equipment. Craftsman tools are easy to love for several reasons. First, they're available at any Sears store throughout the country and the line offers just about anything you could possibly need in the way of hand tools. They also are very well-made, affordable, and guaranteed for life. If anything breaks, wears out, or doesn't function properly, Sears will exchange it for another same or similar tool free of charge with no hassles.

The local NAPA dealer is another wonderful source for tools and equipment, yet it is overlooked sometimes because of the mistaken perception that you have to be a "professional" to purchase gear at a NAPA store. Nothing could be further from the truth. Your friendly NAPA store owner will gladly sell you tools, parts, or gear as readily as he or she will sell them to a garage or repair facility. If the store doesn't have what you're looking for in stock, someone there can order it for you.

When One Is Not Enough

Many tools come in several sizes and types, so you'll want to have more than one in your tool chest. Others, however, are multi-purpose tools, and you'll want to have extras of those

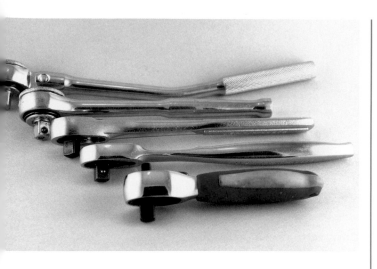

Ratchets come in a wide variety of styles, handle shapes, and sizes. An assortment of ratchets will give you some freedom to select the one that will be the most efficient—and comfortable—for a particular project. Author's Collection

American-made vehicles began using metric standard fasteners, either exclusively or in combination with U.S. standard fasteners. Today, metric fasteners are used exclusively in the vast majority of vehicles found on the road—both domestic and foreign.

Whitworth fasteners, more properly known as BSW (British Standard Whitworth), use a coarse thread that was devised and standardized in Manchester, England, in 1841 by British engineer Sir Joseph Whitworth (1803–1887). Now considered an obsolete thread form, it still can be found worldwide on many types of British machinery, including vintage motorcycles, automobiles, aircraft, and a host of other interesting things. Obviously, Whitworth sockets and wrenches are required for these fasteners.

The various head sizes and thread diameters of these three standards—including conversion charts for them—will be covered in Chapter 15, when different types of fasteners are discussed in more depth and detail.

because what gearhead doesn't need more than one standard wrench, hammer, or screwdriver? Other tools you'll want multiples of include ratchets, sockets, drill bits, and pliers.

The reason for having multiples of the same type of tool is simple. Sometimes you'll use both hands, with a tool in each, to accomplish a task. For example, you may use a wrench to hold onto the head of a bolt while you use another wrench (possibly of the same size) to turn the nut at the opposite end. This is a very common scenario when working on vehicles. Having a few socket sets also makes life easier, and an assortment of screwdrivers is also a must-have for the well-equipped garage.

With few exceptions, it's safe to say that you'll be better off with at least two of every hand tool in your garage. In some instances, more than two tools will be the way to go, but you'll be able to judge what you need as you become more familiar with the type of tasks each implement is designed to do.

U.S., Metric, and Whitworth Standards

The type of wrenches and sockets you use will depend on the standards of the nuts and bolts. The three basic standards are U.S, metric, and Whitworth.

U.S. standard fasteners and the tools used with them are measured in inches or fractions thereof. For example, U.S. standard sockets and wrenches bear sizes such as 3/16", 1/4", 5/16", 3/8", and so forth. Up until about the mid-1980s, virtually all American-made vehicles used U.S. standard fasteners exclusively.

Metric fasteners and the tools used with them are measured in millimeters—5-mm, 6-mm, 7-mm, 8-mm, 9-mm, and so forth. Starting about the mid-1980s, most

CHAPTER 4
DUMBER THAN A BAG OF HAMMERS

Hammers have been around almost as long as man. In fact, stone hammers pre-date stone axes and knives. It was only after bludgeoning small prey to death with an early makeshift hammer that the Stone Age man figured he'd need a way to cut it up and skin it, so the stone axes and knives came about out of necessity, as an afterthought.

In the early scenes of *2001: A Space Odyssey*, director Stanley Kubrick presented his idea on how hammers came to be when one of our primate ancestors picks up a long bone and, probably out of boredom, smashes it down on a pile of other bones, which break apart and fly about. An idea is born. This bone—an early hammer, if you will—would be good for bashing in the skulls of enemies, the ape thinks, which is indeed what happens a bit further into the movie.

In Norse mythology, Thor, the Viking god of thunder, wielded a mighty hammer, named Mjölnir, against giants, monsters, trolls, and other nefarious beings that threatened the common good.

So, as I said earlier, hammers have been around a while, and they've undergone a lot of evolution and development

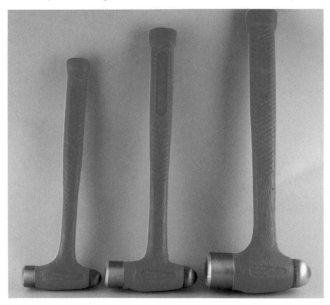

Stanley's Compo-Cast® ball pein hammers are available in five weights, ranging from 8 through 32 ounces. The handles and heads are made of a very strong composite material, with hardened steel hammer and pein striking heads imbedded in them. They are extremely durable, well balanced, and represent a very good value. Courtesy: Stanley Tools

along the way. There are literally hundreds of individual hammer types currently available, but they all basically fall into the main categories outlined in this chapter.

Claw Hammers

The claw hammer is the most well known of any hammer and also the most common, ranging in weight from 1/2 pound to 1 3/4 pounds. Claw hammers have a standard driving head, which is either round or octagonal, and the claws have a sharp radius that gives you more leverage and makes pulling nails easier. Claw hammers always have a smooth striking face, so they can be used for finishing work.

A variation of the claw hammer is the framing hammer, which tends to be longer and heavier, with a more shallow claw radius. Framing hammers range in weight, usually from 1 to 2 pounds, and they can have either smooth or milled striking faces. The idea of the milled face is that it digs into the head of the nail to prevent the hammer from slipping off it. The straighter radius claw is beefier for pulling larger framing nails. Framing hammers usually have some form of shock absorption to reduce fatigue and injury caused by repetitive blows.

Claw hammers and framing hammers are never used for automotive or mechanical work. Their purpose is for construction and woodworking, but they are included here for the sake of completeness and to distinguish their intended purpose.

Pein Hammers

The most common metal working hammer is the ball pein (frequently spelled ball peen), also sometimes called an engineer's hammer or a machinist's hammer. This hammer has a standard flat face and a semi-circular convex face called the pein. These hammers were designed for shaping metal and for setting iron rivets by peining over the edge. The steel head of a ball pein hammer is harder than the head of a claw hammer, so it's less likely to chip on contact, which is why it is used for automotive and machine work applications.

A cross pein or machinist's hammer has a flat face that is either square or octagonal on one side and wedged-shaped on the opposite side. These hammers are often used for blacksmithing and metalworking where the wedge or cross pein face is used for shaping, cutting, or folding the metal.

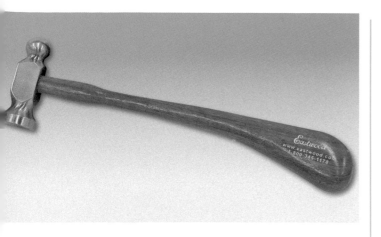

A classic 1-pound ball pein hammer, this finely-crafted hammer has a hardened head and a long, hickory handle, which gives it great balance and shock absorption from the impact of the blow. Courtesy: The Eastwood Company

Sledge Hammers

Sledge hammers have heavy heads that range in weight from 2 pounds to 20 pounds. Sledges weighing more than 5 pounds often have long handles because you need two hands to swing them. A single-handed sledgehammer, usually weighing 2 to 5 pounds with a shortened handle, is also sometimes called a drilling hammer, since they are frequently used to drill into rock and stone. The short handle makes it easier to swing and control the heavy head, up to 5 pounds, in cramped quarters. They have two flat faces and are usually square. Sledge hammers are only used for heavy-duty persuading when working on vehicles or machinery.

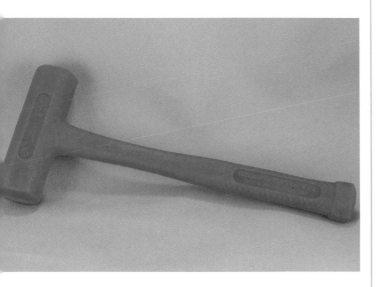

This is one of Stanley's Compo-Cast® dead blow hammers. Dead blow hammers are used when having a bounce or recoil effect from the striking blow is undesirable. These hammers come in assorted weights, are very durable, and are comfortable to use.

Courtesy: Stanley Tools

Dead Blow Hammers

These hammers are made of a medium, soft plastic and filled with lead. They're called dead blow hammers because instead of bouncing, as a rubber hammer does, the movement of the lead causes the full force of the blow to be transferred to the material that is struck.

Although the plastic housing usually won't damage the material that is struck, it is too soft to use on sharp metal. Dead blow hammers can leave a mark on wood or other soft surfaces susceptible to denting. Weights for dead blow hammers range from 2 to 3 pounds.

Rubber Hammers

Rubber hammers have either white or black rubber heads and can be used as a dead blow hammer, but they do have some bounce. Also frequently called rubber mallets, they are used primarily to tap or lightly persuade parts without risk of marring the surrounding surface as a steel hammer might do. However, they can leave a rubber mark on the parts they make contact with. This is particularly true of the black rubber hammers. The common weight range for rubber hammers is from 8 ounces to 32 ounces.

Double-Faced Hammers

These hammers have two faces, each a different softness, and they are frequently a combination of plastic or rubber. These hammers are used for light tapping tasks and the end caps can leave a mark from the plastic or rubber as it rubs off. Double-faced hammers are measured by the diameter of their faces rather than by weight. Common sizes are from 3/4 of an inch to 1 9/16 inches.

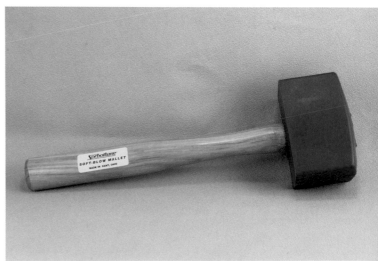

The pliable head of this mallet makes it ideal for soft-blow chores where you'd ordinarily use the heel of your hand. Courtesy: The Eastwood Company

A classic brass tapping mallet, this hammer is used for very delicate work because the soft brass striking surface is fairly gentle. These brass mallets are also ideal for applications where a spark produced from the hammer blow may be dangerous.

Courtesy: The Eastwood Company

Rawhide Hammers

Rawhide hammers are the precursors of the dead blow, rubber, and double-faced hammers, and they are generally used for the same purposes. They can be used on machined parts, and they also have the added advantage of not leaving any kind of mark. Common weights for rawhide hammers range from 1/2 pound to 1 3/4 pounds.

Brass or Copper Hammers

These hammers are normally used if a spark from a standard steel hammer could be dangerous or for tapping on machined parts. Common weights for brass or copper hammers range from 1/2 pound to 1 3/4 pounds.

Mallets

Usually equipped with composite heads and wooden handles, these hammers are used for bodywork, to stretch and form sheet metal. Available as round mallets with flat faces or with teardrop heads, they are measured in head diameter rather than weight. They are typically available in 2-inch, 2 1/2-inch, and 2 3/4-inch diameters for the teardrop style and 2-inch, 2 3/4-inch, and 3 1/4-inch diameters for the round style of mallet.

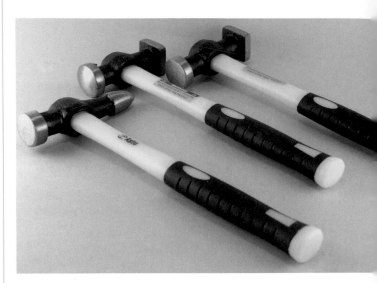

Bodywork hammers with composite handles, cushioned rubber grips, and assorted head styles are relatively inexpensive. The three shown here are basic bodywork hammers, of which there are about 75 different variations. Courtesy: The Eastwood Company

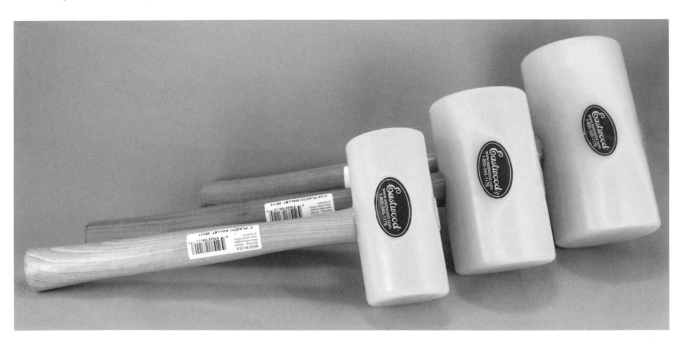

Round composite mallets with wooden handles are measured by their head size rather than by their weight. The three shown above are 2-inch, 2 3/4-inch, and 3 1/4-inch diameters, and they're used for bodywork as well as general light tapping chores. Courtesy: The Eastwood Company

Bodywork Hammers

There are well over 75 different types of hammers used for doing automotive bodywork and sheet metal forming. These include bumping hammers, long pick hammers, shrinking chisel hammers, cross-peen finishing hammers, blunt pick hammers, and straight-cross chisel hammers, to name but a few. Used for specific tasks in doing bodywork and metalworking, their weights and striking faces vary greatly.

A specialty tool useful for metalworking, this hammer has a face that rotates on impact to shrink the metal it comes into contact with and a flat striking head for smoothing.
Courtesy: The Eastwood Company

How many different types of bodywork hammers should I have in my garage? Your answer might come in this interchangeable-head hammer set. The various heads simply snap into the handle and lock in positively. Pushing a release button ejects them. Courtesy: The Eastwood Company

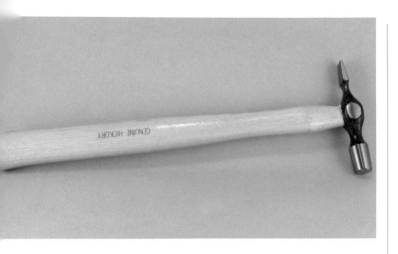

A trim hammer like this is ideal for delicate work such as taking dents and dings out of stainless-steel automotive body trim. Courtesy: The Eastwood Company

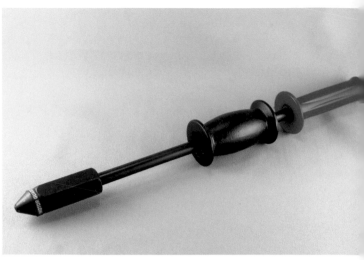

A slide hammer like this is just the ticket for pulling dents out. After a hole is drilled in the dent, a screw bit is inserted into the nose of the hammer, threaded into the hole, and the sliding weight is pulled back sharply to the handle, thus pulling the dent out with the force of the blow. Courtesy: The Eastwood Company

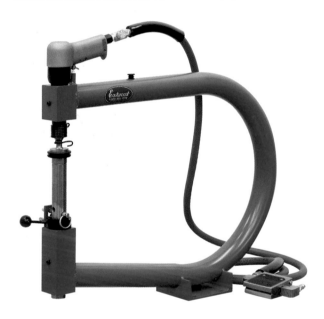

A pneumatic planishing hammer like this one is used for metal forming. The air-driven hammer slams against the metal anvil platform as the metal being worked on is moved about to achieve the desired shape. Courtesy: The Eastwood Company

A ring hammer gets its name from the fact that the user inserts his or her middle finger into the ring and uses the tool for hammering, bumping, or like a handheld anvil. Courtesy: The Eastwood Company

Specialty Hammers

These hammers are special-purpose implements and they include soft-blow mallets, trim hammers, twist-shrinking hammers, ring hammers, pneumatic body smoothing hammers, slide hammers, and pneumatic planishing hammers. Their sizes, weights, and uses vary greatly.

And the Beat Goes On

Often when using a hammer, you need to use a striking surface so that the force of the blow can do its intended job. Some of the most commonly used striking surfaces are listed here.

Anvils

Originally made of stone, anvils made the transition to iron and eventually steel to serve as an essential piece of equipment in every village's blacksmith shop. Usually anvils have a flat striking table with a rounded horn at one end, which is used for forming curves in metal objects, such as horseshoes. Anvils vary in size and weight from a few inches at a couple of pounds to three feet or more in length at several hundred pounds.

A miniature anvil like this one is excellent for working on trim and other delicate pieces where a flat surface for hammering is needed. Courtesy: The Eastwood Company

Unless you'll be doing some serious metalwork, a small anvil about 1 foot long weighing in the 50- to 75-pound range should serve you nicely for most of your pounding tasks. Used anvils are often found for sale at farm equipment and tool flea markets, and the rule of thumb for pricing is generally $1 per pound.

Beater Bags

Made of leather and filled with either sand or metal shot, a beater bag provides a sturdy yet pliable surface on which metal may be beaten to form it into the desired shape. Beater bags are extremely useful when shaping sheet metal or fabricating metal parts, and they come in various sizes. A solid workbench top or a beater bag stand is recommended whenever using a beater bag.

Dollies

Dollies are essentially small handheld anvils used for automotive bodywork. Dollies are used to back body panels while hammering on them to remove dents or form metal. Dollies come in several sizes and shapes; the most common are the general purpose dolly, the heel dolly, the wedge dolly, and the double-ended dolly. Other varieties include egg-shaped, light-duty, spoon-end, shrinking, and toe dollies.

A Pound of Flesh

Whacking your thumb or hand while using a hammer is almost a given—sooner or later, your striking implement will miss its mark and hit you instead. The best way to prevent this from happening, or at least to lessen the frequency of its occurrence, is to be careful and concentrate on what you're doing. It's not a good idea to hammer (or use any tool, for that matter) when there are distractions, poor lighting, or obstacles in the way.

Wearing some hand protection, such as leather work gloves and safety glasses or goggles, is also a good idea when hammering.

This concludes the hammers chapter; hopefully, I've pounded out some valuable knowledge for you.

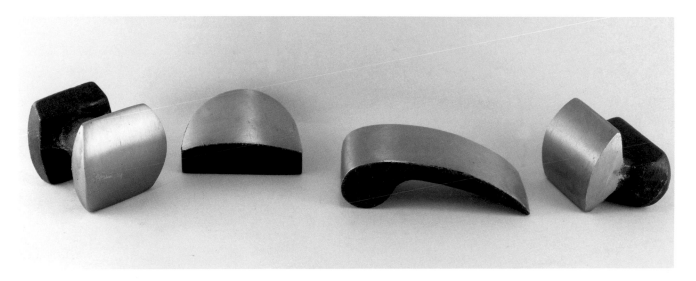

While there are over a dozen variations on these basic dolly shapes, the four shown above are the workhorses of the body and fender trade. Essentially, they are handheld anvils that are used to back the metal piece being struck by various metalworking hammers. Courtesy: The Eastwood Company

CHAPTER 5
PUTTING THE SQUEEZE ON THINGS

That's what this chapter is about—tools and implements that will grab and hold objects. By far, the most common and most useful of all these tools are pliers. King of the compression tools, pliers are never known as a "plier." There is no such thing as a plier. Even if you're talking about a single tool, it's always pliers.

The great thing about pliers is that they give you a tremendous mechanical advantage by multiplying the holding power of your hand several times over. They do this by using a double lever-and-fulcrum effect, with each of the handle/jaw halves pivoting on a fulcrum. In this case, a rivet or bolt holds the two halves together. You've got to love any tool that multiplies your own might so simply and efficiently!

The basic purpose for a set of pliers is to hold, turn, and/or cut wire or objects. There are many types of pliers, however, which are designed for specific tasks. So it's best to know what type you might need for your project before you get started.

Pliers come in an assortment of sizes ranging from 4 inches to 20 inches. Some are available with factory-applied plastic handles, which provide an attractive finish and a comfortable grip. Others come with resilient "comfort" grips made of rubber, urethane, or other cushioning material to make them more comfortable to use.

Pliers can be either a slip-joint or a solid-joint design. Both types can have the capability to cut materials. Here are the basic distinctions between the two types:

• Slip-joint pliers have multiple holes or a tongue-and-

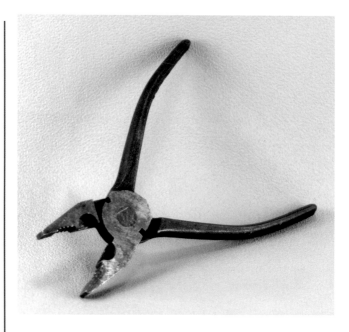

These solid-joint electrician's or lineman's pliers are also very common and they have a cutter built into them for stripping and cutting wire. Author's Collection

groove design that enables you to adjust the tool to the specific size needed for the object to be held.

• Solid-joint pliers are not adjustable because of a solid pin or rivet that is attached to the joint.

Some of the other kinds of pliers include the following:

• Cutting pliers, which come in side, end, or diagonal varieties.

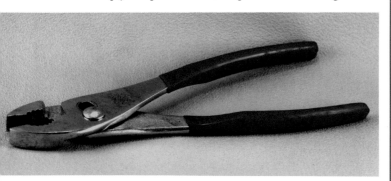

Traditional slip-joint pliers such as these are what most folks think of when they hear the word "pliers." Although these are by far the most common pliers, they are by no means the only type used in the garage. The joint permits the jaws to be expanded by slipping into the other hole in the handle, hence the name. Author's Collection

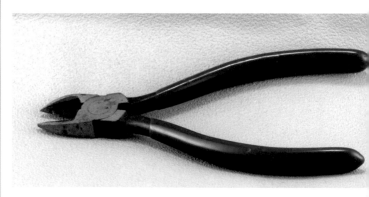

Side cutters, such as these, are probably the third most-used pliers. Primarily intended for stripping and cutting wire and light cable, they frequently have insulated grips for comfort and extra protection against shocks. Author's Collection

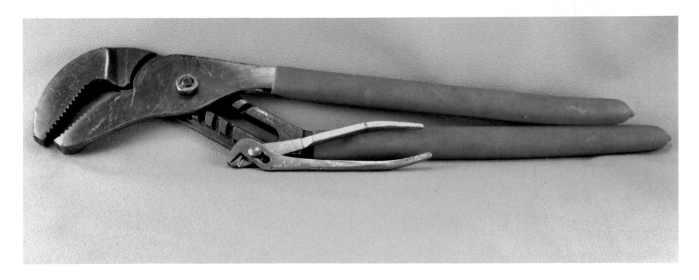

Multiple slip-joint pliers, also known as water pump pliers, permit the jaws to open to several widths, depending on which of the expansion slips is used. These pliers come in very small (4-inch) sizes all the way up to the giant 20-inch size shown here. Some specialty tool houses can even get them in larger sizes on special order. Author's Collection

• Side cutters, available in long-, curved-, and short-nose types with a cutting edge on one side.

• End cutters, with cutting edges on the tips where clean, sharp cuts may be needed. These are ideal for surface cuts on wire, rivets, or bolts.

• Diagonal cutters, which have two cutting edges set diagonally from the joint or handle.

Pliers, Pliers, and More Pliers

Regular slip-joint pliers are commonly used around the house or on small projects. The adjustable jaw-opening fits a greater variety of objects and some have the ability to cut wire. Thin jaw slip-joint pliers are a variation on regular slip-joint pliers with more narrow jaws so they can fit into hard-to-reach areas.

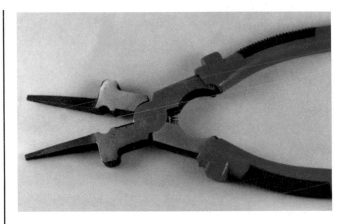

These are MIG welding pliers that have squared, spring-loaded tips for removing welding spatter. The inside surfaces are knurled in two places for installing welding tips. They also have a wire cutter and cushioned rubber grips. Courtesy: The Eastwood Company

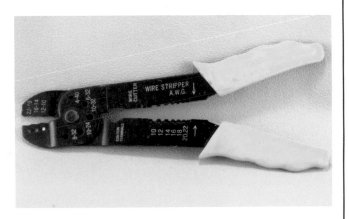

Wire strippers or terminal crimping pliers are handy for doing automotive electrical work and other wiring tasks. The strippers have holes for the most common wire gauges. Author's Collection

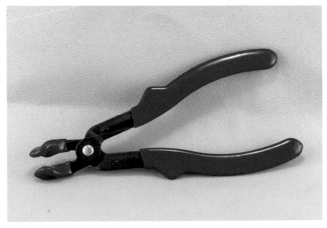

These pliers are specifically designed for removing spark plug boots. Notice the insulated tips and handles to prevent getting a nasty shock from the ignition system if the motor is running. Author's Collection

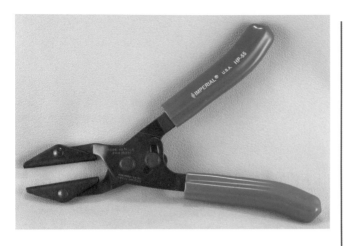

Hose-clamping pliers such as these are handy when working on fuel lines, cooling system hoses, or anytime you need to pinch-off the flow of liquids within a pliable hose or piece of rubber tubing. Courtesy: The Eastwood Company

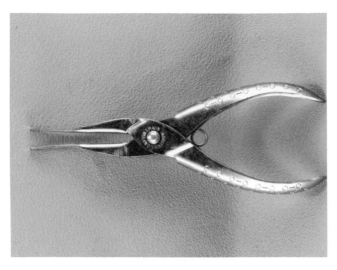

Made specifically for use on radiator and condenser fins, these pliers have long, flat blades that are ideal for such tasks. Courtesy: The Eastwood Company

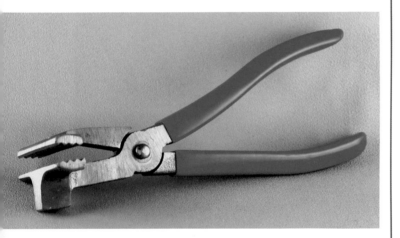

Fabric-stretching pliers like these are another absolute must when doing automotive upholstery work. The wide jaws permit you to stretch the material much more than your bare hands could, yet the stretching force is spread over several inches to prevent tearing.

Courtesy: The Eastwood Company

These wide-jaw (3 3/8-inch) welding pliers are great for bending and folding sheet metal, and the 8-inch long handles give you a lot of leverage. Courtesy: The Eastwood Company

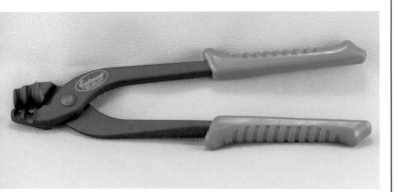

These pliers are specially designed to form brake line and fuel line tubing, and they feature 3/16-inch and 1/4-inch channels to permit bending the tubing without kinking it.

Courtesy: The Eastwood Company

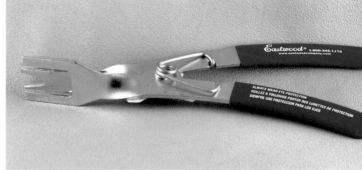

Specifically designed for removing automotive door interior panels without the retaining clip pulling through the backing, the tapered U-shaped jaws easily insert between the door panel and metal inner door surface. Squeezing the comfortable vinyl handles multiplies your force while gently releasing the clip. Courtesy: The Eastwood Company

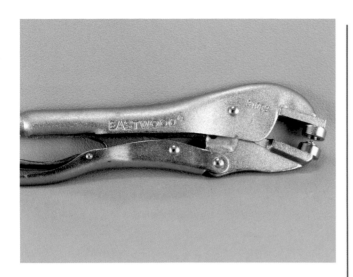

These pliers are designed to create dimples in sheet metal for spot welding, they're adjustable, and they lock into position. Courtesy: The Eastwood Company

Overlap shaft pliers like this three-tool set from Titan increase your leverage so you can work more efficiently with less effort. The handles are also spring loaded, and they feature comfortable soft grips. Courtesy: Genuine Hot Rod Hardware

Multiple slip-joint pliers, also known as water pump pliers, generally have up to eight different adjustment settings with a maximum 4 1/2-inch opening (although larger sizes are not uncommon). Some come with straight or curved jaws, and the most common type are the 10-inch water pump pliers.

Bench vises come in a wide variety of sizes and styles, from the miniature one shown here to huge vises weighing more than 100 pounds. An intermediate 5-inch jaw size vise should serve most garage gearheads well. Author's Collection

Crimper-stripper pliers are used for electrical work, including crimping solderless connectors and stripping insulation from most types of common gauge wire. They also can be used in cutting, holding, and bending wire. They are frequently equipped with sheaving holes that cut common sizes of screws without damaging their threads. Wire strippers are also used for electrical work and feature adjustable stops so the insulation is cut, but the wire is left exposed and undamaged.

More pliers that should have a home in your toolbox include:

• Needle-nose pliers, also known as long-nose pliers, which have a pointed nose for reaching spots that do not have much space. Some are also equipped with side cutters.

• Thin-nose pliers, also known as bent-nose pliers, which have an 80-degree bent angle nose to reach around specific objects.

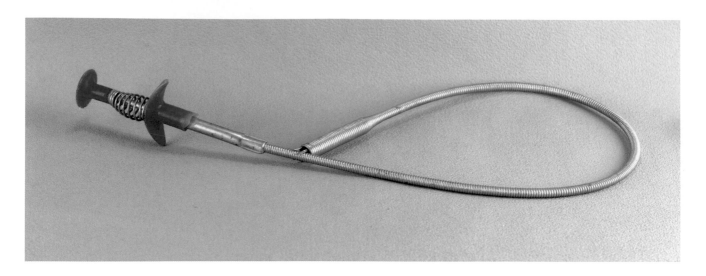

If you've ever dropped a nut, bolt, or other small object into an inaccessible place, then you'll readily appreciate how handy a set of spring-loaded "mechanical fingers" like this can be. Available in various sizes, they're a most worthwhile investment. Author's Collection

• End-cutting nippers, cutting pliers that provide lots of leverage for cutting bolts, wire, and rivets close to or flush with the surface.

• Lineman's or electrician's pliers, which have double-sided cutting edges to cut all types of regular wire and gripping jaws that hold on tightly to any surface or object.

• Fence pliers, which are designed to pull and cut out staples from fencing. These pliers also have two wire cutters and a heavy head for hammering.

• Locking pliers, which are adjustable, vise-locking pliers that can be locked onto an object or workplace, thus freeing up both hands. Usually a one-hand (or sometimes a two-hand) release disengages the locking feature. These are extremely handy since they can be used for a variety of tasks and can do the work of a pipe wrench, adjustable wrench, wire cutter, ratchet, or a clamp. Locking pliers come with metal or cushioned grips and in a variety of sizes and shapes to fit your specific needs.

• Multi-use pliers, which are like the Ginsu knife of pliers. In addition to turning nuts and bolts and holding pipes and other objects, these twist and cut wires, hammer nails and tacks, remove nails and staples, and much more.

• Special-purpose pliers, which are specialty pliers designed for very specific tasks. These include brake-line bending pliers, snap-ring pliers, radiator fin pliers, MIG welder's pliers, welding pliers, and interchangeable-jaw pliers, to name but a few.

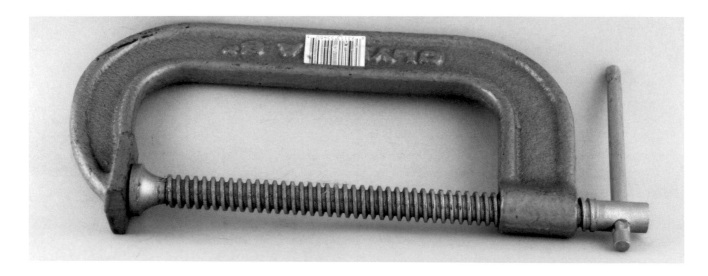

Every garage should have at least one C-clamp for those times when you need to hold a couple of pieces of material together, or to clamp the material onto your workbench to keep it from moving. They're inexpensive and surprisingly handy to have around. Author's Collection

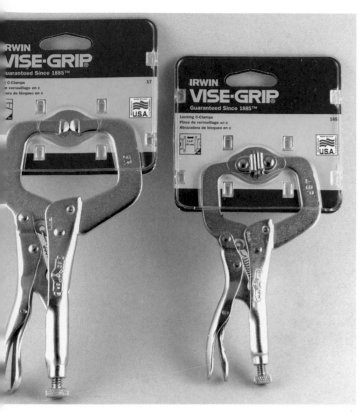

Clamp tip styles vary, so make sure you select the style that is best suited to the project you have at hand. Depending on the project, pointed tips may be the way to go over flat tips. The easy solution is to have an assortment of styles in your tool arsenal, so you're covered regardless of what the project calls for. Courtesy: Irwin Industrial Tools

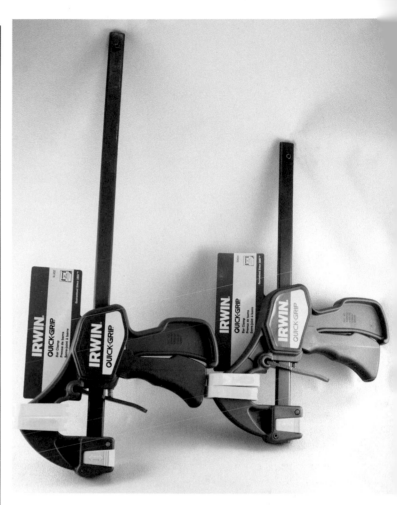

Locking bar clamps like these are available in several lengths, and they're just the ticket when you have larger projects that need clamping. Courtesy: Irwin Industrial Tools

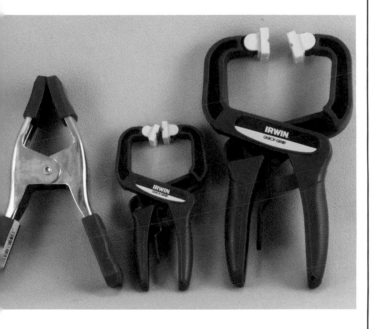

Spring-loaded and quick-grip locking clamps are also handy items to keep in your garage when you need to secure parts or material while working on various projects. Courtesy: Irwin Industrial Tools

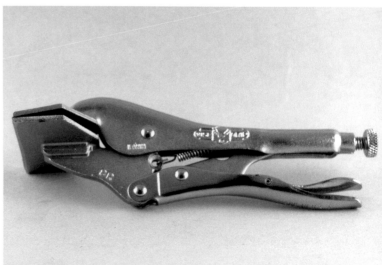

Vise-Grips flat panel holding pliers are great for holding two pieces of sheet metal or other flat material together for drilling, bolting, welding, or other work. Courtesy: Irwin Industrial Tools

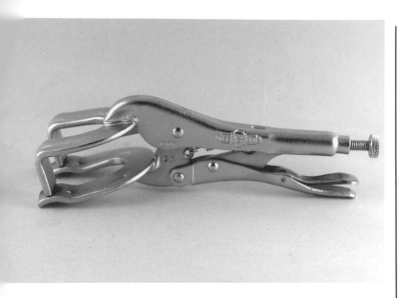

These clamping pliers from Vise-Grips are designed to hold your stock while welding or doing other work on it. The two contact points of the jaws permit clamping several pieces at the same time. Courtesy: Irwin Industrial Tools

These thin, long-nose locking Vise-Grips pliers are excellent for working on parts located in areas that won't permit using standard locking pliers, and they're available with standard or comfort-cushioned grips. Courtesy: Irwin Industrial Tools

More Squeezy-Grabby Thingamajigs

More tools that fit in the squeezing category include:

• Mechanical fingers are spring-loaded, pre-bent "fingers" that extend out of their housing (usually a flexible spring)

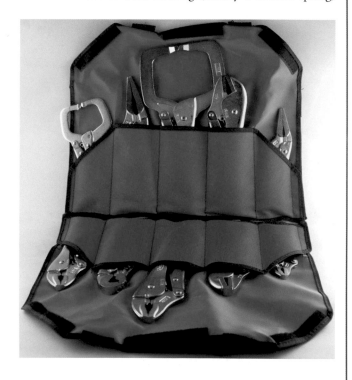

Vise-Grips tools are available in a convenient set like this one that includes a handy and durable tote bag for storage and transport. In addition to including all of the most-used tools, it also saves you money over buying each piece individually. Courtesy: Irwin Industrial Tools

when the end plunger is pushed to grab onto small objects like screws, bolts, or nuts that are otherwise inaccessible by hand. When the plunger is released, the fingers retract, thus grabbing and holding the target object. Mechanical fingers are available in several lengths in both rigid and flexible configurations.

• Tweezers, hemostats, and forceps are available in various sizes and point styles. Tweezers are good for retrieving and holding small parts. Hemostats, also known as surgical vein clamps, are forceps that lock to hold a desired object fast, whereas traditional forceps hold an object while pressure is exerted on the handles, but they do not lock. Various spring-loaded tweezers and clips are also useful for holding or retrieving small objects or parts.

Squeeze Me, Tease Me, Please Me

In addition to the various types of pliers listed above, several other implements can put pressure where you want it.

Clamps are one such device, designed for such tasks as crafting furniture, carpentry, holding molds together, and more. The clamps that most gearheads are interested in make working on various vehicles and machines easier. Among these are the various types of vise-lock pliers and the good old C-clamp. As the name implies, this type of clamp is shaped like the letter C. It has a threaded shaft with a flat-faced gimbal on the end of it that presses the desired object (or objects) against the opposite end of the clamp when tightened.

Vise-Grips are another squeeze-friendly tool, and no garage should be without a decent bench-mounted vise.

There will be times when you need to gently pry something, with gently being the key word. For these special tasks a set of gentle pry tools is the ideal solution. Strong and flexible, they won't mar the surface you're working on. Courtesy: The Eastwood Company

For those times when you need a bit more force to pry things like automotive trim loose, you may want to invest in a pry tool set like this one with comfort-grip handles and stainless blades. Courtesy: The Eastwood Company

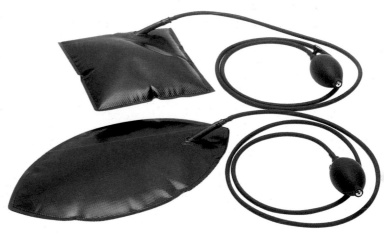

Inflatable dent bags are available in square and football-shaped versions. They're great for popping out dents in bodywork without damaging the paint, and I've used them for other projects as well. Courtesy: The Eastwood Company

Usually made of heavy steel, vises come in various sizes—from very small ones used for delicate work to huge units that weigh upward of 100 pounds. They should always be bolted securely to a stationary surface, such as a heavy workbench.

Vises are marvelous devices for holding items or material steady while you perform such tasks as hammering, straightening, threading, drilling, or filing. Usually equipped with flat steel jaws that are tightened by turning a threaded shaft, some vises can accept different jaw pieces for holding round or cylindrical objects, cushioned jaws for holding the item securely without marring its surface, knurled jaws for digging in to hold slippery items, and more.

Pullers, as you can guess by the name, are used for pulling objects off other objects. For example, removing gears from shafts or pulling a steering wheel off a steering column—and I'm not pulling your leg here! Pullers come in

Tool Tip

A HELPING HAND

There are plenty of times when you wish you had a third hand to make things go a bit easier out in the garage. This is especially true when you're using hog rings to do upholstery work on your vehicle.

The problem is that one hand is busy stretching the fabric, leaving the other hand to fumble with positioning the hog ring in the jaws of the pliers. The solution is to pre-load the hog ring in the jaws and to use a rubber band to keep tension on the pliers handles so the ring won't fall out.

This trick can also be used to hold a nut or bolt in the jaws of pliers when both hands could be better used elsewhere. Not rocket science, just a simple trick that really works.

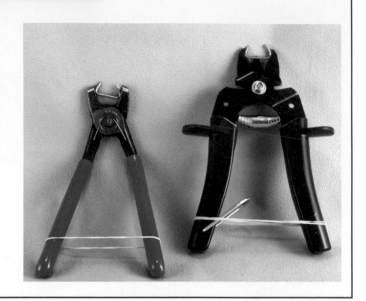

various sizes and configurations for different jobs. Virtually all of them consist of prongs, legs, or jaws that grab the object to be pulled off. The pullers utilize a threaded shaft that exerts pressure on the object's mounting shaft and pulls the object away from and off that shaft.

Presses perform the opposite task of what pullers do. Instead of pulling objects off, they press things (such as bearings or bushings) on or push them out. Presses can run the gamut from small, hand-operated units to large hydraulic presses that can exert tens of thousands of pounds of pressure.

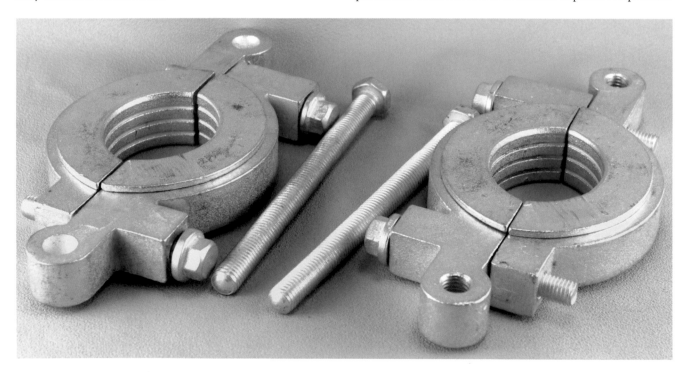

You'll readily appreciate how handy this exhaust pipe tool is if you've ever had to separate a muffler from an exhaust pipe or tail pipe. You merely clamp the round sections around the stem and the pipe, and then turn the long bolts to force the pieces apart. Courtesy: The Eastwood Company

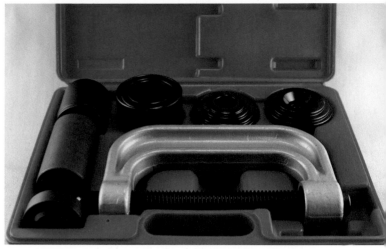

Removing and installing coil springs in a vehicle is all but impossible and dangerous, too, unless you use a quality spring compressor like this one. Insert the tool inside the spring through the shock mounting hole. The "fingers" grab onto the coils of the spring and the threaded rod is turned to compress the spring. Courtesy: The Eastwood Company

This is a multi-use tool kit for servicing ball joints, universal joints, truck brake anchor pins, and for other tasks when press-fitting is required. Courtesy: The Eastwood Company

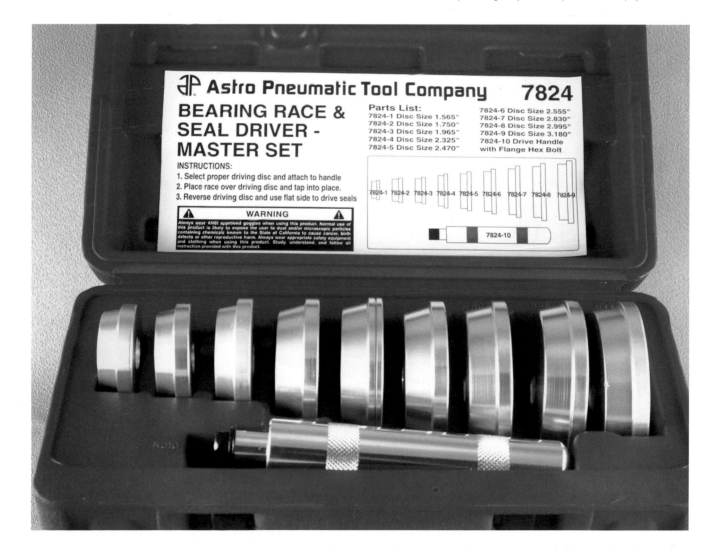

This tool set enables you to install wheel bearing races and seals without damaging the race and axle housings. Courtesy: The Eastwood Company

With this steering wheel remover/lock plate compressor set, you can remove steering wheels on most domestic and imported cars, with or without tilt or telescoping steering columns. The set comes in a molded case and includes four pairs of cap screws, a steering wheel puller, and a lock plate compressor. Courtesy: The Eastwood Company

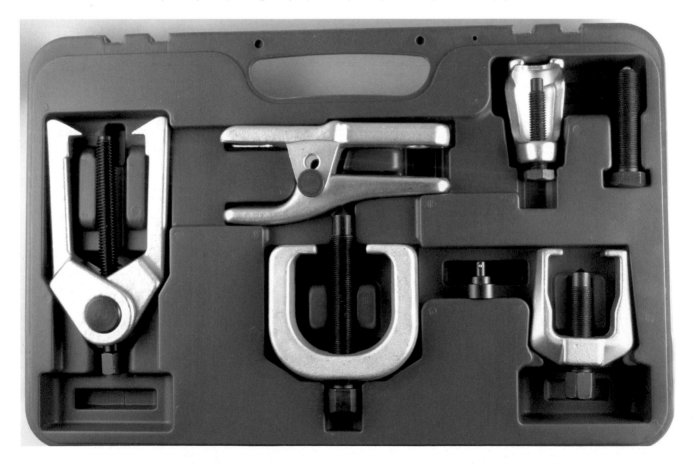

This front-end service kit comes in a heavy plastic case and it has everything you need to remove tie-rod ends, ball joints, and steering linkages without damaging the parts.

Courtesy: The Eastwood Company

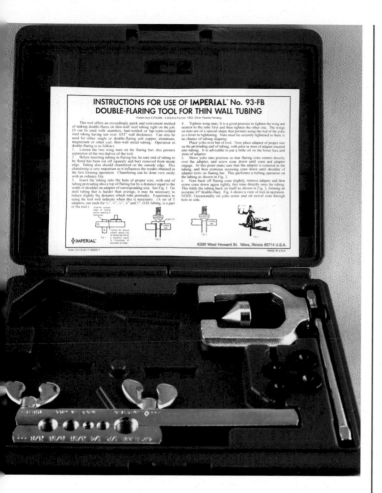

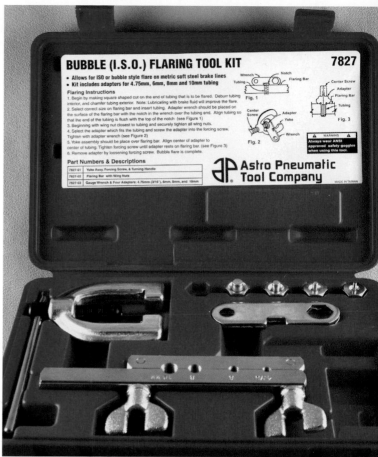

This tool forms SAE single-or double-flares on 3/16-inch, 1/4 inch, 5/16-inch, 3/8-inch, and 1/2-inch outside diameter tubing made of annealed steel, copper, and aluminum.

Courtesy: The Eastwood Company

You can make either ISO or bubble-style flares on metric soft steel brake lines with this tool. The kit also includes adapters for 4.75-millimeter, 6-millimeter, 8-millimeter, and 10-millimeter tubing. Courtesy: The Eastwood Company

Their sizes and configurations vary as greatly as the uses for which they are designed.

Spring compressors come in a variety of types, and the most common for automotive use are coil spring compressors and valve spring compressors. These are used for removing and installing coil springs in the front end of a car or truck, and smaller compressors are used for removing and installing valve springs in engines. Coil spring compressors can be either the internal or external type, with the internal type being a bit easier (and somewhat safer) to use.

Basically, the spring compressor is a threaded rod with hook-shaped brackets at both ends. These brackets are nestled in the coils of the spring at both ends. When the threaded rod is turned, it pulls the upper brackets toward the lower brackets, thus compressing the spring. When sufficiently compressed, the spring can be removed from its mount. When reinstalling the spring, it is compressed with the compressor, inserted into its mount, and expanded gradually by turning the threaded rod in the opposite direction.

Benders—whether they are tubing benders, conduit benders, pipe benders, wire benders, brake line, or fuel line benders—are used, quite simply, for bending material in a uniform way that doesn't cause distortion to the material. These can vary in size and use from handheld units like brake line–bending pliers to electric or pneumatic units that can handle large-diameter or thick materials.

Brakes are also benders, but used primarily for bending sheet metal or other flat metal stock that needs to be formed without distorting the material at the point of the bend. Again, these can range in size from small handheld benders and flanging pliers to large industrial-grade brakes used for sheet metal work.

Shrinkers and stretchers, used for forming curves and flanges in metalworking, either shrink metal to make it conform to compressed shapes or stretch it to conform to an expanded shape. Shrinkers and stretchers can be manually, electrically, or pneumatically powered and vary in size and power.

CHAPTER 6
MAKING THE CUT

Like hammers, cutting implements date all the way back to Stone Age man. The first cutting edge probably happened serendipitously when one rock fell upon another and chipped a piece off. Our early ancestors, upon examining the chipped fragment, found that its edge was sharp, and the idea that it could be used to cut something was born. By repeatedly striking one rock against another to remove more and more fragments, a defined sharp edge was produced and, thus, the first knife came about. It was just what the doctor ordered for skinning and dismembering the prey these early folks had just killed with their hammers.

Several hundred centuries later, mankind entered the Age of Metals. Starting with the Bronze Age, stone cutting implements quickly fell to the wayside when knives were fashioned from bronze. The blades of these early knives were keener and smoother than their stone predecessors and, what's more, could easily be sharpened by drawing them across a stone when the edges became dull.

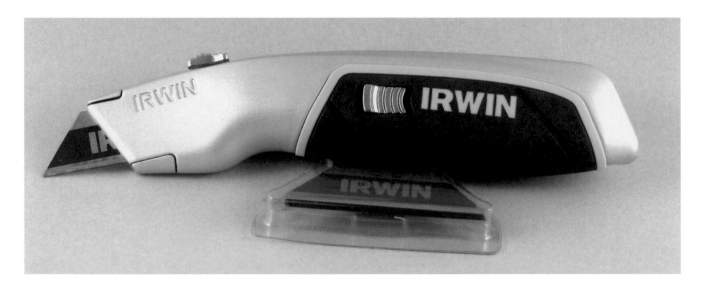

You'll probably use utility knives more than any other cutting implement in the garage, so it pays to have at least one good knife available. This deluxe model from Irwin features an easy-open handle that doesn't require a screwdriver for blade changing. The company's bi-metal blue blades stay sharp for an incredibly long time, too. Courtesy: Irwin Industrial Tools

A panel-separating knife like this one is used for prying welded panels apart after the spot welds are drilled out. The extremely sharp and hefty Sheffield steel blade is tapped with a hammer to separate the panels. Courtesy: The Eastwood Company

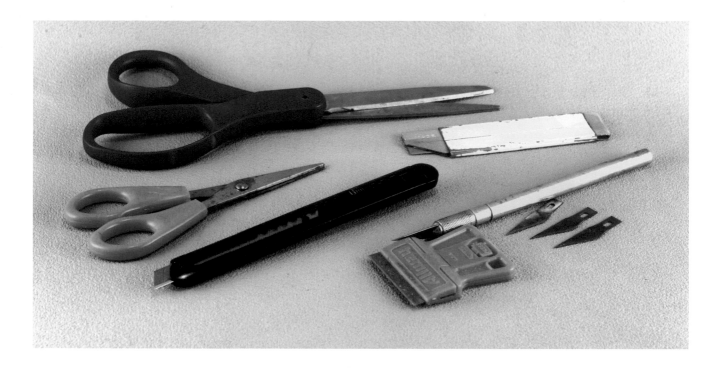

It's a good idea to keep an assortment of cutting tools available in your garage, including scissors, box cutters, hobby knives, razor blades, a pen knife, and perhaps an old steak knife, among other things. You never know when you may need to cut a piece of twine, duct tape, rope, or whatever, so it's best to be prepared. Author's Collection

Time, and progress, marched on, and the Iron Age heralded even greater improvements in implements with cutting edges. Knives, axes, swords, pikes, and other implements that could cut, chop, or impale improved greatly from

A wire stripper is a handy tool for stripping and cutting stranded wire for easy and simple splicing. This tool strips and cuts 12- to 22-gauge single or multiple stranded wire. It automatically adjusts to the wire size, and it has a built-in wire cutter.

Courtesy: The Eastwood Company

this metal, which was much harder than bronze. A bit further on down the timeline, craftsman discovered that by adding carbon to molten iron an even harder metal—steel—could be produced. Steel made even sharper and more durable cutting edges than iron. Could it get better than this?

Well, yes. Modern metallurgy has given us remarkable alloys that can be made into incredibly sharp edges that don't get dull for a long, long time. The end result is that when it comes to tools used in the garage, these ultra-sharp edges help us to do more work with less effort in a shorter time and, to quote Martha Stewart, "that's a good thing."

Living on the Edge

It helps to think of "cutting edge" in a broader context than the simple blade. Indeed, lots of tools have cutting edges. For example, drill bits have cutting edges, as do augers, reamers, scrapers, snips, shears, and scissors, to name but a few. Awls, ice picks, punches, and other implements have points that pierce, which is also a form of cutting. So thinking that cutting edges are found only on blades is limiting, to say the least. Learn to think "outside the box," as it were.

The main purposes for a cutting edge are to separate, trim, smooth, perforate, or puncture material. Many tools serve these purposes and this chapter explores them—starting with drills and other implements that make holes, and I promise, it won't be *boring*!

If you have a lot of twist drill bits to sharpen, you may want to consider investing in an electric sharpener like this Drill Doctor, which does an excellent job. With a price tag of over $100, however, it may not be a practical choice if you don't do a lot of drilling.

Courtesy: The Eastwood Company

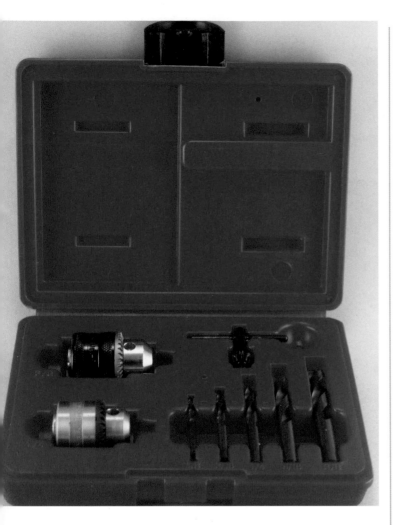

This handy kit converts your 1/4-inch and 3/8-inch ratchet into a right-angle drill. It's ideal for drilling holes where there's not enough room for an electric drill. It's also reversible. The kit includes two Jacobs chucks (one 1/4-inch drive, 1/4-inch capacity, and one 3/8-inch drive, 3/8-inch capacity), a chuck key, and five high-speed steel drill bits (1/8-inch, 3/16-inch, 1/4-inch, 5/16-inch, and 3/8-inch). Instructions are in the kit's durable molded plastic case.

Courtesy: The Eastwood Company

You Know the Drill

Or at least you will by the end of this chapter! Drills have been around for a very long time. In fact, ancient Egyptian doctors routinely used drills to make holes in their patients' skulls to do brain surgery (ouch!). Thankfully, our uses for drills here are confined to inanimate objects, and the materials today's boring implements are made from are literally state-of-the-art.

To drill a satisfactory hole in any material, the correct type of drill bit must be used; it must be also used correctly and it must be sharp.

A set of high-speed steel twist drill bits is usually sufficient for most of the tasks you'll be performing in your garage. However, for more sophisticated jobs/material, others bits will be required—perhaps larger bits or those designed for a specific material/purpose.

Quality drill bits can be expensive, so take care of them. Keep them in a case or box if possible, rather than allowing them to roll around loose in a toolbox where the cutting edges may be damaged. Another reason for keeping them in a case or special box called a drill index is that you won't have to go hunting for the appropriate bit when the need arises. It will be right there in the index when you need it (provided, of course, you put it back when you're done using it).

Below are some of the various drill bits available.

Twist Bits

Usually referred to as twist drills, these are the most common drilling tools used with either a corded or cordless electric drill. The front edges cut the material, and the spirals along the length remove the debris from the hole and tend to keep the bit straight. They can be used on wood, metal, plastics, fiberglass, and similar materials.

Most twist bits are made from either:

• High-speed steel (HSS). These bits are suitable for drilling most types of material because the steel stands up to high temperatures without dulling or losing its cutting edge.

• Carbon steel. These bits are specially ground for drilling wood and should not be used for drilling metals since they tend to be more brittle and less flexible than HSS bits.

Twist drills are usually available in 1/32- to 1/2-inch (approximately 0.8–12 mm) sizes. Designed for drilling relatively small holes, the smallest of these bits can be thin and brittle, so you should apply only light pressure when drilling with them.

Twist bits are also available coated with titanium nitride (TiN), and these are easily identified by the gold-like color. They're often simply called titanium bits. This coating increases the hardness of the bit and adds a self-lubricating property. The coating is only really effective when metal is being drilled, since it has little effect when drilling other materials.

Titanium nitride bits cannot be sharpened without destroying the coating (although if the drill needs sharpening, the coating will probably have already been destroyed). Forming the correct angle at the tip is important for efficient cutting, and for this reason you should always use a sharpening jig when sharpening these bits.

Screwdriver Bit Drills

Designed to fit in rechargeable screwdrivers, these bits have a hexagonal shank. They are ideal for drilling pilot holes, but are limited by the power and speed of the screwdriver motor.

Burrs

Generally made of carbide, burrs are used for accurate removal of metal when shaping, leveling, porting, engraving, or detailing cast iron, steel, and other metals. Burrs come in various shapes including cylindrical, ball, cylindrical radius end, tree-shaped radius end, and flat end. Burrs are usually used with high-speed handheld die grinders, either electric or pneumatic.

Diamond burrs are more expensive, but they cut faster than carbide burrs and generally last longer, making their extra cost worthwhile if you do a lot of work that requires their use.

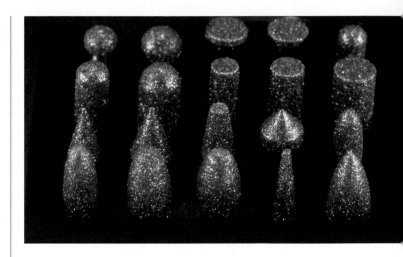

Burrs impregnated with diamond dust like these last much longer than standard carbide burrs, even though they're a bit more expensive. If you do a lot of work requiring burrs, the added expense will pay off in the long run. Courtesy: The Eastwood Company

Drill Presses

Indispensible for drilling straight, perpendicular, precise holes, drill presses are relatively inexpensive and widely available at Sears, Lowe's, Home Depot, or any home improvement store. They are available in single- and multi-speed units and come designed to either sit on a benchtop in your garage or stand independently on the floor. No garage shop should be without a drill press.

Reamers

Reamers are tools used to enlarge and true holes. A reamer consists of three parts: the body, the shank, and the blades. The shank has a square tang to allow the reamer to be held with a wrench for turning. The main purpose of the body is to support the blades.

The blades of a reamer are made of steel that is hardened to such an extent that they are brittle. Because of this, it is extremely important to be careful when using and storing the reamer to prevent the blades from chipping.

When reaming a hole, turn the reamer in the cutting direction only. This is very important, since turning it in the opposite direction may cause the blades to chip or dull prematurely. Be sure to use steady, even pressure as you turn the reamer to prevent "chatter," which may produce scores or other undesirable marks on the hole.

When not in use, be sure to store the reamer in an oiled cloth to prevent blade rusting and to protect the blades from damage. Keeping the reamer in a protective case is the best option.

Primarily used to enlarge holes to precise sizes by gradually removing small amounts of material as they are turned, some reamers are fixed-diameter while others are adjustable.

A set of carbide burrs is useful for jobs like porting intake manifolds and other chores where removing metal with precise control is required. Courtesy: The Eastwood Company

A pair of reamers that both feature hardened steel blades. They're used for enlarging and smoothing holes. Courtesy: The Eastwood Company

Adjustable reamers can be adjusted by loosening one nut and tightening the other to change the diameter of the cutting edges on the blades or splines.

Punches

Punches come in a variety of sizes and types but, ultimately, their purpose is to put holes or indentations in metal.

The most common punch found in the garage is the center punch. With a hardened sharp point, the center punch

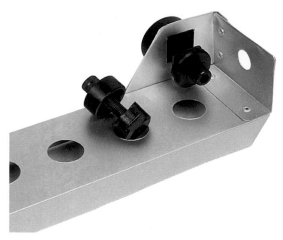

Sheet metal hole punches are available in assorted sizes. They're ideal for cutting clean, concentric holes in sheet metal without distorting the surface. Courtesy: The Eastwood Company

is struck with a hammer to create a dimple, which serves as the center for a hole to be drilled, hence its name.

Other punches include stamping punches, which are frequently used in metalworking to stamp holes of predetermined sizes and shapes in sheet metal. Some stamping punches are lever operated with a platen on which the sheet metal rests. A stamping die lowers down onto it to pierce the metal until it mates with the receiving die underneath. Other punches rely on a drilled pilot hole through which a cutting die with threaded shaft is inserted. On the opposite side of the metal, a receiving die is tightened on the shaft with a wrench until the hole is cleanly punched through.

Awls

Similar to ice picks, awls are used for piercing materials, but they usually have rugged handles attached to hardened shafts and points to withstand being struck by a hammer. Similar in function to center punches, awls are generally used when deep piercing of a material is desired.

A center punch has a tip of hardened steel. It is useful for punching a hole in sheet metal or creating a dimple for a drill starting point. Courtesy: Stanley Tools

An awl is an excellent tool for piercing soft materials and for scratching. Courtesy: Craftsman Tools

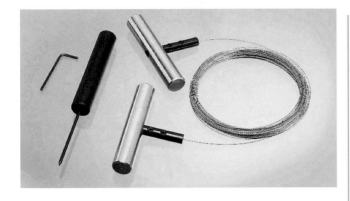

This windshield removal kit consists of a roll of cutting wire, two steel handles for pulling the wire, and a hardened-tip awl for making a starting hole in the windshield gasket.

Courtesy: The Eastwood Company

Cutting Wire

Cutting wire is used primarily for cutting through the gasket material or mounting adhesive that holds windshields in place. Cutting wire is usually braided and has sharp edges that cut through the rubber, silicon, or butyl tape when run back and forth using a sawing motion. An awl is usually used to create a starting hole through which the cutting wire is inserted to start the process.

Hacksaws

Hacksaws have a narrow blade stretched in a steel frame for cutting metal. These blades are rated in the number of teeth per inch; the more teeth per inch, the finer the cut will be. Generally, the blade of a hacksaw is designed for cutting when

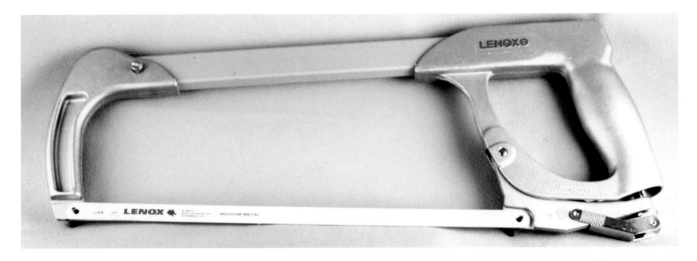

This is a high-tension frame hacksaw from Lenox that features a comfortable grip. It will easily accommodate gloved hands and storage for up to five 12-inch blades in the handle.

Courtesy: Lenox/American Saw & Mfg. Co.

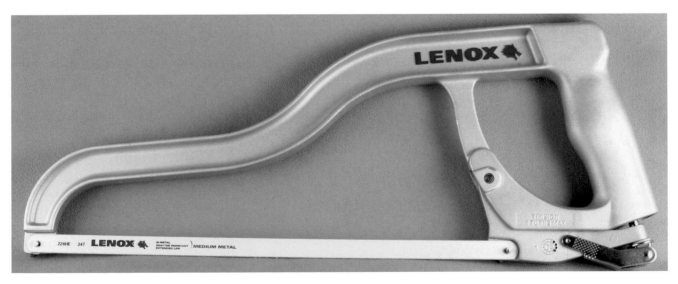

Designed to fit into tight spots, the low-profile tip of this saw easily handles close-quarter cuts. Courtesy: Lenox/American Saw & Mfg. Co.

it is pushed. Therefore, more force is used when pushing the hacksaw than when pulling backward during the return stroke. Cutting metal using a hacksaw is easier and safer when the material being cut is fixed in a vise.

Reciprocating Saws

Reciprocating saws are extremely useful for a variety of automotive restoration jobs when fitted with a metal-cutting blade. They are extremely portable and available in corded, battery-powered, and air-powered models. Common brands include Milwaukee Sawzall (the original) and Porter Cable. Reciprocating saws generally do the work of a hacksaw much faster. See Chapter 13 for more details.

Utility Knives

As the name implies, utility knives are used for many tasks in the garage. While there are several variations, there are two basic types of utility knives: the fixed-blade type and the retractable-blade type.

Fixed-blade utility knives are less expensive due to the fact that they have no moving parts; in effect, they are made up of a replaceable blade sandwiched between two handle halves that are held together with a screw.

Retractable-blade utility knives have a multiposition locking lever usually located at the top of the handle that permits the blade to be extended and locked in place in various positions. For obvious reasons, the ability to retract the blade completely when it is not in use is more desirable and safer than using a fixed-blade knife. The added mechanism for moving and locking

the blade does add to the price, yet you don't have to spend a great deal of money for even the most sophisticated utility knife.

Most utility knives, both fixed- and retractable-blade varieties, provide space within the handle for storing extra blades. Since utility knife blades are double-ended, they can be reversed to use the opposite end when the initial end becomes dull.

Disposable plastic utility knives with segmented snap-off blades are also available, although they are not as rugged or as reliable as the traditional metal-handled utility knives.

Scrapers

Generally speaking, scrapers are made to remove unwanted material by scraping across the surface. Scrapers come in various shapes and sizes, and they are designed for different tasks. For example, a long-handled scraper that uses a single-edge razor blade could be used for reaching inaccessible areas for removing paint or inspection labels; other scrapers may be designed and used for removing gasket material or other such debris-removal tasks.

Box Cutters

Box cutters are primarily intended for cutting open and/or cutting apart corrugated cartons or cardboard boxes. Literally nothing more than a razor blade holder with a sliding metal cover that doubles as a handle, box cutters are inexpensive, albeit crude, cutting devices that do their job well with a minimum of technology or glamour. Box cutters are like the sharks of the garage cutting tool genre: simple, straight forward, and efficient at what they do.

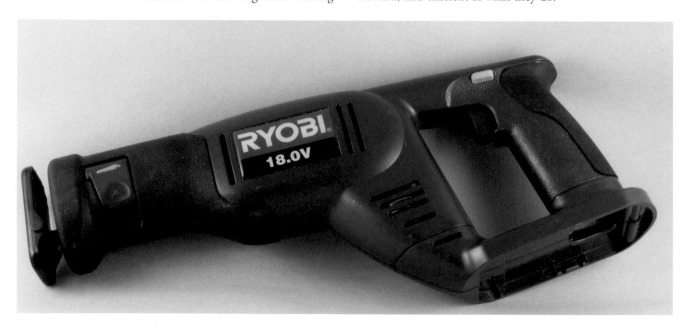

This battery-powered reciprocal saw is used for heavier cutting jobs than the saber saw can handle. Courtesy: Ryobi

Nibblers

Hand nibblers use compound leverage to cut metal easily, accurately, and with less distortion than snips or shears. Nibblers use hardened steel blades and can usually start in the middle of a sheet metal panel using a small (1/4-inch) starting hole.

Pneumatic nibblers are also available for heavier-duty sheet metal cutting tasks, and nibbler attachments are available for turning your electric drill into a power sheet metal cutter. Unless you intend to do a lot of work with sheet metal, a hand nibbler will suffice for most tasks.

Panel Knives

Also more accurately known as panel separating knives, these hefty-bladed tools are used to separate panels with spot-welds that have already been drilled out. The cutting edge of the knife blade is inserted between the two panels and the heel of the blade is struck with a hammer to force the blade deeper between the panels until they separate. The blades of panel knives are usually made of hardened Sheffield steel for durability.

Snips

Snips are metal-cutting tools that have two handles, which intersect via a pivot point with two opposing blades at the cutting end. Snips are generally spring loaded so they stay in the open position until the handles are squeezed together to cut. Snips

A good set of scrapers like these with stainless-steel blades are a boon for removing gasket material, cleaning up the mounting surfaces on heads and manifolds, and lots of other garage chores. Courtesy: The Eastwood Company

Below: This is a nibbler and it's used for cutting sheet metal, especially where tight curves or intricate shapes make it impractical to use snips. While this is a manual nibbler, they are also available in electric and pneumatic versions as well. Courtesy: The Eastwood Company

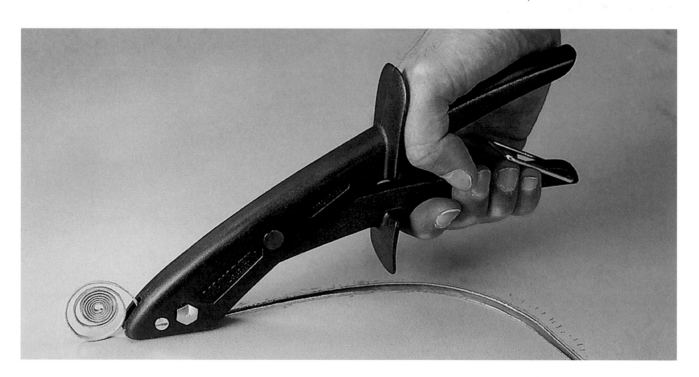

Tinner snips are used for cutting light sheet metal in a straight line. There are a wide variety of other snip styles for different tasks as well. Courtesy: Irwin Industrial Tools

come in a variety of styles for various tasks, among which are the following:

• Aviation snips owe their origin to the aviation industry, where they were developed for cutting sheet aluminum in the production of aircraft. Aviation snips use compound leverage and hardened blades to cut sheet metal up to 24-gauge (26-gauge stainless steel). Aviation snips are available in configurations for left cuts, right cuts, and straight cuts. Better aviation snips have cushioned handles for more comfortable operation.

• Bulldog snips, which are designed to notch and trim metal work, are also spring loaded and usually feature cushioned handles.

• Offset snips are designed to make cutting straight lines easy, but they can also cut angles and curves efficiently.

• Utility snips are general-purpose snips with compound cutting leverage, spring-loaded handles, and cushioned grips.

• Tinner snips feature precision-ground edges on the blades to ensure a tight grip on each cut for superior cutting quality.

Cut-Off Machines

Though these tools are covered in more depth in other chapters, pneumatic cut-off tools with carbide blades (see Chapter 12) and electric chop saws (see Chapter 17) are also staples of the well-equipped garage.

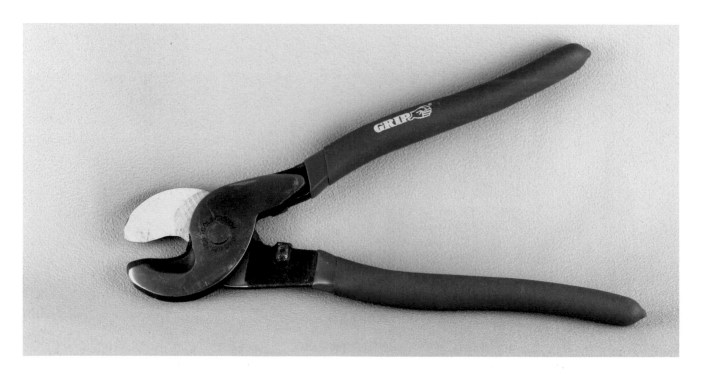

Heavy-duty cable cutters like these are just what you'll need to cut thick stock like battery cables and multi-cable harnesses. Courtesy: The Eastwood Company

A chop saw like this one uses a carbide blade. It's used for cutting thick metal stock, such as steel tubing and solid plate. Courtesy: Ryobi

Power Saws

These, too, are covered in more depth in their appropriate chapters, but certainly pneumatic reciprocating saws (see Chapter 12) and both corded and cordless-rechargeable reciprocating and saber saws (see Chapter 17) have myriad uses in the garage, too.

Shears

Shears can best be described as large, heavy-duty scissors for cutting sheet metal. Shears come in varying sizes and have hardened blades. Like scissors, they are operated using the fingers and thumb to open and close the opposing blades as you work your way through the length of the cut.

Hobby Knives

Similar in size and heft to a surgical scalpel, hobby knives use replaceable blades that are available in a variety of shapes and are held in place by a threaded collar that tightens down on a slotted mandrel into which the blade is inserted. The handles are generally thin, straight, and made of aluminum. The blades are extremely sharp, and these knives are especially good for doing delicate trim work, such as cutting stencils and other tasks where sharpness and precision are the rule of the day.

Scissors

Every well-equipped garage should have at least one decent pair of scissors for general cutting of tape, twine, string, and other such materials that may be required in the course of working on projects. A pair of scissors with long stainless-steel blades and molded plastic grips will serve nicely for most tasks.

Miscellaneous Cutters

It never hurts to have some miscellaneous cutting implements in the garage if you need to cut something out of the ordinary. For example, you might find it useful to keep a nail clipper around if you break or tear a fingernail. An old pen knife comes in handy for cutting rope or twine that may be too hefty for scissors, and a retired steak knife and/or a linoleum knife may be useful for stabbing and slicing material like jute padding if you're installing carpeting in a vehicle. In short, if it cuts, it may have a use for something you'll be doing in the garage at some point, even though it may not be immediately evident right now. Like they say in the Boy Scouts, "be prepared!"

CHAPTER 7
GET TIGHT, GET LOOSE

The vast majority of mechanical assemblies consist of various components. The components are attached to each other by fasteners that cause the pieces to press against each other hard. Likewise, the majority of these fasteners are threaded items such as nuts, bolts, and screws. Concurrently, with the way these fasteners were invented and have evolved, tools for tightening and loosening them have also been developed and have evolved on a more-or-less parallel path.

The most common fasteners used in mechanical assemblies are bolts, nuts, and screws. Bolts usually (but not always) have hexagonal heads, as do nuts. Screws usually (again, but not always) have round heads and a slot or other recess to accommodate the appropriate driver tool.

Nuts and bolts are most often tightened and loosened using wrenches, sockets, and nut drivers; likewise, screws are driven tight or loosened using screwdrivers. There are myriad varieties of these tools and each have uses at which they excel. Let's explore these tools and what they're used for.

Wrenches

Wrenches—the English call them spanners—are hand tools made for tightening or loosening bolts, nuts, or anything that needs to turn. Solymon Merrick patented the first wrench in 1835.

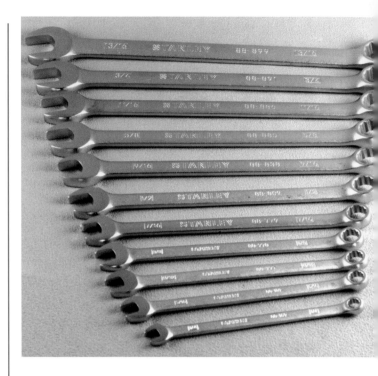

A set of high-quality combination wrenches, both SAE and metric, is a mandatory staple of any well-equipped garage. Courtesy: Stanley Tools

Irwin's automatic adjusting wrench is great for jobs when you only have one hand free to use the tool. Courtesy: Irwin Industrial Tools

A set of stubby GearWrenches like this one will serve you well for jobs where a full-size GearWrench is too big to do the job. Courtesy: The Eastwood Company

An interactive, open-end wrench set like this one is very useful for applications where you only have about 30 degrees of swing to rotate a fastener. Courtesy: The Eastwood Company

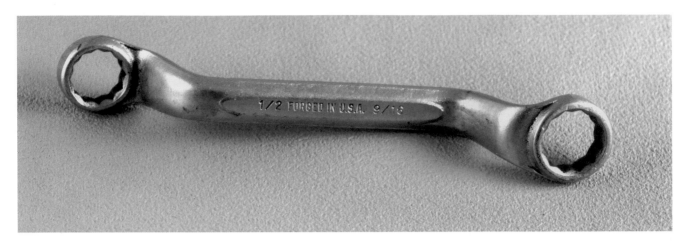

Offset box wrenches like this one are useful for reaching nuts and bolts in inaccessible locations. This particular wrench was my dad's, and it had plenty of miles on it even before I was born!
Author's Collection

With the advent of the Machine Age and the invention of threaded fasteners, among which bolts were the earliest, it became evident that a tool would be required to tighten and loosen these new fasteners; hence, the wrench was invented. Originally a metal handle with a fixed-span jaw at one end, wrenches were made to fit specific-sized bolts. Since there was no standardization of sizes among the foundries producing threaded fasteners during those early days, you would need quite an assortment of single-size wrenches to accommodate the various bolts you might encounter.

The idea of a wrench with jaws that could be expanded or contracted to fit assorted size bolt heads was attractive, and the pipe wrench or "monkey wrench" was invented by Charles Moncky around 1858. This was really a leap in tool development since one tool now could do the job of many on various-sized fasteners.

As bolt sizes finally became standardized, a small complement of single-size wrenches was all that was needed to service all of the common-sized bolts in use. Evolution of the single-size wrenches continued further, outfitting the opposite of the wrench with a "box" end that completely encircled the head of the bolt for a better grip and to enable more torque to be used for tightening. This was the birth of the combination wrench.

A bit further down the line, someone took the idea of the box wrench a bit further by elongating it into a cylinder with a square-drive hole at the opposite end, and the socket was invented. A drive bar with a mating square end could then be used to twist the socket, enabling even greater torque to be applied to the bolt.

Continuing this evolution, someone came up with the idea of creating a handle with a square-drive post that utilized a ratchet-and-pawl mechanism to drive a socket with a back-and-forth motion. This innovation eliminated the need to

Line wrenches like these are excellent for use on brake and fuel line fittings. Courtesy: NAPA

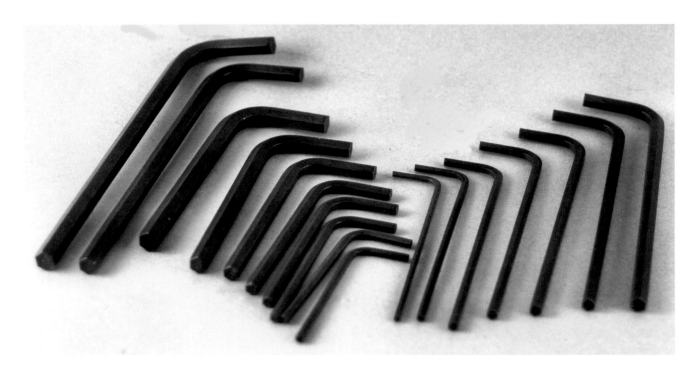

Allen wrenches are available in both SAE and metric configurations, and they are another essential component of a well-equipped garage. Author's Collection

remove the drive head and reinsert it to advance the turning of the fastener. The ratchet was now on the scene. But wait—it gets better still!

Yet another bright person looked at the ratchet and said, "Hmm—that could really be useful if you could incorporate it into a box wrench." And, lo and behold, Robert Owen Jr. (1881–1956) invented the ratchet wrench and received a U.S. patent (number 1,072,980) on September 9, 1913. More innovations continue to produce tools that are more efficient and comfortable to use for tightening and loosening fasteners. So now that you have a little background on wrenches, let's explore the various types that you'll be using in your garage.

Open-Ended Wrench

The open-ended wrench is the most common type of wrench used for mechanical work, and it usually has a single or double end. The head has its jaws offset by about 15 degrees from the run of the shaft, so the spanner can be turned over to engage different flats of a nut when working in confined spaces. A variation

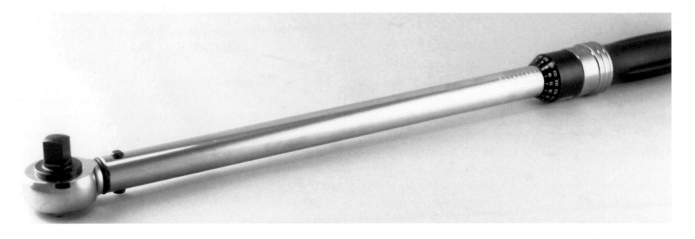

A quality torque wrench is an absolute must when rebuilding an engine or for other projects where tightening the fasteners to a precise torque is mandatory. Torque wrenches are available in 1/4-inch, 3/8-inch, and 1/2-inch drive sizes, and the click type (shown above) is the most accurate. Courtesy: The Eastwood Company

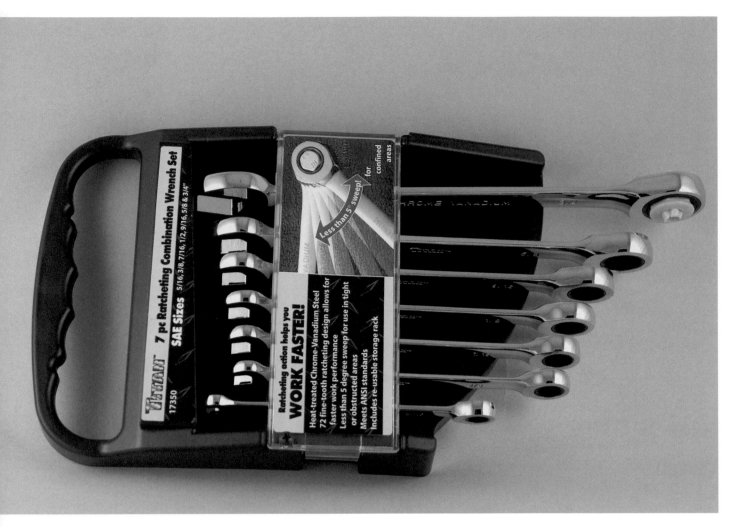

Also available in SAE sizes, these ratchet combination wrenches are among the most useful tools you can have in your garage. You'll be surprised at how often you reach for them.

Courtesy: Genuine Hot Rod Hardware

of the straight open-ended wrench has one head set at anything up to 90 degrees to the shaft, which may have a slight curve. These wrenches are designed for working in confined places.

Box Wrench

As the name implies, the box wrench (called a ring spanner in England) usually has a completely enclosed head, and may have 6 or 12 flats. A 12-flat box wrench engages the corners of the nut and can be used on both hexagonal- and square-headed bolts. A 6-flat box wrench is normally shaped to fit against all 6 sides of hexagonal nuts, and it provides a very tight fit that permits considerable force to be applied. Having 12 flats is more desirable since it permits you to get a "bite" on the bolt in more confined work spaces than would be required for a 6-point wrench.

Box wrenches are stronger than open-ended wrenches, but they need access to fit over the nut, which is not required by open-ended wrenches.

Offset Box Wrench

Among the most useful box wrenches are those with offset heads, which permit using them with bolts and nuts in awkward or hard-to-access places. They provide room for your hand to move without hitting the work piece.

Line or Split Box Wrench

The line wrench, also called a split box wrench, is a hybrid that has a section of the box removed so the 6- or 12-point jaws can be located like an open-ended wrench. These are usually used when working on fuel or brake line fittings when it is necessary to pass over the line itself, hence the name.

Adjustable Wrenches

The obvious advantage of an adjustable wrench is that it can work on a whole range of nut sizes within the capacity of its jaws. The most common version has jaws set at an angle of 15 degrees to the shaft, but other angles are also available. I'm not

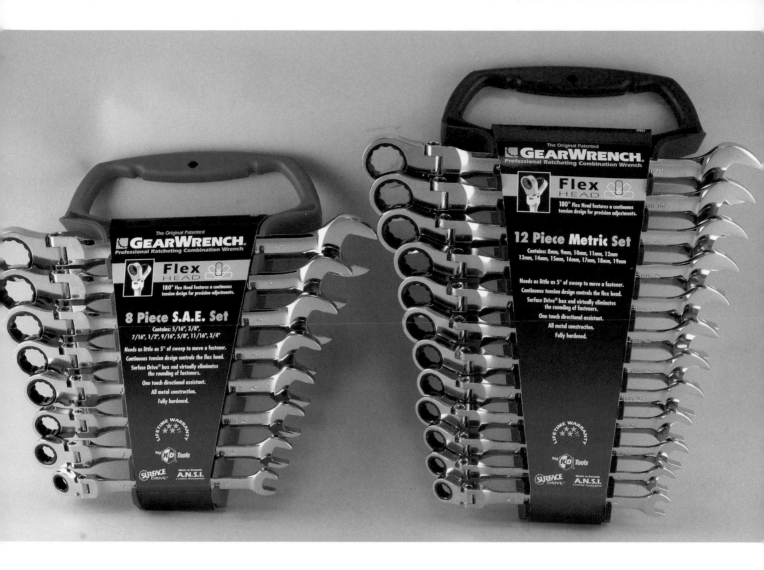

The GearWrench was the original ratcheting combination wrench, and its manufacturer made a good thing even better when it introduced the new Flex-Head GearWrenches in both SAE and metric sets. Courtesy: NAPA

a big fan of using adjustable wrenches, and I opt for open-end or box wrenches whenever I have a choice. There are, however, those times when an adjustable wrench is the tool of choice.

When using an adjustable wrench, it is important to adjust the jaws so that they have a good fit on the nut. The most common adjustable wrenches use a worm screw located close to the opening jaw, which has a rack engaged with the screw. This setup makes it easy to adjust with the finger and thumb of the hand holding the wrench. A variation of the adjustable wrench rarely used in automotive work is the pipe (or monkey) wrench.

Allen Wrenches

Allen wrenches—also known as allen keys or hex keys—are simple hexagonal-shaped rods with right-angle bends. They are designed to fit into the head of a bolt that has a matching hexagonal-shaped recess in the head. They are often found where space clearance is limited, such as for securing exhaust headers to an engine. Hexagonal wrenches are also available with T-shaped handles, which provide rapid spinning capability.

Torque Wrenches

Torque wrenches are used to tighten nuts and bolts to a specific torque. The older type of torque wrenches utilized a pointer attached to the turning point. The pointer was suspended over a scale mounted in front of the handle; as the handle was turned to tighten the nut/bolt, the arm was deflected and the pointer moved across the scale indicating the torque being applied.

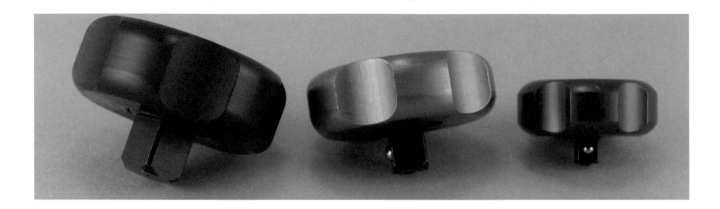

These Ratchet Buddies are very useful for starting a bolt by hand and then attaching a ratchet to finish the job without having to remove the Buddy in the process. Courtesy: The Eastwood Company

While this was better than just guessing at the torque, these older torque wrenches were nowhere near as accurate as today's "click" torque wrenches. With these, you simply dial up the desired torque and keep tightening the nut or bolt until the wrench makes a clicking sound, indicating the desired torque has been reached. More accurate still are the latest digital-electronic torque wrenches. These are basically the click type with electronic read-outs. Torque wrenches are normally made to work with sockets.

Ratchet Wrenches

Ratchet wrenches are box wrenches that have a ratcheting mechanism built into them. The mechanism permits you to turn a nut or bolt without removing the wrench head to reposition it. To change direction, you simply turn the wrench over.

Most ratchet wrenches have an open end at the opposite side to make them more versatile, and some ratchet wrenches have flexible heads that permit accessing nuts or bolts in hard-to-reach places. Stubby versions are also available for working in tight quarters.

Sockets

A socket is a cylinder with either 6 or 12 contact points at one end and a square hole at the opposite end designed to lock into various types of handles, the most common of which is the reversible ratchet. Sockets are available in sets, offering a range of head sizes, extension drive bars, and handles. The most common socket drive sizes are 1/4, 3/8, and 1/2 inch, with larger sizes available for heavy-duty applications, such as working on trucks and construction equipment. Sockets are generally required when torque wrenches are used to tighten nuts and bolts. Aside from wrenches, sockets are probably the most used tools in garage work.

Screwdrivers

It is unconscionable to think of a garage without at least a modest complement of screwdrivers, since these are indispensable tools.

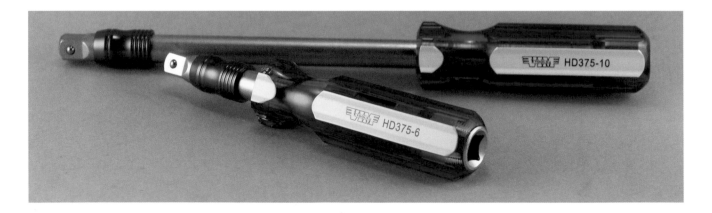

These locking hand-drive extensions with handles can be used by their handgrips. They allow you to start threads by hand, and then tighten them with a ratchet or air tool without even removing your socket from the fastener—they're great time and work savers. Courtesy: The Eastwood Company

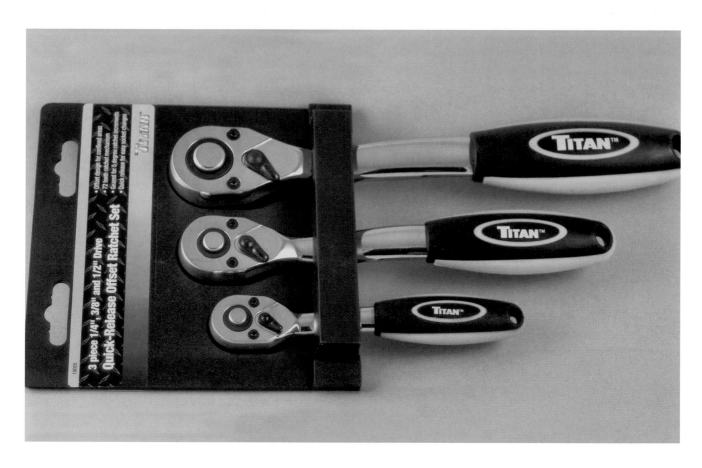

This Titan three-ratchet set includes 1/4-inch, 3/8-inch, and 1/2-inch drive ratchets with comfortable padded grips. Direction reversal is as simple as flicking the top-mounted lever with your thumb. Courtesy: Genuine Hot Rod Hardware

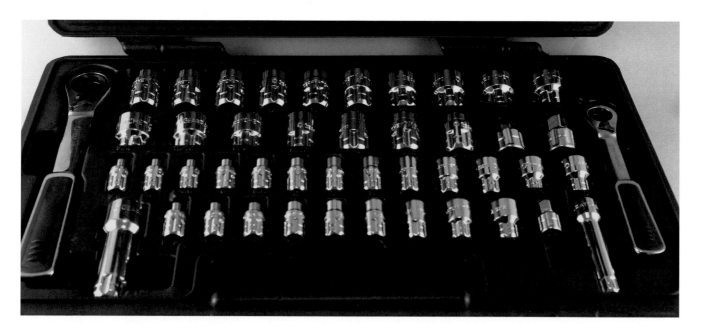

GearDriver also put a new spin on the traditional ratchet/socket arrangement by introducing its GearRatchets in both 3/8-inch and 1/4-inch drive with pass-through extensions. This 46-piece set includes both SAE and metric Vortex sockets. Courtesy: NAPA

A set of quality sockets and at least one ratchet with a few extension bars are absolute essentials in any garage. These sockets have the sizes laser-etched into them for easy visibility. Courtesy: Craftsman Tools

The flat-bladed bit for the carpenter's brace was invented in 1744, and it was the precursor to the first simple screwdriver. Handheld screwdrivers first appeared after 1800. They have remained basically unchanged, except for improvements in the blade, tip shapes, and the comfort and materials of the handles.

Types of Screwdrivers

Flat-bladed screwdrivers are used for working with slot-head screws and are available in sizes from very small (jeweler's screwdrivers) to very large with blades 1/2-inch wide or more.

Keeping your sockets organized will increase your productivity in the garage, as you'll spend less time looking for the size you need. A rack like this one makes organizing them easy.

Courtesy: The Eastwood Company

Purchasing a complete set of sockets makes more economic sense in the long run than purchasing them one piece-at-a-time. This high-quality set from Husky features a black chrome finish and laser-etched sizes and both shallow and deep sockets as well as combination wrenches in both SAE and metric sizes. Courtesy: Husky Tools

Phillips screwdrivers are used for working with cross-head (known as Phillips) screws that have an cross-shaped slot. Phillips screwdrivers were originally designed in the 1930s for use with mechanical screwing machines, intentionally made so the driver would ride out under strain to prevent over-tightening.

Pozidriv screwdrivers are similar to Phillips, but they have better resistance to slipping out of the head of the screw being turned.

Hexagonal or Allen drivers are used with screw heads that have hexagonal holes.

Robertson drivers are used with fasteners that have a square hole in the head and are usually driven by a special power-tool bit or screwdriver (used for decking and other home construction, they are rarely, if ever, used for automotive or mechanical work).

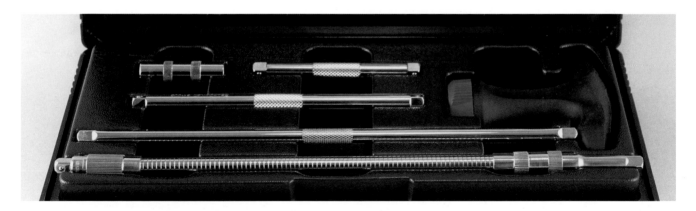

Another option for driving your 3/8-inch sockets is this six-piece GearDriver T-handle driver set that features a fine-tooth ratcheting mechanism and a variety of interchangeable shafts. Courtesy: NAPA

You can tell by looking at the thickness of these deep metric sockets that they are designed for use with an air ratchet or pneumatic impact wrench. When purchasing, go with a name brand like these Stanley sockets because they carry a lifetime guarantee. Courtesy: Stanley Tools

What do you do when the head of a bolt's points are rounded so badly that a traditional socket just spins helplessly around it? You use one of the damaged hardware removers in this 13-piece twist-socket set and a 3/8-inch drive ratchet to get the offending fastener extracted. Courtesy: The Eastwood Company

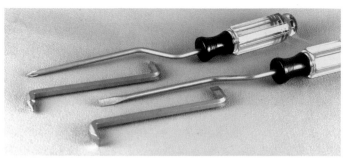

Offset screwdrivers in both flat blade and Phillips tips can help you get at fasteners that traditional straight-blade tools can't reach. Courtesy: Craftsman Tools

Torx drivers are used with fasteners that have a splined head socket, common on late-model cars for such applications as headlight adjustments.

Tamper-proof torx are similar to torx, but the drive socket has a projection the center to prevent a standard torx driver being inserted.

Offset drivers can be flat-bladed or Phillips, and they feature an offset for accessing screws in hard-to-reach places.

Right-angle screwdrivers have heads bent 90 degrees to the shaft for reaching fasteners where traditional straight-shaft flat-blade or Phillips screwdrivers don't have sufficient clearance to work.

Other Noteworthy Tools

In addition to the various types of sockets and ratchets and wrenches and screwdrivers, there are some other tools that you'll probably want to include in your garage arsenal. They include the following:

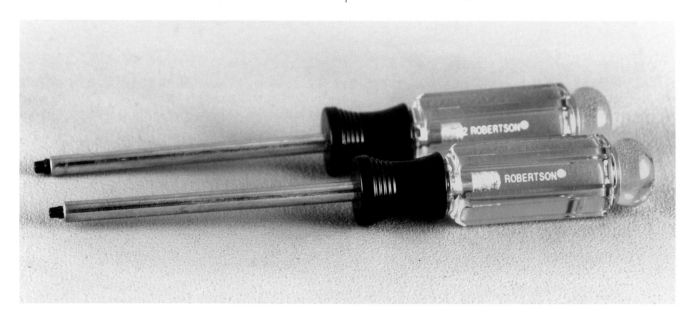

Used mostly for carpentry projects such as driving deck screws, Robertson drivers like these are seldom used for mechanical and automotive fastening, although you may run into some of these square-hole fasteners with some obscure foreign makes. Courtesy: Craftsman Tools

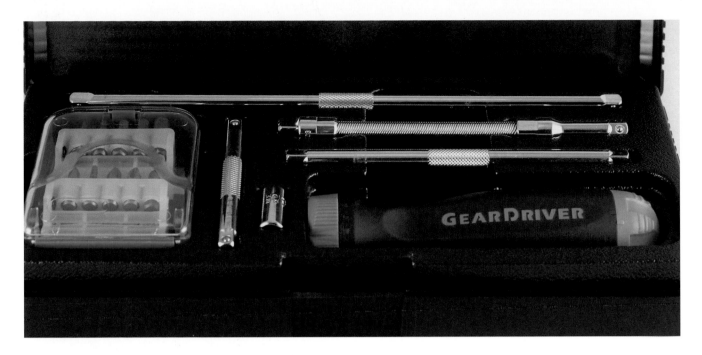

The advantage of ratcheting screwdrivers is that you don't have to release the handle to progressively drive the screw in or out. This 26-piece set from GearDriver includes a total of 20 various bits. Courtesy: NAPA

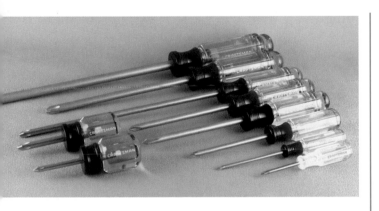

Philips screwdrivers come in three point sizes, with No. 1 being the smallest and No. 3 the largest. You get all three sizes in varied handle lengths with this Craftsman set. Courtesy: Craftsman Tools

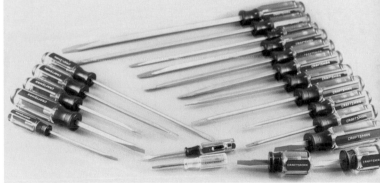

There's no substitute for a good screwdriver, and you can't go wrong if you purchase quality tools like these Craftsman screwdrivers. Like all Craftsman tools, they are unconditionally guaranteed for life. Courtesy: Craftsman Tools

• Crows feet are described as a hybrid combination of an open-end wrench with a ratchet drive. These are available in various sizes and are used for special applications where it is advantageous to have the flexibility of grabbing a nut or bolt with an open-end wrench, but the torque and leverage of a ratchet are desirable.

• Extension bars are extensions that attach between the ratchet and socket to provide additional length and reach for the tool.

• Breaker bars are heavy bars with a socket drive at the end that provide extra leverage over and above that which a ratchet alone could deliver for additional torque in "breaking" loose stubborn nuts or bolts, hence the name.

• Nut drivers can best be described as handheld sockets, since they combine the best of both worlds with the handle of a screwdriver and a socket at the end of a shaft. These are very handy for light-duty work (they are popular with electricians), where the fastener doesn't have to be too tight. They are also useful for quickly starting a fastener and driving it the majority of the way for final tightening by a wrench or socket.

• Specialty wrenches are usually special-purpose wrenches designed to do a specific job. Examples of these are distributor adjustment wrenches that feature a long offset end for accessing the adjustment nut underneath some automotive distributors.

Tool Tip

SWITCH NUT SPANNER

Have you ever tried removing the headlight switch nut or the wiper switch nut from a GM or Ford vehicle from the 1960s or early '70s? Spanner nuts were frequently used by American car manufacturers during this period and removing them can be a real pain if you don't have the right tool.

So, basically, you have three options here:
- You can "tough it out" and use a pair of needle-nose pliers.
- You can spend about $15, including the shipping, to order a spanner nut remover from a catalog.
- Or you can spend less than $2 and make one for yourself in under a half hour.
- If you chose option three, then good for you! Here's how to make your switch nut spanner:

Step 1: Go to the local Home Depot, Lowe's, or plumbing supply and purchase a 1/2-foot length of copper pipe. The smallest I could find was a 1-foot length pipe and it cost about $1.59. Whatever size you find, measure and mark the tubing 4 inches from one end.

Step 2: If you have one, use a tubing cutter to cut the copper pipe at the 4-inch mark. You can also use a hacksaw if you don't have a tubing cutter.

Step 3: Use a straight edge and a black ink marker to mark both sides of the tubing at the half-diameter point.

Step 4: Here's the tubing with the ink marks on it. You'll be removing all the metal that *is not* covered with black ink.

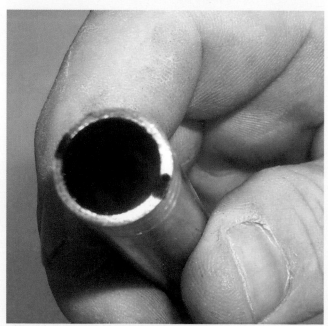

Step 5: Put the tubing in a vise to hold it securely and use a Dremel with a cutting wheel to cut notches approximately 1/8-inch deep on both sides of the two black marks.

Step 6: This is what it should look like when you have the notches cut into the pipe.

Step 7: Now use the cutting wheel to remove the sides of the pipe at the _outside_ of the notches. The pieces you're cutting off will resemble parentheses.

Step 8: After removing these sections, you should have two prongs remaining, as shown in this picture. These prongs fit depressions in the nuts and they're what gets the job done.

Step 9: Drill a 1/4-inch hole through the pipe about a half inch away from the unnotched end.

Step 10: Insert the blade of a small screwdriver into the holes to act as a handle and your new spanner wrench is ready to use.

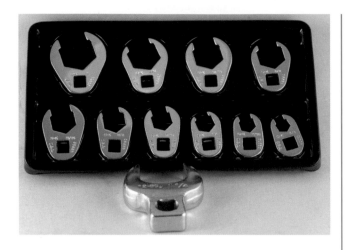

Crows feet wrenches, a cross between an open-end wrench and a socket, are just what you'll need for some special applications. Courtesy: The Eastwood Company

This specialty wrench is used for removing the ignition switch collet on older General Motors vehicles. It's not something you'll use everyday, but when you need it, you'll be glad you have it in your toolbox. Author's Collection

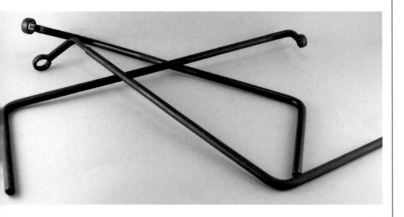

Specialty wrenches, such as these distributor bolt wrenches, are designed for specific tasks at which they excel. Courtesy: The Eastwood Company

Yet another specialty wrench, this spanner is designed to remove the collets from the headlight, wiper, and blower switches in older GM vehicles. Author's Collection

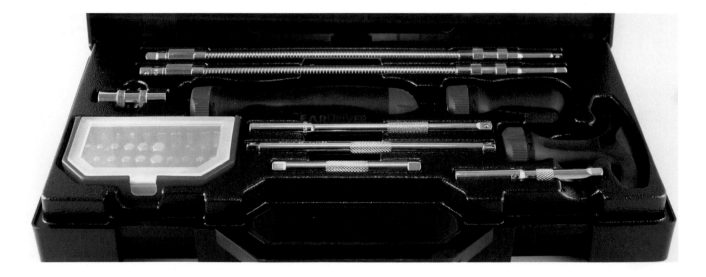

This 40-piece master set includes a standard GearDriver handle, a T-handle, several shafts, and 30 drive bits. It's also a money saver over purchasing individual sets to get all these items. Courtesy: NAPA

Nut drivers are basically handheld sockets that have handles on them, and GearDriver takes the traditional one-piece nut driver to the next level by adding its GearForce fine-tooth ratcheting mechanism to the handle. This deluxe set features both fractional and metric socket sizes for added versatility. Courtesy: NAPA

• The Ratchet Buddy ™ set consists of 1/4-, 3/8-, and 1/2-inch drive discs with indentations to make them easy to hold. Each disc has a square socket drive on one side and a receptacle for a ratchet of the same drive size on the other side. These are very useful for starting a bolt by hand and then attaching a ratchet to finish the job to the desired tightness without having to remove the Buddy in the process.

• Hand drive extensions are also very useful tools to have, since they function both as hand-starters and extension bars by providing a socket drive at one end and a ratchet receptacle at the other end of the grip. These come in sets of two in both 3/8-inch and 1/2-inch drive sizes.

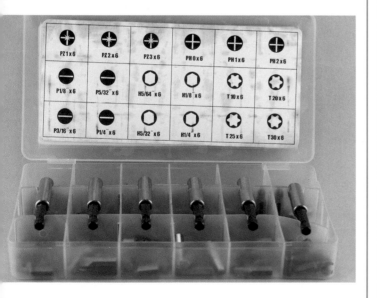

It's also a good idea to have an assortment of extra bits of all types on hand, since the bits will eventually wear and get dull from repeated use. Courtesy: The Eastwood Company

Tool Tip

JUST A LITTLE LEVERAGE

Good old Archimedes—the ancient Greek philosopher and the father of physics—knew the value of a lever. One of his famous quotes is: "Give me a lever long enough, and a place on which to rest it, and I will move the world."

Chances are pretty good that you don't want to move the earth, but if you've ever had to loosen and remove a stuck, rusted bolt, you'll appreciate what some additional leverage can do to make the going a bit easier.

A 3-foot long piece of 1-inch inside-diameter PVC pipe makes a dandy extension lever. Slip it over the handle of your ratchet or combination wrench and get the extra leverage and torque you need for those stubborn bolts.

Another simple, elegant, and cheap solution—what's not to love?

CHAPTER 8
SCRAPE IT TO THE LIMIT

In the garage world, abrasion (wearing, grinding, or rubbing away) generally revolves around removing some type of material—paint, coatings, metal, whatever—by various frictional means.

The earliest abrasion occurred when the first wave hit the primordial shoreline, carrying with it grains of sand that pelted the rocks and ground as it was hurled by the onrushing waters. No one knows for sure how or when early man caught on that he could smooth, sharpen, and shape things by using abrasives such as sand combined with friction (rubbing), but somewhere early in our history this discovery was made and improvements to the materials, tools, and techniques used for abrading have continually gotten better and more efficient.

Lots of tools and implements are useful in the garage for grinding, rubbing, polishing, and buffing, but the great grand-daddy of them all is sandpaper, so that's what this chapter will start with.

Sandpaper
Sandpaper commonly describes abrasive grit glued on to flexible backing sheets that smooth many types of material. Real sandpaper, backing paper covered with grains of sand, is no longer available; it's been replaced by backing sheets of various material covered with glass, aluminum oxide, silicon carbide, garnet, or other special grits. Generally, the terms

sandpaper and glasspaper are used generically to cover all types of grit attached to a backing sheet. To simplify things, however, I'll use the term sandpaper herein to generally refer to sheet-type abrasives.

Each type of grit has different characteristics that make each most suitable for specific applications. An understanding of the types of grit is essential so that the right type is selected for a particular job.

Various sizes of grit are available for all types of grit material and the grit size is referred to by a number that represents the number of holes per linear inch in a sieve screen. They range from 40 (very coarse) to over 400 (very

This Dura-Block sanding block set contains just about every shape and size of sanding block you'll need for any of your garage projects. Courtesy: The Eastwood Company

Here's an abrasive disk and pad setup that uses Velcro to attach the pad to the disk, which attaches to the buffer/polisher via an arbor bolt arrangement. The advantage of this arrangement is that the pad has an uninterrupted uniform abrasive surface.
Courtesy: The Eastwood Company

Sanding blocks come in lots of shapes and sizes, and they usually utilize sheet sandpaper, but this round sanding block will readily take adhesive sanding disks. Its knob-like handle also provides a sure and steady grip. Courtesy: The Eastwood Company

Before you spend too much time learning about various garage abrasives, some precautionary words are in order. Anytime you're removing material using abrasives you're putting your body and health at risk, and this is far from an exaggeration.

Abrasion causes fine particles to fly about, sometimes at very high speed, and these particles can cause serious injury, or even blindness, if they hit your eyes. For this reason, safety glasses or goggles should always be worn during these tasks.

These same particles, some microscopic in size, will also play absolute havoc with your lungs and respiratory system. In addition to being irritants, some may very well be toxic and/or carcinogenic. A good quality respirator will only cost you a few dollars—well worth protecting your health and well being.

Work gloves, a shop apron, and long-sleeved apparel are also good clothing items to wear whenever you're using abrasives in the garage. Remember the old adage, "an ounce of prevention is worth a pound of cure." If you take the proper precautions and use good judgment when using abrasives, your body will thank you for it.

---

fine). Good quality sandpaper will have universal-sized grit. The size of grit is used to classify the sandpaper into the various grades is indicated below:

Grit Size	Grade
40-60	coarse
80-100	medium coarse
120-150	medium
180-220	fine
240 and higher	very fine

Individual sheets of sandpaper are normally marked on the reverse with the grit size (i.e., 120) and/or with the grade (i.e., medium). Sandpaper is most commonly available as closed coat (completely covered with grit); however, open coat (where only 50 to 70 percent of the backing is covered) is often available for most types of sandpaper on special order. Closed-coat sandpapers cut faster, but are more likely to clog (the spaces between the grains become clogged with waste material produced by sanding) than open-coat sandpapers.

Backing Materials

Three types of backing materials are commonly available:

• Ordinary paper is an adequate material for most sandpapers. The quality of paper varies depending upon the intended method of use and price. Sandpaper designed for use with power tools generally has a tougher quality of backing paper than that intended for hand sanding.

• Waterproof paper is essential where the sandpaper is to be used with a lubricant. The back of this type of paper usually has a darker, glossier appearance.

• Cloth is generally used where a high degree of flexibility is required when using the sandpaper.

Backing Adhesives

Backing adhesives may be water soluble or waterproof. Most common sandpapers use a water-soluble adhesive since they are usually not intended for use with a lubricant.

No matter which of these types of adhesive is used, it is important that the bond between the grit and the backing material is strong enough to prevent excessive separation when being used. As you would surmise, sandpapers produced for power tools tend to have a stronger grit/paper bond than sandpapers made for hand use.

Formats

Sandpaper is available in a number of formats, each of which is usually available in several grades, including the following:

• Sheets, normally 8.5x11 inches in size, are sold for the Do-It-Yourself market in packs of four or more sheets, either of the same or mixed grades. These sandpapers are usually only suitable for hand sanding.

These abrasive cleaning pads mount to the buffer/polisher via an arbor bolt—note the hole in the center of the pad. Courtesy: The Eastwood Company

This 7-inch disc cleaning/stripping system uses the popular and efficient Velcro mounting.

Courtesy: The Eastwood Company

An assortment of good files should be in the tool chest of every serious gearhead, and this assortment should include general-purpose, bastard cut, half round, hobby rasp, round (also called rat tail), and triangular files in assorted sizes. Courtesy: Craftsman Tools

If you have a mini die grinder that can accept 2- or 3-inch surface conditioning discs, this 60-piece set is a great way to get an assortment of discs at a super good price.

Courtesy: The Eastwood Company

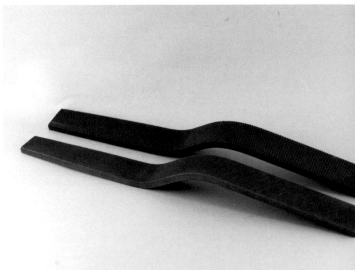

These slapping files are primarily used for shrinking high spots in sheet metal, although they can also be used for traditional filing chores to remove material quickly. Courtesy: The Eastwood Company

- Rolls, available in a number of widths, are sold by linear length, and each roll is of a single grade. Although rolls are produced for use with power tools (like orbital sanders), they can also be used for hand sanding.
- Discs are for use with rotary sanders or other power tools. The discs are used with a stiff but flexible backing disc. The sanding disc is fitted to the backing disc either by a central securing screw/dished washer or by a self-adhesive backing. Various disc diameters are available, and the diameter of the sandpaper disc should always match the diameter of the backing disc.
- Belts are used with belt sanders. Various widths and lengths are available to suit each belt sander on the market.
- Specials are designed to fit several new power sanding tools that are now available with non-standard "footprints." With unique pre-cut shapes, special sandpaper can be attached to the tool by a self-adhesive backing.

• Sanding sponges, also called flexible abrasive blocks, are usually soft and flexible rectangular blocks with grit on four faces. Sometimes they can have the same grit on all of the surfaces, while other variations provide two faces of one grade of grit and a different grade of grit on the other two faces. The blocks aren't very durable, but they certainly can come in handy for sanding irregular surfaces and shapes.

While sandpapers for power tool use can be used for hand sanding, the reverse does not apply. Hand sandpapers will not last very long if used with a power tool.

Types of Grit

Glasspaper is generally composed of quartz granules on a paper backing, and is an inexpensive and relatively soft abrasive for sanding painted or raw metal and other materials. It wears quickly and is usually used to produce a rough finish before sanding to a smooth surface. Glasspaper is usually only available with non-waterproof adhesives/backing paper.

Aluminum oxide is a man-made material suitable for shaping, sanding, and polishing hard metal such as iron and steel. It cuts much faster and lasts longer than glass or garnet papers. It's available with non-waterproof, cloth, or waterproof backings. The cloth backing provides lots of flexibility and it's suitable for heavy-duty applications such as rust removal and metal shaping.

Silicon carbide paper, also known as "wet and dry" paper, is suitable for both dry and wet sanding. It's good for sanding soft metal like brass and aluminum as well as fiberglass and plastic. It is also fast-cutting and almost as hard as diamond, but it is brittle so the coarser grades will wear fast if used on hard metal.

When used with water, it yields a very fine sanding of paint between coats and can also be used with mineral oil for smoothing and polishing metals. The lubricant helps to keep both the abrasive and the surface cool, and it floats away sanding waste while preventing the formation of fine, airborne dust. The wet slurry that forms has to be wiped away while you're working so you can see what you're doing.

"Wet" sanding with water is used extensively during vehicle body painting because it can create a very smooth surface for each coat of paint. It's not at all uncommon to wet-sand both the base color coats and the top clear coats to achieve an extremely smooth finish that looks like it is under glass.

Garnet paper is natural crushed rock and is an excellent abrasive. It is easily recognized by its bright green color. Highly favored in the past and still used extensively in Europe, it has largely been replaced by aluminum oxide grits here in the United States. Although the natural garnet grit lasts about twice as long as the quartz grit used on glasspaper, it doesn't last as long as aluminum oxide.

Other Abrasives

In addition to sandpapers, you're likely to use several other abrasive materials in your garage. Although the list of all of these materials can be quite lengthy, the most common and popular among them are detailed below.

Steel wool cuts rather than abrades the surface, producing very fine finishes. As the wool is used, small pieces of it break off and mix in with the sanding dust. It is particularly good for removing light surface rust and bringing up luster on bare metal surfaces such as stainless steel.

Steel wool is graded by number, starting at a very coarse 5 through to a series of zeroes, with 0000 being the finest. Steel wool can be very effectively used to "sand" complicated shapes, such as metal castings. One caveat in using steel wool is that it breaks up into tiny slivers of metal that can find their way into mechanisms, bearings, and oilways, and wreak havoc.

A handheld media blaster is ideal for small jobs. It can use sand, glass beads, or other blasting media. The media resides in the reservoir right under the handle, so no suction hose is required. Courtesy: Craftsman Tools

Blasted Abrasives

If your car has ever been caught in a sandstorm, then you are fully aware of how abrasive sand can be when propelled at high speed. That's pretty much the principle behind sand blasting or, more correctly put, abrasive blasting, since abrasives other than sand are now commonly used with compressed air to blast them onto the work surface. Since sand was the first material used for blasting, it's only appropriate that we start with it.

Sand, cheap and readily available, has been the favorite blast media for several decades. The use of sand as a blasting media, however, has inherent risks which should not be taken lightly. (See the sidebar at the beginning of this chapter and make sure you wear appropriate eye and respiratory protection.)

Glass beads are an all-purpose abrasive for all types of metals and many plastics. They are best used on softer metals like aluminum and brass. This media is great for cleaning pistons, engine blocks, and light rust removal with minimal dust. As with sand, when using glass beads, be sure to wear appropriate respiratory protection.

Crushed walnut shells (yes, you read it correctly) are ideal for cleaning internal parts since any of the soft abrasive material left in the working part will break down with minimal damage. Walnut shells are also great for gentle paint and carbon removal from ferrous metals.

Aluminum oxide is a preferred all-purpose abrasive for all types of metals and many plastics. Best on softer metals like aluminum and brass, aluminum oxide is great for paint and rust removal as well as for cleaning pistons and other internal engine parts.

Blast Cabinets

Media blasting cabinets are available in a wide variety of sizes, from small blow-molded plastic units that sit comfortably on a workbench to large free-standing units capable of holding large parts such as wheels and doors inside them.

The advantages of using a blast cabinet are that you can media-blast small parts while keeping the mess of the abrasive blasting contained within the cabinet. Most cabinets also have a collection container at the bottom of the cabinet that catches the spent blast media and permits it to be reused.

In addition to confining the blasting media, blasting cabinets also keep the garage clean and neat and keep the particulates generated from entering your respiratory tract. Blast cabinets also have viewing windows that protect your eyes as well.

Vibratory Tumblers

Vibratory tumblers offer thorough, gentle cleaning automatically. Rust-cutting media is inserted in the tumbler's bowl along with the parts to be cleaned, and an electric motor creates an oscillating vibratory action within the bowl, removing

This is a battery terminal cleaning brush. The sharp, abrasive bristles scrape the surface of the terminals to remove slag and oxidation; the blades at the opposite end are for scraping the terminal cable clamps. Clean, shiny terminals are essential for good electrical conductivity. Courtesy: The Eastwood Company

rust and other debris from nuts and bolts without rounding edges. After de-rusting is completed, a brilliant luster can then be achieved by using a dry shining media. Vibratory tumblers work more quickly and are quieter than rotating tumblers.

Rasps and Files

Rasps and files are hand tools that are used for smoothing and shaping metal when other edge-cutting tools won't do the trick. A rasp is a coarse file with sharp, pointed projections. Rasps are most frequently used for the shaping and removal of softer materials such as plastic body filler, while files are usually used on metal. Both rasps and files come in various shapes, such as flat, round, triangular, and slightly curved. Rasp teeth are very coarse to remove material quickly, while the teeth on files can range from coarse to very fine.

Slapping Files

Slapping files have been used for decades for removing dents and smoothing body work on hand-fabricated panels. The serrated face of the slapping file works in two ways. It shrinks the stretched metal and highlights high/low spots that require hammer and dolly work. When used as a slapping hammer, with a dolly, the files shrink metal to remove high spots. The files can also be used to remove metal. Slapping file teeth are available in medium and coarse cuts.

Sanders

Available in both pneumatic and electric versions, sanders can be oscillating, orbital, or straight-line. They can use sanding pads, discs, belts, or sheets of abrasive media. Generally used for aggressive removal and surface prep of metals prior to painting, power sanders are never used for final finishing after painting.

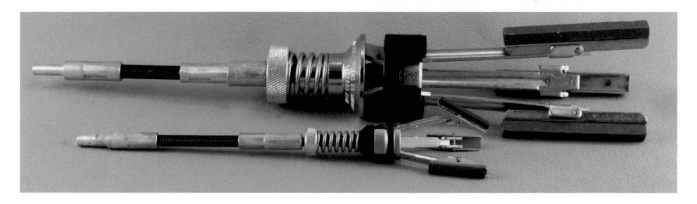

These are hones. The larger one at the top is an engine cylinder hone, while the smaller one is for brake cylinders. The abrasive stones are on spring-loaded arms that help maintain contact with the target surface. Courtesy: Craftsman Tools

Bench Grinders

These are essentially bench-mounted electric motors with shafts on each end that accept abrasive wheels of varying coarseness and size. They are primarily used for the removal of metal for shaping and smoothing. When outfitted with wire wheels, they are effective for parts cleaning and rust removal. When fitted with softer wheels, they can be used for polishing as well.

Wire Brushes and Wire Wheels

Used primarily with bench grinders, wire brushes and wire wheels provide a fast means of removing paint, rust, and other surface coatings from small objects that can be held against them. Usually having bristles made of steel or brass, they are used for the aggressive removal of unwanted material. Eye protection should always be worn when using wire brushes or wheels.

Buffers

Either pneumatic or electrically powered, buffers are used for polishing and waxing the finishes on vehicles. They are also used with abrasive discs for paint removal and metal preparation prior to painting. Some buffers use an arbor and mandrel mounting system for attaching their wheels, while others rely on adhesive and/or Velcro attachment arrangements.

Abrasive Wheels

Abrasive wheels are available in a wide variety of materials, grits, diameters, and mounting mechanisms. Used primarily for paint removal and surface preparation, abrasive wheels are used with power buffers, either pneumatic or electrically powered. While some use arbor/mandrel mounting systems, others use adhesives or Velcro attachment arrangements.

Hones

Hones are whetstones made of fine gritstone, usually attached to spring-mounted legs that expand to keep the stones in contact with the surface being worked on. Most hones are used for breaking the glaze and smoothing the surface of engine cylinders. Smaller hones are used for conditioning and

This handheld electric grinder removes material in a hurry, and its side-mounted handle is reversible so it can accommodate left- or right-handed users. See Chapter 17 for more coverage on power tools. Courtesy: Black & Decker

These pneumatic palm sanders include a 3-inch model on the left and a 6-inch model on the right. Their small size and shape make them ideal for sanding applications where control is of the utmost importance, such as shaping body filler. Courtesy: The Eastwood Company

A very special item, this MBX tool is available in both electric (shown) and pneumatic versions. It can clean and strip a surface in an amazingly short time without causing any damage to the surface, and it works around irregular shapes, such as protruding nuts and bolts, without a problem. It can also remove pinstriping tape, vinyl appliqué, and other materials in record time without damage to the surface. Courtesy: Monti Tool Company

resurfacing brake cylinders. Both cylinder and brake hones are usually powered by electric drills to achieve a satisfactory rotational speed for the removal of material.

Die Grinders

These handheld power tools can be powered either by electricity or compressed air, and some of the newer cordless models use rechargeable batteries for power. Especially well-suited for fine detail work such as engraving, shaping, and porting cylinder heads, die grinders come with a variety of bits and accessories, including flexible shafts (which add to the versatility of these very handy tools). Most die grinders have multiple-speed motors that can reach or exceed 30,000 rpm. As with any power tool, wearing eye protection while using die grinders is an absolute must.

Specialty Abrasive Tools

The MBX power tool, available in both pneumatic and electric versions, uses unique, proprietary bristled belts to clean and remove material without loading up or shedding. The tool operates at 3,500 rpm with excellent stability and control, and no perceptible vibration. The MBX Power Tool is terrific for removing rust, corrosion, paint, undercoating, and more from many surfaces. It can produce a surface on cast iron, steel, sheet metal, and aluminum that looks like it was abrasive blasted. A rubber belt is also available for the tool for pinstripe and vinyl removal.

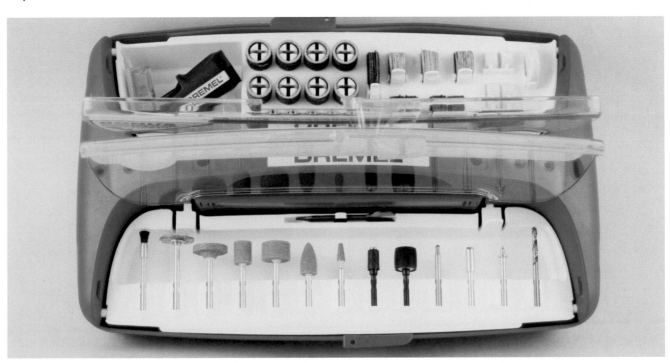

Dremel makes a plethora of abrasive wheels, stones, sanding cylinders, and other abrasives that work with its 1/8-inch chuck electric mini die grinder. Courtesy: Dremel

CHAPTER 9
I'M GONNA TAKE YOU HIGHER

Ever since the very first vehicle was built, man has had the need to gain access to the underside of it for maintenance, repairs, or improvements. Because of this, gearheads have also needed a way to elevate their vehicle. Necessity being the mother that it is, the jack came into existence.

The Elevation Sensation

There are lots of ways to lift your vehicle or other heavy objects in your garage, and we'll explore many of them in this chapter. But before we do, let me give you some sage advice: Do not EVER get under a vehicle that is supported by a bumper or scissor jack alone. These devices are intended solely to get a wheel off the ground so you can change a flat tire—period! The following is a true story that illustrates how foolish and stupid acts like that can turn into potential tragedies.

In my late teens, I endeavored to remove the four-speed transmission from my Chevelle Super Sport so I could replace the clutch. I did the job right on the street in front of my house while the front of the car was supported only by a cinder block on one side and a bumper jack on the other.

Paraphrasing one of the more memorable lines from the Humphrey Bogart movie, *The Treasure of the Sierra Madre*, I reasoned, "Jack stands? I don't have no jack stands! I don't need no stinkin' jack stands!"

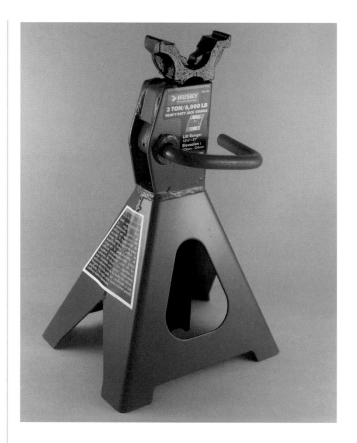

Jack stands are another item that you shouldn't skimp on, since your life may well depend on how sturdy they are when you're under your vehicle. Again, overkill is a good thing with a jack stand like this Husky unit rated at 6,000 pounds (3 tons). Courtesy: Husky Tools

A well-made hydraulic floor jack, also called a trolley jack, is an absolute essential for elevating a vehicle to work on its undercarriage. In the case of jacks, bigger is better. This unit is rated at 3-ton capacity, making it more than adequate for most vehicles.

Courtesy: The Eastwood Company

Wheel chocks like these are an absolute must anytime the front or back of your vehicle is elevated because they will prevent it from rolling or rocking. These units are made of lightweight plastic, they're sturdy, and they don't take up much storage space.

Courtesy: Mid America Motorworks

This is a typical scissor jack that came as standard equipment with a car I bought a few years back. It is compact and efficient for lifting a vehicle to change a flat. However, it is labor intensive, has limited elevation, and isn't the most stable lifting solution. For these reasons, I recommend that you keep it in your trunk and use it only for changing the occasional roadside flat. Author's Collection

Bumper Jacks

Thankfully, these aren't supplied or used anymore. Popular through the mid-1960s, bumper jacks were supplied with many new cars. They consisted of a pedestal into which a toothed shaft was inserted. A ratchet-and-pawl type mechanism held a bracket that hooked onto or under the car's bumper. The lug wrench doubled its duty as the lever to raise the mechanism until the tire that needed changing was off the ground. By flipping a lever on the ratcheting mechanism, the jack could be lowered back down, again using the lug wrench as the handle. To say these bumper jacks were unstable is a big understatement.

Scissor Jacks

Supplied as standard equipment with all Corvettes from 1953 through 1996 as well as some other cars, these compact jacks use a screw shaft to elevate the lifting platform by turning the shaft with the lug wrench. While efficient for changing a flat tire, they are definitely not the lifting mechanism of choice for elevating a vehicle to work on the undercarriage. Their maximum lift and stability is limited.

I figured that with the money I saved on jack stands I could buy a couple of used tires at the junkyard. Needless to say, if it wasn't for Divine Providence (or sheer luck, depending on your personal belief system), I could have easily been crushed to death. And, if that had happened, you wouldn't be reading these pearls of wisdom right here and now. And, oh, what a shame that would have been—for both of us!

Seriously, though, many of the OEM jacks manufacturers put in their cars are unsafe, and they can also be very difficult to use. They fail more often than you'd care to believe, resulting in serious injuries. In the United States alone, hospitals treat more than 10,000 auto jack–related accidents annually, with five percent of those accidents resulting in amputations (according to the National Highway Traffic Safety Administration). Need I say more about not getting under a vehicle supported by a jack alone? Without a doubt, nothing can put a damper on your day like having a 2-ton vehicle fall on you. Ouch big time!

One more thing, and I can't stress this enough: When it comes to lifting devices and vehicle supports, do not be penny wise and dollar foolish! As I mentioned in Chapter 3, you get what you pay for when it comes to jacks and jack stands. Go the extra bucks to get sturdy, well-made equipment that exceeds your lifting and load capacities. After all, it's your life at risk when you're under an elevated vehicle, so get the very best you can afford.

A cushioned jack pad provides a soft lifting point for your hydraulic trolley jack, and it protects the surface being lifted. This is especially important if you have a show vehicle with a really pristine undercarriage. The cushioned pad simply drops into the jack in place of the stock lifting platform. Courtesy: The Eastwood Company

GoJaks are the ideal solution for moving a vehicle without starting the engine or pushing it. Each GoJak elevates a single wheel, and the sturdy casters enable a single person to move the car without much effort. It's even possible to totally rotate the car. Courtesy: GoJaks.com/T&L Industries, Inc.

Hydraulic bottle jacks are alternative lifting solutions to trolley jacks and scissor jacks. They're particularly useful when you only need to elevate a single wheel or one side of the vehicle. Be sure to purchase bottle jacks that exceed your lifting needs, like this 6-ton (12,000-pound) unit. Bottle jacks are also just the ticket for elevating a vehicle that's on a drive-on lift when you need to work on brakes or suspension components. Courtesy: Husky Tools

Folding plastic sawhorses like these are very handy for numerous jobs where you need to elevate whatever you're working on, and they fold flat and store easily on or against a wall.

Courtesy: Storehorse/The Lehigh Group

Hydraulic Floor Jacks

Also called trolley jacks, these are the workhorses of the automotive world. A good floor jack is capable of lifting the entire front or rear of a vehicle to a height of 20 inches or more. A hydraulic piston does the lifting when pumped by using a long handle that also steers the jack. While these jacks are sturdy and usually very reliable, they should never be used as the sole support for an elevated vehicle that you have to go under to work on. Regardless of how good a trolley jack is, they have been known to fail occasionally. All you need is one failure while you're under the vehicle to completely ruin your day.

Lifting Cushions

Various types of lifting cushions are available for the lifting platform of your hydraulic trolley jack, and these are especially useful if you're concerned about marring the undercarriage of your vehicle. A friend of mine has a vintage Chevy muscle car whose undercarriage is almost entirely chromed, including the rear end and banjo cover, and he wouldn't think of jacking up this car without using a lifting cushion on his jack. The one he prefers has a soft rubber cushion that simply drops into the lift platform hole of his jack. These cushions are relatively inexpensive and can be just the ticket for protecting the undercarriage of your prized vehicle.

Bottle Jacks

These small hydraulic lifting devices are really mighty mites capable of lifting several tons. Like the other lifting mecha-nisms discussed so far, their primary purpose is to get the vehicle off the ground and to a usable working height, but they shouldn't be used as the sole support for the vehicle once it is elevated.

Jack Stands

These don't lift, but rather support the vehicle once it is already at the desired working height. A pair of sturdy jack stands is essential equipment for any well-equipped garage, and two pair are even better, especially if you need to have the vehicle entirely suspended both in the front and rear. Like virtually all other aspects of garage gear, jack stands come in varying price ranges and you get what you pay for. Even the best jack stands are comparatively inexpensive compared to other equipment, so don't skimp here. Get stands that exceed the weight capacity you will need. It never hurts to have more strength than you need when it comes to jack stands.

Electric Vehicle Lifts

Not too long ago, having an electric vehicle lift in your garage was considered a luxury enjoyed only by the well-heeled hobbyist or car buff, but things have changed. The price on these lifts has come down considerably, and a lot of folks have realized that there are some considerable advantages to having a lift in their garage. In addition to making it easy to work on your vehicle's undercarriage, a lift can pro-vide double the parking space in your garage by enabling you to stack your vehicles. Most lifts are wide enough to accom-

STRUCTURAL SUPPORT

If you're considering installing a hoist in your garage, you should definitely consult a structural engineer to assess the need for any reinforcements required to support the weight of an engine or anything else you may want to lift. The engineer's fee will be modest and should be considered money well spent.

modate a second vehicle underneath the one that's elevated and that certainly doesn't detract from their appeal, at least for most of us gearheads.

Consumer lifts are available in two basic styles: the two-post style, which makes contact with the vehicle's frame, and the four-post style, which has runways that the car's tires sit upon. The two-post style must be anchored to the concrete floor of the garage, while the four-post style is basically free-standing, and you can even get a caster kit to permit moving the lift around. The four-poster lift has several inherent

advantages, among which are the ability to keep the vehicle's suspension "loaded" (i.e., the weight of the car is sitting on the tires, just as it is when it's on the ground). If you need to work on the brakes, shocks, or other components that require the wheels to be elevated, bottle jacks do the trick nicely. They allow you the convenience of having the vehicle elevated to a comfortable working height.

When considering the purchase of a lift for your garage, you first want to think about the lift's electrical requirements. Most garages have 120-volt AC outlets with 15-amp service. This is adequate for most electrical vehicle lifts. Unless your garage has 220-volt electrical service, avoid lifts that have 220V lifting motors or you'll incur the additional expense of having an electrician run a 220 line into the garage to accommodate it.

Weight capacity is another factor you'll want to consider seriously. Let's say your current vehicle weighs 2,400 pounds. Surely, a 2-ton capacity lift will be adequate for this vehicle. But what if you purchase something a bit heavier in the future, say a vintage Cadillac, a truck, or some other vehicle that tips the scales at 4,200 pounds? This lift may be able to handle it, but

These Rhino Ramps offer a very shallow incline that's ideal for low vehicles like late-model Corvettes. The ramps are made of sturdy plastic, are lightweight, and are easy to store on a hook mounted to a wall in the garage. Best of all, they won't dig into your driveway or rust like steel ramps. Courtesy: Mid America Motorworks

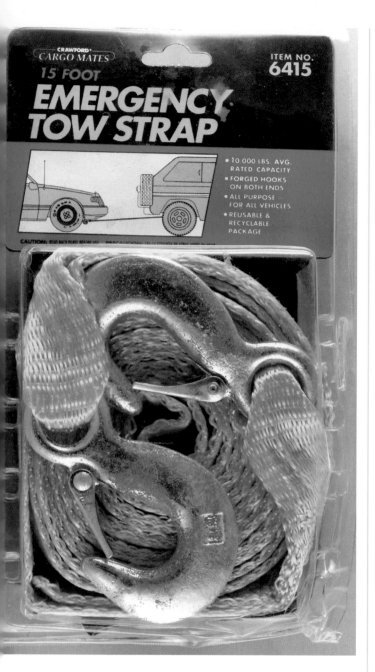

You never know when you may have to do an emergency tow, so it pays to have a sturdy tow strap like this one, rated at 10,000 pounds. Courtesy: Crawford/The Lehigh Group

collapsing, thereby bringing the vehicle down on you with tragic (and very probably fatal) results. In addition to a positive locking mechanism, your lift should also have a deliberate release mechanism that has to be consciously released before the lift can be lowered.

If you're serious about playing in your garage, an electric vehicle lift is a worthwhile investment that will serve you for many years to come. Plus, it has the added benefit of giving you room to store a second vehicle in the same space formerly occupied by only one, so what's not to love?

Mid-Rise Lifts

As the name suggests, these are lifts that rise to about half the height of full vehicle lifts, elevating either the front or rear of the vehicle about 3.5 feet off the ground. Used mainly for front-end and suspension servicing, they are compact and hydraulically operated. They can also function as service lifts for ATVs, snowmobiles, jet skis, and other recreational draft. Their maximum lifting capacity is generally in the 1,500-pound range.

Hoists

Usually suspended from overhead girders or beams, hoists can be either manual or electrically operated. Manual hoists usually have a series of pulleys that carry lifting chains. The pulleys work in series to multiply the mechanical advantage, much the way gears in a transmission multiply the driving force to produce more torque.

It is extremely important that the beam or girder the hoist is attached to is strong enough to support the weight of the item being hoisted. For example, the typical 2x8 beams of a garage are not sufficiently strong enough to support the weight of a small-block Chevy engine. Attempting to lift the engine will result in the beam starting to sag, crack, and ultimately fail, which results in the engine crashing dangerously to the floor. A transverse steel girder I-beam is the desirable mount for any garage hoist that will be lifting more than a couple of hundred pounds.

Body Slings

These are nylon slings with hooks on their four ends designed to lift the body off the chassis when doing a frame-off restoration. The central lifting ring of the sling is attached to a hoist, which, in turn, lifts it (and the body) off the chassis.

Ramps

Drive-on ramps are the simplest and least expensive vehicle lifting devices. Stamped steel ramps are readily available at almost any auto parts store, and they are very inexpensive. They are simply placed in front of the front or rear tires, and

that's a big if. Are you willing to stand under it and work on the vehicle, knowing it exceeds the rated capacity? I wouldn't be. That's why when it comes to lifts, as in boxing, the heavyweights rule. You're only looking at a couple of hundred dollars more for a lift rated at 3 or even 4 tons over one that's rated at 2 tons. Go for the extra bucks and get the heavy-duty model.

Perhaps the most important feature of any lift is its locking mechanism. You want to be sure that there's a positive locking mechanism that will absolutely prevent the lift from

the vehicle is driven up them to elevate the desired end. The downside of these stamped steel ramps is that they have a tendency to dig into the blacktop of your driveway once the weight of the vehicle is upon them, and this is particularly troublesome in hot weather when the asphalt is soft. Their incline is also rather steep, making them unsuitable for use with vehicles that have low ground clearance.

Rhino Ramps are made of a lightweight composite plastic, and their angle of incline is relatively shallow. That's why they are well-suited for Corvettes and other vehicles with low ground clearance. Another added plus is that their underside is waffled to distribute the vehicle's weight, thus preventing dig-in on the driveway surface. And since they are made of a composite material, they don't rust.

Race Ramps take things to the next level. These composite ramps feature a solid bottom so driveway dig-in is a non-issue. They also don't rust, and the 65-inch versions yield a total of 12.5 inches of elevation with a very shallow incline, making them the ramp of choice when ample elevation is needed for vehicles with low ground clearance. A pair of Race Ramps weigh only 30 pounds and they store vertically on a wall, thanks to included hanger straps.

Wheel Chocks

Whenever you have your vehicle on ramps, or even on a lift, it's a good idea to chock the wheels to prevent your car from rolling. Chock the unelevated wheels, since the vehicle will have a tendency to roll downhill. In other words, if the front of your car is on ramps, chock the rear wheels and vice versa. While you can use a couple of pieces of 2x4 as chocks, commercial wheel chocks are much more efficient and lightweight. They are a good investment that you should purchase at the same time you buy your ramps.

GoJaks

GoJaks will not only lift your vehicle's tires off the garage floor, but they will allow you to move the vehicle about with minimal effort. Each GoJak surrounds one tire. A hydraulic lever causes the cradle rollers to move in toward the tire, thus lifting it off the floor in the process. When all four tires are off the ground, the heavy-duty casters on the GoJaks permit the vehicle to be moved, swiveled, and even turned 360 degrees within its own radius. GoJaks are an ideal solution for vehicles under restoration or otherwise unable to move under their own power. A handy storage rack is also available for the GoJaks so you can stow them when they're not in use.

Portable Electric Jacks

A modern variation on the hydraulic floor jack, the portable electric jack is small and light enough to carry in

Canvas universal tie-downs are available in 5- and 10-foot lengths and they're great for securing cargo in transit or keeping your trunk lid from bouncing when you have an oversize load aboard. Courtesy: Crawford/The Lehigh Group

the trunk of your vehicle, and it takes the drudgery and effort out of changing a flat on the road. The jack's lifting platform can be simply positioned under the chassis, with the power leads connected to either the battery or the cigarette lighter socket (with the optional cigarette lighter adapter). By pushing a remote control switch, the jack is activated, and *voilà*, the side of the vehicle goes up, giving you access to both tires on that side of it. After changing the flat, you put the remote switch in the down position and the tires return to earth.

Winches

Winches are electric motors with cables and hooks that are used to pull heavy loads, such as vehicles, onto trailers, flatbed trucks, and so forth. Winches can also be used for various pulling jobs around the garage, such as pulling a dented frame straight when mere muscle alone can't get the job done, or pulling a non-running vehicle into the garage from the driveway. Winches vary in strength, mounting, capacity, and power requirements (battery or A/C). As with other tools, don't buy cheap, since you get what you pay for.

DRIVEWAY SAVERS

The scenario goes like this: it's a hot summer day and you have to do some kind of service on one of your vehicles and it requires lifting one or both sides of it off the ground.

Being safety-minded, as you should always be, you place jack stands under the frame to provide a sturdy and stable platform for the vehicle to rest upon.

You finish whatever your task was, jack up the vehicle, and remove the jack stands. But lo and behold, there are scars in the blacktop from where the jack stands dug into it. Unsightly, to say the least, and you're going to have some explaining to do when your significant other sees what you've done.

Well, there's an easy way to prevent the base of your jack stands from digging into the blacktop of your driveway, especially in hot weather. Put a small square of 1/2-inch thick plywood between the base of each jack stand and the driveway. It's a simple but very effective—and reusable—solution.

Come-Alongs

Basically, come-alongs are hand-powered winches that use a ratchet-and-pawl arrangement to wind a cable tight using a hand-operated lever. The come-along has a hook on one end of its frame and another hook on the cable. The frame is hooked to a stationary point and the cable is hooked onto the object to be pulled. The lever is then ratcheted back and forth to retract the cable, which, in turn, pulls the attached object. Releasing the pawl lever permits the cable to be slackened.

Tow Straps

While this isn't exactly a lifting device, it deserves to be mentioned here. Towing a vehicle had traditionally been done using a tow chain in the past, but there were several disadvantages to chains. First, they're heavy and noisy. They also make sparks when they come into contact with the roadway, which is very dangerous if there's a gasoline leak. Lastly, they rust and are messy. Fortunately, today's synthetic fibers are lightweight and stronger than their steel counterparts, so they're a natural choice for towing straps.

Conservatively rated at 10,000-pound capacity, tow straps are up to pulling any passenger vehicle and, with a 15-foot length, there's enough slack for maneuverability and safety between the two vehicles. Best of all, they don't weigh much and they don't take up a lot of space, making them easy to stow in the garage or in the trunk of your car.

When Lifting is Not the Gameplan

There are times when you want to prevent items from being lifted or shifting while in transit, and here are a few items that can help you achieve that end.

Canvas Tie-Downs

Available in various lengths, these are basically straps with tightening mechanisms that permit you to hook both ends and remove the slack to keep the secured item from moving. They are very handy for securing the trunk lid when you have cargo to transport that prevents it from closing. They're also useful for transporting motorcycles, ATVs, and other items. Inexpensive and easy to stow, they make a great addition to any garage.

Bungee Cords

These familiar fabric-covered elastic stretch cords with hooks on both ends come in various lengths and colors. Used for just about every securing use you can think of, bungee cords are essential equipment in any garage, and you should keep a couple in the trunk of your vehicles, too.

Rubber Tie-Downs

Similar to bungee cords but made of thick, flat rubber, these tie-downs are for heavier duty applications and they come in various lengths. They offer more holding strength than bungees, and their hooks are heftier as well. Useful for applications where heavy-duty holding power is required, these should always have a home in your garage.

CHAPTER 10
HOW DO YOU MEASURE UP?

At some point while working on your vehicle, your project can become a numbers game. Whether you want to know something simple, like what your current garage temperature is, or more complex, such as a precise torque measurement, you can know all the vital statistics in your garage with some of the following tools.

Calipers

Calipers are precision hand tools used in conjunction with a scale to measure diameter or thickness. There are three basic types of calipers: vernier calipers, which have a sliding scale along the top and bottom; dial calipers, which have a dial that displays the measurement via a pointer; and electronic digital calipers, which have an LCD digital display of the measurement.

Calipers can be used to measure either inside or outside dimensions, and they can have either a dial-type (analog) or digital readout. Typical uses for calipers include measuring the inside diameter of cylinders and the thickness of brake drums and rotors.

A Vernier caliper like this one is especially useful for measuring the thickness of disc brake rotors to establish if they have enough thickness left for turning on a lathe.

Courtesy: The Eastwood Company

This 8-inch digital caliper measures OD, ID, and depth. It has an all stainless-steel body, reads in inches or mm down to .0005, has a 1/4-inch tall LCD display, and comes with a protective plastic foam-lined case. Courtesy: The Eastwood Company

There are lots of times when you'll want to make sure things are straight, such as when you're hanging storage cabinets in the garage, and this laser line level is just the tool to use. It even has a stud finder built into it. Courtesy: Stanley Tools

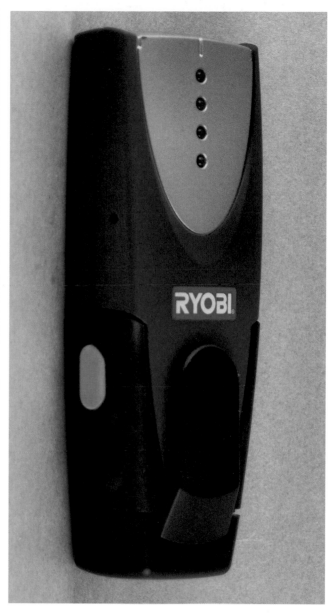

An inexpensive electronic stud finder like this one is a good thing to have in your garage for finding studs on which to hang racks, hooks, brackets, clocks, pictures, or even cabinets.
Courtesy: Ryobi

Torque Wrenches

Torque wrenches are used to tighten nuts and bolts to a specific torque (or tightness), and they give readouts of the specific torque measurements. (Please refer to Chapter 7 for more information on torque wrenches).

Micrometers

Micrometers are precision instruments used to measure distances between surfaces in thousandths of an inch. Micrometers are used to measure outside diameters, inside diameters, the distance between parallel surfaces, the depth of holes, slots, counterbores/recesses, and the distance from a surface to some recessed part. There are other uses of micrometers, but those mentioned above are the uses you are most likely to encounter for a micrometer in your garage. Micrometers are available in analog (dial-type readout) and digital readout (electronic) versions, with the digital models being easier to use.

Levels

Used to check for plumb and/or straightness, the level has a place in every garage. The spirit level, which has a vial of liquid with some air trapped in it (also called a "bubble stick"), is the most common type of level. When the air bubble is equidistant between the two ends of the vial, it is level.

Achieving a level plane is important when mounting cabinets, hanging fixtures, and myriad other uses in the garage.

Scales

A good scale is a handy piece of equipment to have in your garage. Scales can be either analog (dial-type readout) or digital. They are useful for several tasks. These include determining the weight of an object before suspending it from a hanger to make sure you are not exceeding the hanger's rated capacity, weighing scrap metal or other recyclables, and checking the overall weight of various objects found in the garage.

Thermometers

Thermometers indicate the temperature of an environment or an object. It's good to have a decent thermometer mounted in the garage to tell you the overall ambient temperature. A good immersible thermometer is useful for taking the temperature of liquids such as engine coolants.

Infrared thermometers that are capable of measuring temperature without making contact with the object are especially useful for tasks such as checking engine temperature and taking the cabin temperature when checking the efficiency of a vehicle's air conditioner.

Tape Measures

Tape measures come in varying lengths and every well-equipped garage should have at least one with a minimum length of 12 feet. The handiest tape measures have a belt clip on them and are self-retracting.

The new battery-powered tape measures are particularly handy because they extend their tape with the push of a

It's good to know how cold or warm it is in your garage, so a wall-mounted thermometer should be on your mandatory gear list. You can also mount a second one outside if you want to know what the temperature is outside your vehicle oasis.

Courtesy: Mid America Motorworks

button. The steel the tape is made from is a bit thicker and wider than usual, which helps to keep the tape from kinking while it is extending. A retraction button pulls the tape back into the case quickly.

Rulers

Rulers come in a variety of sizes, materials, and styles, and it's always a good idea to have a couple of rulers on hand in your garage. Good choices include either a plastic or wooden 1-foot

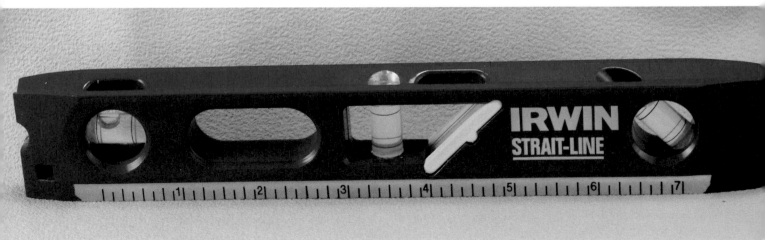

Good, old-fashioned torpedo levels, or bubble sticks as they are more commonly known, are simple yet functional tools for checking the straightness and levelness in your garage.

Courtesy: Irwin Industrial Tools

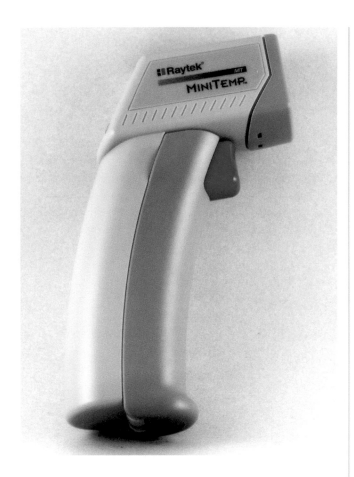

This is a professional-grade infrared non-contact thermometer with digital readout. Under-hood temperature variances are most often indicative of larger-scale mechanical and/or electrical malfunction. Designed specifically for automotive diagnostics, this tool enables you to detect and diagnose these problems quicker, easier, and safer. The portable unit's "SmartSight" feature utilizes two lasers, which merge to provide a single 1/2-inch focal point and optimal working distance. Courtesy: Mid America Motorworks

This pocket-sized non-contact thermometer is a great troubleshooting tool to spot engine, ignition, cooling system, brake, and tire problems. It has laser sighting, so you don't have to make contact with hot spots. It also has a digital display readout. The 6:1 target spot ratio reads temperatures from 0 to 500 degrees Fahrenheit (-18 to 260 degrees Celcius). You can also use it to check the operating temperatures of household appliances, HVAC systems, and electrical components. Courtesy: Mid America Motorworks

A four-piece measuring tape set like this one from Titan is handy and economical to boot, since there are times when the 12-foot tape will do the job and other times when the 33-foot unit is the one you'll want to use. Courtesy: Genuine Hot Rod Hardware

This AutoTape uses four AAA batteries to power its auto-extending 25-foot tape measure. Simply press the forward arrow and the tape advances as long as you hold the button down. Pressing the back arrow automatically retracts the tape. Courtesy: Black & Decker

While you probably enjoy whiling away the hours in your garage workshop, it's a good thing to have a clock out there so you'll know when it's time for a break or to call it a day. You can get a utilitarian timepiece or you can add a bit of pizzazz with something classy and easily visible like this Corvette clock from Mid America.

Courtesy: Mid America Motorworks

ruler and a yard stick. A folding 6-foot carpenter's ruler is also a good choice, as is a gradated 2-foot T-square or an aluminum sheetrock square that has a 4-foot ruler as its spine.

Feeler Gauges

Feeler gauges are more accurately called thickness gauges, and they come in two main styles. One is the blade style, which consists of blades of metal of varying thicknesses with their values stamped or printed upon each blade. The other is the wire style, which uses wires of various thicknesses also with their values stamped above each of the various wire thicknesses.

Feeler gauges are used to check the gap between two surfaces, such as the gap between the center and side electrodes of a spark plug, the gap between ignition points, and other small gaps that require accurate spacing.

Laser and Sonic Measures

These handheld devices enable you to take measurements up to 50 feet. They will determine the square and cubic interior room measurements in both feet and meters for paint, flooring, and realty estimates. Generally equipped with stud finders, they are a boon to locating beams for hanging brackets, shelves, cabinets, and other items on the garage wall. Their measuring capabilities help you to determine how much material will be required for covering the floor,

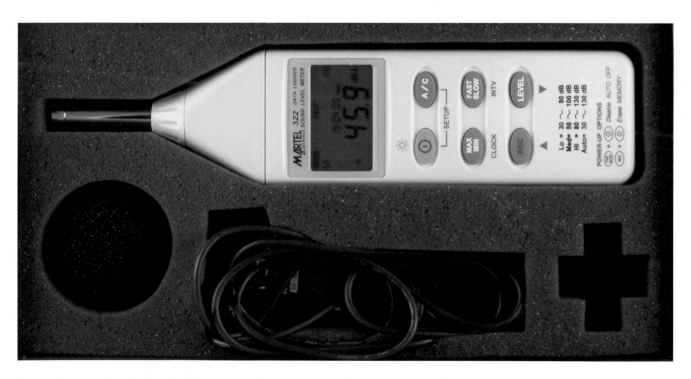

A sound level meter, or decibelometer, is used for taking measurements of ambient sound. Especially useful for measuring the increase in volume of the exhaust system both inside and outside the vehicle after making performance modifications, this Martel Model 322 will also do double-duty for other sound measurements, such as your stereo system's maximum output. The data can also be recorded and downloaded to a PC for comparison and analysis. Courtesy: Martel Electronics Corporation

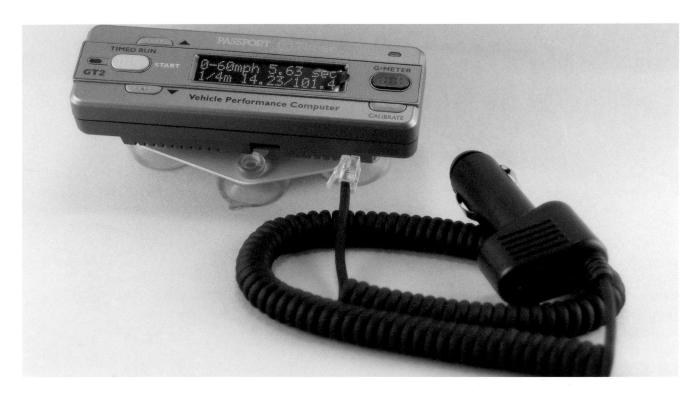

This G-meter measures G forces for acceleration, braking, and cornering, as well as other measurements. It is powered via a cord that plugs into the vehicle's cigarette lighter, and it can store measurements from several runs for downloading and analysis. Courtesy: Mid America Motorworks

walls, and other areas. Built-in lasers also assist in mounting items squarely.

Sound Level Meters

A sound level meter, also known as a decibelometer or decibel meter, measures the volume of sounds. Useful for getting measures of the volume of exhaust systems, in-vehicle stereo system output, and other auditory measurement chores, a good sound level meter should be capable of storing readings from several trials for later comparison or analysis. High-end sound level meters are also capable of interfacing with a personal computer for downloading and analyzing audio data collected.

Clocks

Time to get started; time to take a break; time to knock off: these are all things that a clock will tell you. As essential as pliers, screwdrivers, and wrenches, a good clock is an indispensable piece of garage gear. It doesn't have to be fancy or elaborate, just accurate and visible from a distance to be functional and useful.

Calendars

While not absolutely essential, it's good to have a calendar in the garage to help you keep track of what day it is and also to

Another G meter, this high-end G-Tech Pro SS unit can download saved data to your PC for detailed comparison and analysis. Courtesy: Mid America Motorworks

provide a sense of scheduling for various tasks you're already involved in or planning to undertake. The size and style is entirely your choice. Many gearheads prefer the "pin-up" type often available for free from major tool and auto parts suppliers. But there are a number of other cool car calendars out there (many from Motorbooks, the publisher of this book, in fact) that are more suitable for family viewing.

CHAPTER 11
SHEDDING SOME LIGHT ON THE SUBJECT

In addition to the ambient light that streams in through the windows and open door(s), you'll undoubtedly need a little more illumination when you're out working in your garage. Whether it's overhead electric, incandescent, or fluorescent, basic lighting is key to making the time you spend out in the garage more productive.

General Lighting

Fluorescent lighting is the route most folks take for illuminating their garage, and for several good reasons. These reasons include that the fixtures and bulbs are inexpensive, they're readily available, and the cost of operation versus the amount of light produced is considerably less than incandescent lighting.

In figuring how much light you get from a certain bulb, you can check the number of lumens the bulb produces. The chart below shows the number of lumens the most popular types of bulbs produce.

Lamp	Lumens
60-watt incandescent bulb	850
150-watt soft white incandescent	2,780
40-watt cool white fluorescent	3,050

This flashlight comes as part of the Ryobi rechargeable tool ensemble, or it can be purchased separately. Since it uses the same 18-volt battery as the other tools in the set, you can count on getting several hours of illumination between charges from it. Courtesy: Ryobi

These two tripod lights both feature LED-based illumination and tripod bases for hands-free operation. The larger one has three light ranges, while the smaller one is pocket-sized and even has a handy key ring on it. Both units throw an astonishing amount of light for their sizes. Courtesy: Stanley Tools

This cordless LED inspection light isn't just another flashlight by a long shot. It has an array of 30 high-intensity LEDs that are arranged in a shatterproof, shock- and water-resistant housing that provides an intense flood of non-glare light. The Ni-MH battery provides up to six hours of operation on a single charge, and it has a short recharge cycle. An integrated hanging hook is perfect for working under the hood, or you can lay it flat for an ideal light source under the vehicle. Courtesy: The Eastwood Company

As you can see from the chart, the 40-watt fluorescent bulb emits almost four times as much light as a 60-watt incandescent lightbulb. It also uses a lot less electricity, to boot.

But in addition to luminance, you also want to have light that renders colors accurately, so this is another important consideration. If you're working on the paint or upholstery of a vehicle, having a light source that accurately renders color is of utmost importance. The Color Rendering Index (CRI) is a numerical system that rates the color-rendering ability of fluorescent light compared with natural daylight, which has a CRI of 100. A bulb with a CRI of 91 shows colors more naturally than a bulb with a CRI of 62. Most standard "cool white" fluorescent bulbs range 60 to 75 CRI.

The important factor is how colors look when illuminated by the lightbulb. An incandescent bulb has all the colors of the rainbow, so all colors of your vehicle and other items in your garage will be properly rendered if viewed under an incandescent lightbulb. The CRI for incandescent lamps is a perfect 100. Well-designed fluorescent bulbs have a CRI of 80, which is considered very good. The best you'll find with a standard fluorescent lighting system is about 85 CRI. That's well below the CRI of an incandescent bulb. However, some brands of "daylight" fluorescent tubes, although a bit more expensive, rate as high as 95 CRI, which is really excellent. The chart below will give you a better picture of the CRI for different types of light sources.

Light Type	CRI
Incandescent bulb	95–100
Normal fluorescent tube	75–85
Cool white fluorescent tube	62
"Daylight" fluorescent tube	93–95

Life Expectancies and Costs of Operation

The easiest way to compare the economics of incandescent vs. fluorescent lighting is to consult the variables in the following chart.

Incandescent	Fluorescent
Ten 75-watt incandescent bulbs produce 11,700 lumens	Four 40-watt fluorescent bulbs produce 12,600 lumens
Each incandescent bulb produces 750 hours of light	Each fluorescent bulb produces 20,000 hours of light

For an equal amount of light produced for one full year, the fluorescent bulbs will yield an average savings of $171.81 over incandescent bulbs (source: www.lightathome.com/lightingproducts/energysavings.htm).

Droplights: The Heat Factor

Heat is frequently a byproduct of electric lighting, especially when it comes to incandescent lights. The heat generated from lighting is not desirable, though, and, in some instances, it can be downright dangerous in the garage. For example, let's say you're using an old-fashioned droplight that has a lightbulb encased in a wire cage, and there's a spill of gasoline or another flammable liquid in your garage. If the droplight accidentally falls to the floor, the bulb could shatter, creating a flash as its tungsten element comes into contact with the air. Then the fuel could ignite, creating an absolute disaster in a matter of seconds. It's not the type of scenario any of us want to encounter, for sure.

Halogen bulbs produce an enormous amount of light, but, like incandescents, they also produce a great deal of heat. Additionally, halogen bulbs are fairly fragile when it comes to sustaining bumps and shocks from rough handling. The oil from your fingers can also cause the bulb to fail if it gets on the glass surface. That, coupled with the expense of halogen lighting, makes it less than an ideal work light solution.

Fluorescent work lights don't produce much (if any) heat, so they're comfortable to work with even when they're in close proximity to your body. By nature, however, fluorescent tubes are on the fragile side and they don't tolerate rough handling or dropping well. If you're going to use a fluorescent work light, make sure you get one that totally encases the fluorescent tube in a clear plastic housing. With this protective housing, the tubes won't make a huge mess when they shatter, sending razor-sharp shards of glass all over the place. The plastic encasement contains the mess and makes safe cleanup considerably easier and less time consuming.

Flashlights

Just about everyone has at least one flashlight somewhere in the house and/or garage, and these venerable workhorses have served us well for the better part of the last century. But progress has spawned improvements in flashlights, just as with everything else.

While you can still get a cheap flashlight for a couple of bucks that will adequately help you find the keyhole in your garage door lock on a dark night, the newer versions use LEDs rather than conventional bulbs. These provide more light with less battery drain, so in the twenty-first century you may want to spend a few dollars more for an LED flashlight. It will last longer and cost less to operate for the long haul.

Lanterns

No, I'm not talking about kerosene or propane lanterns here, but the large handheld lights that use big square batteries. These flashlights-on-steroids are great for throwing a large amount of light, and most of them can illuminate a wide area for a decent distance.

Like conventional flashlights, however, they use incandescent bulbs that eat up battery power in a hurry. Your local home improvement center may sell a one-million candle-power lantern that is rechargeable for under $20, and this is a good investment for your garage. Of course, it's wise to keep the charger plugged in all the time so the lantern is fully charged when you need it. While these are a bit cumbersome to use as work lights, they most certainly have their uses.

LED Work Lights

So you want a work light that's durable, doesn't generate a lot of heat, throws a lot of light, and is cheap to operate, huh? Well, step right up, sonny—what you want is an LED work light. That's right, the light emitting diode (LED, for short) is the answer to your work light wishes.

LED lights have an enormous life expectancy—something on the order of 100,000 hours or more before they eventually fail. And because they consume such a minute amount of electricity, they're extremely economical to operate. They also don't give off any heat and their light is very bright. One more bright note: white LED lights generate light that is just about the same color as daylight. So if you're starting to get the warm and fuzzies about the LED light, that's perfectly understandable.

Yet the biggest advantage LED work lights have going for them is their durability. You can drop them, bang them around, or have stuff fall on them, and they'll keep working.

A novel idea, indeed, this baseball cap has two white and two red LEDs built into the brim. The batteries are located on the adjustable headband at the rear of the hat, along with discrete switches for each pair of LEDs. Courtesy: Panther Vision

These lighted safety glasses provide plenty of working light, thanks to their exclusive 1 3/4-inch ultra-high output LED technology. Courtesy: Panther Vision

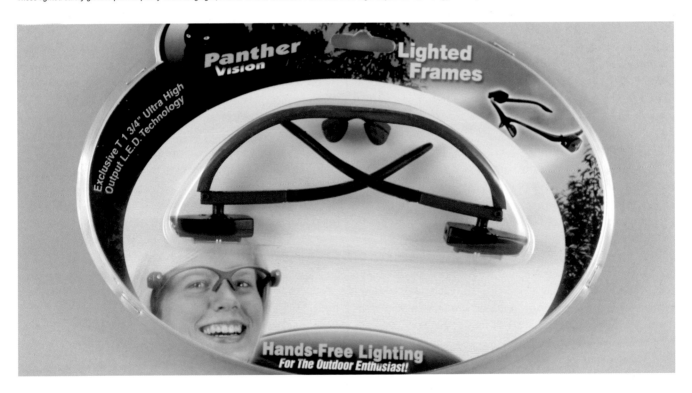

The dual LEDs on these lighted frames can be individually aimed to give either concentrated or wide light distribution and, since they don't have any lenses, they weigh less than the lighted

glasses. Courtesy: Panther Vision

Specifically intended for folks who already wear glasses, these center clip-ons provide a lot of hands-free illumination with minimal weight. Courtesy: Panther Vision

In fact, a couple of brands of LED work lights are guaranteed indestructible. You can drive over them with your vehicle, immerse them in water, or do your worst to them, and they'll still work (or the manufacturer will replace them at no charge). Now that's my kind of work light!

Corded or Cordless

Various work lights come in both corded (AC power) and cordless (rechargeable or battery power) varieties, and each variety has its inherent benefits and disadvantages.

On the plus side, corded lights simply plug into any available wall or extension cord outlet and, as long as there's juice flowing, you have light. The obvious disadvantage is that there may be times when you're not near an outlet, or the extension cord won't reach as far as you need it to. There may also be occasions when you're working outdoors and the weather (e.g., rain) may make it imprudent to use any electric device that's connected to household AC power.

Cordless work lights are battery powered, and these batteries may be disposable alkaline cells, rechargeable NiCad or NiMh cells, or built-in rechargeable batteries. Portability is the biggest advantage of these cordless work lights, since they can go anywhere you need light without the cumbersome umbilical of an AC power cord. The disadvantage is that, sooner or later, the batteries will need to be replaced or recharged. Of course, when you run out of juice, you won't be getting any light from these cordless lights. The amount of time you'll get usable light from a cordless light depends on the light itself, the candle power of its output, and the strength of the batteries that power it. There's no hard and fast rule that states two double A rechargeable cells will give you a certain number of minutes of light.

There's also an economic factor you'll want to consider here as well. When using a corded work light, you're pretty much paying for the light and a few cents per hour to operate it (aside from the cost of a bulb if it needs to be replaced). With cordless work lights, you have to consider the cost of batteries. If you're using disposable alkaline cells, this can suck up some serious cash over time if you use the light frequently. Likewise, rechargeable cells and a charger will set you back some cash initially, but in the long run will be more economical than using disposables. Cordless work lights with integrated rechargeable batteries are the most expensive of the bunch. As is often the case, when the integrated battery reaches the end of its useful life, so does the light, since the battery can't be replaced. All of this information is certainly worth thinking over before purchasing a work light or lights for your garage.

These Lynx lights attach using Velcro to just about anything you can think of—tools, hats, work surfaces, you name it. They come with a handy carrying case, too, for versatile hands-free lighting that goes wherever you do. Courtesy: Panther Vision

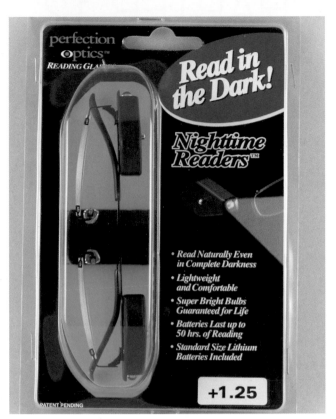

These nighttime reading glasses are great for reading in bed without disturbing your partner, but they're also excellent for working under the dashboard or in other dark spots where you need both light and magnification to see what you're doing. These are available in various magnification strengths, too. Courtesy: Panther Vision

Look, Ma, No Hands!

There are countless times when you'll wish you had a third hand to hold a light on your work. I know I've had more than my fair share of these occasions, particularly when working on inaccessible areas such as the underside of a dashboard. I wish I had a dollar for every time I had a battery-operated penlight clenched in my teeth while doing this kind of work. That's why I was really happy to find out about a whole slew of hands-free lighting solutions that are now available, which include the following:

• **Pocket lights:** battery-operated lights that simply clip onto your pocket or collar and usually have a flexible neck so you can direct the beam onto your work.

• **Pen lights:** slim battery-powered flashlights that you can hold in your teeth if necessary to direct the light where you want it while working with both hands.

• **Clip-on lights:** battery-powered lights that have clips, clamps, or fasteners to hold them in a stationary position to keep your work area illuminated.

• **Head lights:** an elastic headband that holds an LED light that can be aimed up or down to light up your desired work area. Very lightweight, they throw a surprisingly large amount of light for so small a package.

• **Wearable lights:** come in a wide variety of styles that include illuminated eyeglass frames, clip-on frames, and even hats with LEDs built in.

• **Tripod lights:** LED flashlights that have tripod-stands built into them to permit you to aim the light where you want it to shine.

Utility Lights

Utility lights are rechargeable flashlights that usually come as part of a rechargeable tool set, and they use the same rechargeable battery as the other tools in the set. Generally they emit a good amount of light and, because they are powered by a high-capacity power cell, they have excellent light duration between charges.

CHAPTER 12
A BREATH OF FRESH (COMPRESSED) AIR

In my years as a gearhead, I've really come to like working with air tools. Why? Well, there are a number of reasons, including the following:

- Air tools have a better power-to-weight ratio compared to electric tools.
- They're safer than electric.
- They don't require the cooling-off period needed by some electric tools.
- They have simpler design and construction.
- They're more powerful.
- They're not damaged by stalling.
- They're more rugged and reliable.

Like just about everything else in life, though, air tools have a downside, too. They require an air compressor for power, and compressors are inherently noisy and consume considerable amounts of electricity.

Regarding the noise level, you have three options: 1) deal with it; 2) turn up the stereo really loud; or 3) wear hearing protectors or ear plugs (the best of the 3 choices). That being said, there is still no substitute for air tools when it comes to a large number of garage jobs.

How Air Tools Work

For some reason, most folks who are into all things mechanical have a pretty good handle on how most electric tools work, yet find the mechanisms that power air tools shrouded in mystery. So let's talk a little bit about the nuts and bolts of air tools.

All air tools fall into two basic categories: ones that use rotational power, such as drills and ratchets, and ones that use percussive power, such as air hammers and reciprocating saws.

Rotational power comes from an air motor. An air motor works by creating a flow of air over a rotor in a cylinder. This air flow causes the rotor to turn and produce a torque proportional to the pressure of the air supply.

Percussive power is produced by applying air to either side of a piston in a cylinder so the piston is propelled either forward and/or backward. That motion produces a force on the object the piston comes into contact with.

There, the mystery is solved. That wasn't so hard to understand now, was it? OK, now that you understand the mechanisms involved, it's time to look at the source of all this power, which is, of course, compressed air.

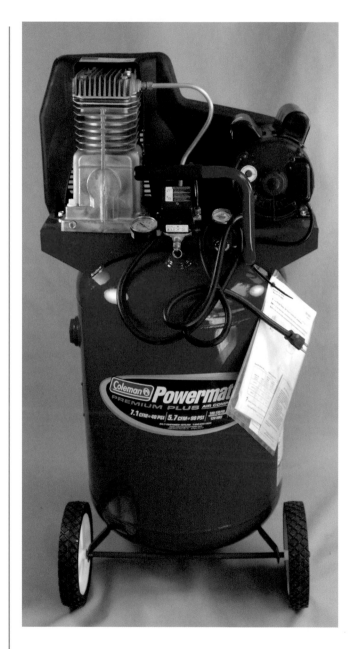

A good air compressor that is capable of delivering the power you'll need (with a large enough tank) is the first piece of equipment for your pneumatic gear arsenal. This vertical unit from Coleman Powermate has maximum pressure of 100–130 psi and delivers 7.1 cfm @ 40 psi and 5.7 cfm @ 90 psi. It has 5 peak horsepower, and its air tank has a 27-gallon capacity. A compressor like this should serve the needs of even the most ardent garage gearhead.
Courtesy: Coleman Powermate

A tool caddy like this drapes around a vertical air compressor and has pockets to hold extra chucks, blow guns, inflation needles, extensions, and other accessories. It keeps everything you use frequently with your compressor close at hand, and it saves space, too.

Courtesy: Coleman Powermate

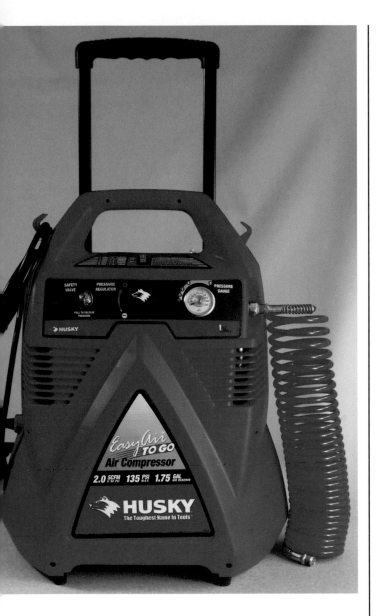

If you anticipate lighter pneumatic power needs and you want a compressor light enough to travel with, perhaps you should consider this Husky unit. It puts out 2 cfm @ 90 psi, has a maximum pressure of 135 psi, and has a 1.75-gallon reserve tank. While it isn't what you'd want to paint a vehicle with in your garage, it's certainly up to inflating a raft, air mattresses, pumping up a flat, and powering low-demand air tools. Courtesy: Husky Tools

Putting the Squeeze on Air

Air compressors hold compressed air in their tanks until it is ready to be used. The amount of force the air is released with is controlled by a regulator.

Air compressors can have either vertical or horizontal tanks, and they can have one or more compressing cylinders. They can also be electrically powered (which is what most folks want in their garages) or they can be powered by a small gasoline engine, which is useful if you have to take the compressor on a job site for vehicle repair, construction, or other purposes.

Compressors are rated on their motor power, tank capacity, maximum output pressure, and the volume of air they can move. The motor power is measured in horsepower (1 horsepower, 2.5 horsepower, etc.), and the tank capacity is measured in gallons (5 gallons, 10 gallons, etc.). The output pressure is measured in pounds-per-square inch or psi (90 psi, 120 psi, etc.), and the volume of air is measured in cubic-feet-per minute, or cfm. This last measure is probably the most important, since most air-powered tools specify a minimum cfm volume required for satisfactory operation.

For the average hobbyist who uses air tools occasionally, a compressor with a 10-gallon tank and at least 90 psi of output should be sufficient. On the other hand, if you intend to paint a vehicle, you'll want a much larger tank (30- to 50-gallon capacity) and pressure output of 120 psi, so you'll have a plentiful supply of uninterrupted air.

Generally, the larger the compressor is, the larger the motor is, and, consequently, the more electrical power it will need. If you only have 12-amp electrical service in your garage, don't buy a 15-amp compressor because you'll be snapping the circuit breaker every time you turn the compressor on. (See the section on electrical power for your garage in Chapter 2.) And, as you've probably figured out by now, the larger the compressor, the higher the price will be. This is not to say that you should buy something small that won't be adequate for your current and future foreseeable needs, but at the other extreme you don't need a large commercial compressor that is capable of supplying five or six mechanics working with air tools simultaneously. For even the hard-core wrenches out

Compressor oil is the lubricant that will keep your compressor and air tools working smoothly for trouble-free operation. Adequate lubrication is crucial, so always keep a quart on hand. Don't be afraid to use it! Courtesy: Coleman Powermate

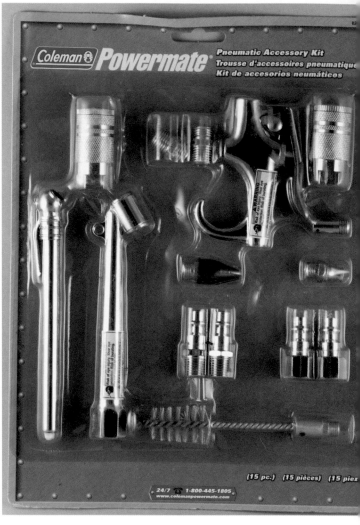

A pneumatic accessory kit is a good way to get the items you'll need and save some money over individual purchases at the same time. Courtesy: Coleman Powermate

there, a 30-gallon compressor putting out 120 psi and 7 to 9 cfm should be more than adequate for anything you would want to undertake in your garage.

Compressors can be oil-lubricated or oil-less, depending on their design. They also can be direct driven or belt driven. These are all features that vary with the manufacturer and model. The important thing is to get a compressor with enough "oomph" to do the work you want it to do.

Got Oil?

Oil-lubricated compressors are significantly quieter than most oil-less compressors and, if taken care of, can literally last a lifetime. You will need to change the oil periodically (once per year is usually enough for home shops, but follow your manufacturer's directions), and you'll need to install a high-quality inline filter because of small amounts of oil that get in the air. Life expectancy generally runs anywhere from 2,000 to 6,000 actual pumping hours between rebuilds, and they generally feature all cast-iron construction for durability and noise reduction.

Oil-less compressors are designed with a low-friction coating on their moving parts to eliminate the need for oil. These compressors are generally less expensive than their oil-lubricated counterparts. Because there is no residue

Don't skimp when purchasing an air hose. The best ones are only a few dollars for a 50-foot length. Make sure you get a hose that's rated at 300 psi, is shielded, and has a highly visible color so you won't trip over it in the garage. Courtesy: Coleman Powermate

from any lubricating oil, the air they produce is cleaner (although you should still use an inline filter). On the downside, these compressors are really loud (89 decibels and higher) and generally have duty cycles of 50 percent or less. Oil-less compressors are usually made of aluminum to reduce weight.

Two-Stage vs. Single-Stage

Single-stage compressors take air into their cylinders at atmospheric pressure and compress it with a single stroke of the piston directly to the desired pressure. The air is then passed through a cooler (called an aftercooler), which removes some of the heat generated by compression. This type of compressor is most commonly used for applications where the pressure requirements are not in excess of 150 psi. In other words, it will serve nicely for just about any home garage workshop.

Compressor efficiency varies with pressure, being lower at higher pressures. At high pressure or above 130 psi, the efficiency of a single-stage compressor falls off rapidly and a two-stage compressor should be used. Note that single-stage efficiency (55 percent to 70 percent) is lower than that of two-stage compressors (75 percent to 80 percent).

The dual-stage compressor builds to the maximum tank pressure faster and with less strain on the motor. It accomplishes this by having one piston pump air into a smaller volume cylinder and then compressing that with another piston before it goes into the tank. A single-stage two cylinder compressor has two cylinders; a dual-stage two cylinder compressor has four cylinders.

Two-stage air compressors provide a reliable air source in commercial, industrial, and automotive applications. These units are more efficient, compressing air to a higher pressure

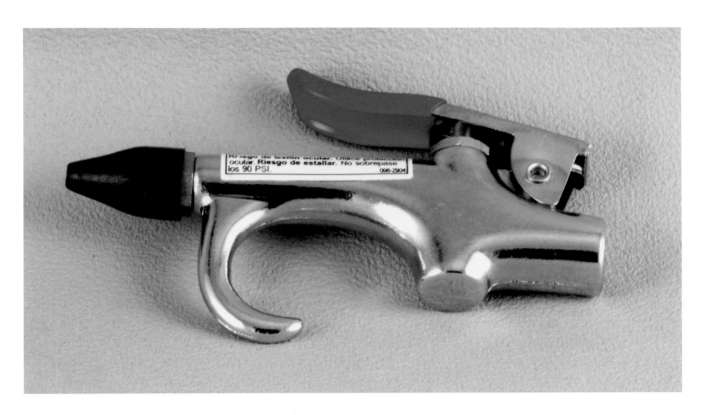

An air blow gun comes in very handy for blowing away loose dust, leaves, loose rust, and other debris, so it's definitely an accessory you'll want to have on hand in your garage.

Courtesy: Coleman Powermate

You'll need quick couplers to quickly attach and detach the hose to and from the compressor and, on the opposite side of the hose, to attach and detach your air tools. They're available in galvanized finish and, for a little more money, solid brass. Personally, I prefer the brass units because they don't rust in damp environments. Courtesy: Coleman Powermate

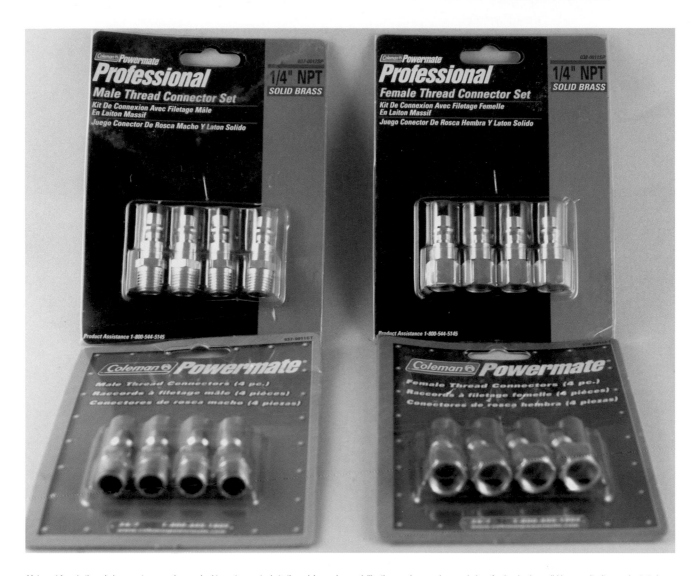

Male and female threaded connectors are also required to mate your tools to the quick couplers and, like the couplers, you have a choice of galvanized or solid brass units. It never hurts to have a few spares on hand, either, because you'll need them as your pneumatic tool collection grows. Courtesy: Coleman Powermate

than single-stage compressors. This allows more air to be stored for future use while generating less heat, reducing wear, and extending compressor life. The downside is that dual-stage compressors are more expensive than single-stage units.

Duty Cycles

The duty cycle of an air compressor is the percentage of the time it is designed to run before it must rest and cool off. Each manufacturer lists the duty cycle in the specifications of that compressor.

How often the compressor will be running and resting can be calculated by figuring what cfm will be used (a combination of nozzle orifice size and psi), the tank size, pressure cut on, and maximum pressure. Some compressors are listed as continuous duty (100 percent duty cycle). For

these, you can expect to pay more than others that have less than 100 percent duty cycles.

Compressors generate a lot of heat while in use, and the heat is tough on the pump components. These components will wear out quickly if the compressor runs all the time. If you don't want to over work your compressor and risk burning it out, you must get a compressor that is capable of delivering about 50 percent more air than the tool you're running will demand.

For example, if a person is using an media-blasting gun with a 3/32-inch nozzle requiring 5 cfm at 40 psi to blast glass, then the compressor must deliver about 7-8 cfm at 40 psi in order to meet the usage criteria of 50 percent excess air capability. As the nozzle enlarges to 1/8-inch wide, the same compressor should deliver about 12-13 cfm at 40 psi.

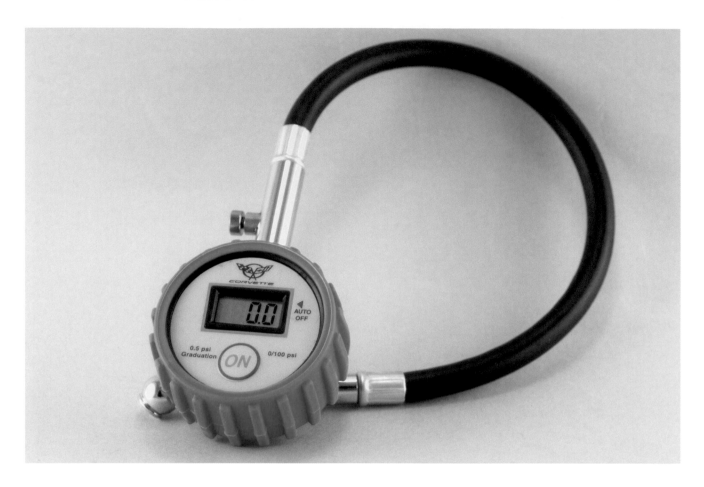

A good tire gauge is an essential piece of gear to monitor the pressure in your vehicle tires. Available in analog or digital versions (shown), they're inexpensive and can save you lots of money by extending the life of your tires. Courtesy: Mid America Motorworks

Let's Accessorize

There's more to pneumatic tools than just buying a tool and a compressor. You're going to need several other items to make everything work the way it should, including the following:

• An air hose, the essential link between the air compressor and the tool it powers. I recommend getting at least one 50-foot air hose made of PVC with a 3/8-inch diameter rated at 300 psi. As far as color goes, yellow or orange is preferable because these highly-visible colors help keep you from tripping over the hose while it's in use. Other desirable features in an air hose include solid brass fittings and a spiral reinforcement under the "skin" to help prevent kinks. A hose covering that is oil- and abrasion-resistant is another good feature to look for.

• Quick couplers, which come in both male and female varieties. They enable you to connect and disconnect the hose and air tools quickly. Because they are spring-loaded, you merely pull the collar back and push the male end into the female end, release the collar, and you're ready to do work. It's advisable to have connectors mounted on each of your air tools, so you don't have to constantly swap them. Having each tool equipped with its own connector enables you to save time and effort by changing tools in a matter of seconds.

• Compressor and tool oil. If you have an oil-lubricated air compressor, you'll want to have compressor oil on hand to keep the reservoir filled to the prescribed level. And even if you have an oil-less compressor, you'll still need compressor oil to keep your air tools well-lubricated. Virtually every air tool has a lubricating hole into which you should squirt a few drops of oil prior to each use. Well-lubricated air tools work better and last longer.

• Compressor tool caddy, a canvas apron, if you will, that drapes around a vertical air compressor and has pockets to hold extra chucks, blow guns, inflation needles, extensions, and other accessories. At under $15, these caddies are very handy for keeping your frequently used pneumatic accessories readily available without taking up additional valuable workbench or counter space.

• Blow gun. No, we're not talking about the hollow pipes the natives use in the Congo to shoot small monkeys and other prey for dinner out of the treetops! A pneumatic blow gun is a small handle with a trigger on it that, when pressed, emits a powerful jet of air. These are very useful for blowing off loose dust, rust flakes, and other debris from your vehicle.

• Air chuck, a fitting that attaches to a quick coupler. It is used for inflating tires or other items with similar inflation valves (e.g., portable air tanks).

• Inflation needle, a thin needle that attaches to an air chuck. It's used for inflating footballs, basketballs, soccer balls, and other items that have a very small inflation port.

• Air driers, the desiccant dryers are used to remove water vapor from the compressed air system.

• Filters, used to protect the desiccant air dryer from oil vapor and contaminants.

A retractable air hose reel makes keeping your air hose stowed when not in use and readily available when you need it. The reel can be mounted on a wall stud or ceiling beam near the compressor, and the hose retracts with a simple tug, keeping it off the floor and out of the way when you're not using it. Courtesy: The Eastwood Company

• Pressure regulator. While virtually all air compressors have built-in regulators, it is often desirable to have a separate regulator attached directly to your air tool so that you can provide fine air control for the spray gun or air tool. Regulators with built-in gauges are the way to go, since they let you see what the air pressure is at a glance.

• Tire gauge. I'll bet you know what this is, and what it's used for, right? This handy tool that measures the air pressure

HARD AIR LINES

Most of us start out with a neoprene hose connected directly to the air compressor. After a while, the hose gets to be a bit of a hassle. It seems that the hose is always in your way. It picks up dust and dirt from the garage floor, so you can't handle it without getting your hands dirty, and, more often than not, it's not quite long enough to reach where you need it. And that's to say nothing of what a pain spooling the hose after using it can be.

Some folks like the retractable reels, but they aren't always a total solution. Reels still have a single outlet, and you have to pull the hose from one end of the shop to the other, so you have the "rubber snake" draping across the floor again. The more you use your compressor, the more you'll want to install "hard" air lines around the perimeter of your garage.

With hard lines, you can place an outlet or coupler every few feet along the wall. Like compressor tanks, the bigger the air lines the better. You'll want a huge volume of air coming out the end of the air line, and only a larger line can provide that. I strongly advise you to use 1/2-inch lines because a smaller diameter won't delivery the volume you need.

You also should use metal pipes rather than PVC to help remove moisture from your air lines. When the compressed and heated air strikes cold metal pipes, the moisture in the air condensates, which is much easier to remove from metal lines.

Putting a lot of U-turns in the air lines also helps to minimize moisture in the lines. Water, being heavier than the air, has a hard time making all the turns. It gets trapped in the pipes and can be removed by opening drain valves you install in the lines.

If you have basic soldering skills, you can use 1/2-inch copper pipe with soldered joints. Optionally, you can use 1-inch inside diameter iron pipe with threaded ends, but this will cost you a bit more than the copper tubing. You'll also have to settle for stock lengths unless you have a pipe threader or are willing to pay additionally to have them threaded. Use standard drain valves to remove any accumulated moisture in the lines and standard hanger clamps to attach the lines to the walls.

(based on information from Ultimate Garage Handbook *by Richard Newton, MBI Publishing Company, ISBN: 0-7603-1640-6)*

If you do a lot of mechanical work, then you'll find a good 3/8-inch drive air ratchet to be indispensable. This handy tool really speeds up disassembly and reassembly for tasks that you'd normally use a manual ratchet and socket set for. Courtesy: Stanley Tools

in your tires, comes in both analog and digital varieties, and in different shapes and sizes.

• Portable air tank, available in 5- and 10-gallon sizes. These provide a convenient way of taking compressed air with you wherever you go. These tanks are equipped with pressure gauges, hoses, and air chucks. They're very handy for inflating flat tires, air mattresses, rafts, or other items that rely on compressed air to enable their usefulness

• Hose reel. One of my least favorite tasks is winding and storing the air hose attached to my compressor when I'm done using it. I've eliminated this pain-in-the-butt chore by getting a self-winding air-hose reel. With this nifty device, I can just give the hose a tug when I'm done using it, causing the reel to retract the hose automatically. No fuss, no muss—a very worthwhile investment.

• Air tool rack, which is very handy for keeping your air tools conveniently located for immediate use. The rack mounts on the wall or to the underside of a wall cabinet. It's made of heavy stainless steel so it won't rust, and it can be locked to prevent unauthorized access to your air tools.

You can also save quite a bit of money by purchasing an accessory kit that contains all of these items, plus a few addi-

tional accessories like a wire brush for cleaning your air tool equipment. These accessory kits usually contain a few quick connects and other useful items, too.

A 3/8-inch drive pneumatic impact wrench is another "must have" staple of any well-equipped air tool complement. This tool delivers a bit more "oomph" than an air ratchet, and its gun-like shape permits bracing it with two hands for those stubborn fasteners. Courtesy: Stanley Tools

This heavy-duty pneumatic saber saw easily cuts through aluminum, steel, plastic, and fiberglass up to .080-inch (14 gauge). It's ideal for body shop repair, muffler, and exhaust work. It has an adjustable blade guide that increases blade life, and it cuts straight and tight radius curves on flat and curved surfaces at the rate of 10,000 strokes per minute. Courtesy: The Eastwood Company

A mini die grinder like this one is another handy air tool. This particular one has a comfort-grip palm trigger and comes with two different sized chucks for added versatility. Courtesy: Coleman Powermate

Air Power Punch

Air tools come from a wide variety of manufacturers and in many styles and capacities. As with all other tool categories, you're best advised to stay with the name brands. Though they don't cost a king's ransom, air tools are an investment that you'll want to spend wisely on—buying a quality air tool now for a couple of bucks more than the bargain-basement, no-name brand will pay off with trouble-free service for many years to come.

That being said, here's what you can expect to find in the realm of pneumatic power tools:

• Impact wrench, a heavy-duty air ratchet that delivers a tremendous amount of torque with a hammering action at the same time. Available in 3/8-inch and 1/2-inch drive (and larger sizes, too), the latter is most often used in torqueing lug nuts and doing exhaust system work. A decent impact wrench is an essential part of any garage owner's pneumatic tool set.

• Reversible air drill, available in 3/8-inch and 1/2-inch chuck sizes. These are real work- and time-savers, since they are much faster and more powerful than their comparable electrically powered counterparts.

• Air hammer, also sometimes called an air chisel. This tool causes the bit inserted into it to pound against the surface it is applied to. With a flat bit inserted, it is indeed a hammer,

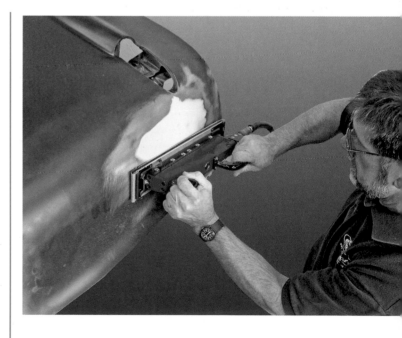

A straight-line pneumatic sander works great on plastic fillers at any stage of hardening and feathers with ease and smoothness. It has a two-handle configuration for comfortable operation and balance. Its dual-piston design provides efficient power and prevents stalling while delivering a 1-inch stroke at 2,200 strokes per minute.

Courtesy: The Eastwood Company

A pneumatic air hammer is great for dislodging stubborn exhaust components and, when a chisel blade is inserted, it can also cut through exhaust pipes, mufflers, and the like in short order. The spring collet keeps the blades seated while in use. Courtesy: Husky Tools

but it can cut through metal when a chisel bit is inserted. It's a heavy-duty tool for heavy-duty jobs.

• Cut-off tool, a very handy tool that you'll probably use more often that you expect. Cut-off tools usually use 3-inch abrasive wheels and are great for slicing through sheet metal, steel rods, muffler clamps, exhaust pipes, and other metal-cutting chores.

• Air ratchet, available in both 1/4-inch and 3/8-inch drive sizes. They greatly speed up the tasks of tightening or loosening nuts and bolts. Simply turning a knob on the top of the ratchet reverses its rotational direction.

• Orbital sander, available in various sizes. The sanding pads of these tools rotate in a variable elliptical orbit, hence their name. They are very useful for paint removal and other automotive body work, so every gearhead needs at least one orbital sander in his garage.

• Die grinder, available in 1/4-inch and 1/8-inch chuck sizes. Using various bits, they can be used to grind, file, cut, drill, sand, polish, de-burr, smooth, and shape (as well as a host of other tasks).

• Right angle die grinder, an air-powered die grinder with the chuck at a 90-degree angle to the handle. The angle makes this tool handy for accessing hard-to-reach parts.

• Buffer/polisher, uses a soft polishing bonnet rather than a sanding pad. It is most useful for buffing out newly painted finishes and polishing.

• Pneumatic cutting shear, quickly cuts sheet metal up to 16-gauge and leaves a smooth, clean edge. Its uses are limited to sheetmetal forming and body work.

• Air nibbler, used for cutting sheet metal and body panels. An air nibbler leaves the metal smooth and free of burrs and distortion. This is a nice tool to have if you do a lot of sheetmetal work, but it is a luxury item that can easily be substituted with a hand nibbler for limited applications.

• Pneumatic file, an air-powered filer that provides increased control over hand filing and requires a lot less effort. Air files are great for enlarging holes, cleaning up edges, and smoothing metal work prior to painting. They are usually supplied with four file blades (flat, round, triangular, and bastard cuts), and they typically deliver 9,000 strokes per minute.

• Air palm sanders, available in 3-inch and 6-inch sizes. These sanders are lightweight and powerful, delivering 10,000 rpm with no load. Since they are controlled directly by the palm of your hand, they offer excellent precision for sanding delicate areas.

If you're just starting to build your air tool collection, you may want to consider purchasing a starter set like this one from Coleman Powermate that contains every tool and accessory you're likely to need for some time to come. Courtesy: Coleman Powermate

• Spray guns, covered in more detail in Chapter 16. Air-powered spray guns are the defacto standard for vehicle painting and painting anything when a professional finish is desired. Available in gravity-fed and suction-feed types, spray guns come in a wide variety of styles and price ranges.

• Hot coat guns, also covered in more detail in Chapter 16. Hot coat powder coating guns are similar to spray guns, but rather than spraying paint, they spray powder for powder coating.

• Air saber saw, can cut through aluminum, steel, plastic, fiberglass, and other materials up to .080-inch thick at the rate of 10,000 strokes per minute. Medium-coarse (24 teeth per inch) and fine (32 teeth per inch) blades are available and can be changed in just a few seconds.

• Abrasive blasters, available in both cabinet and handheld versions. Abrasive blasters can use sand or other abrasive mediums, and they're great for removing paint, rust, powder coating, and other finishes, as well as restoring bare metal to like-new condition.

• Straight-line sander, a pneumatic sander that oscillates its sanding surface back and forth in a straight line. This tool is excellent for quickly removing paint or body filler from flat surfaces and it delivers a 1-inch stroke at 2,200 strokes per minute.

CHAPTER 13
AN ELECTRICAL EXPERIENCE

It's hard to believe when you think about it, but 150 years ago there was no such thing as electricity: no electric lights, no refrigerators, no air conditioners.

Electrical power is so much a part of our lives that we scarcely give it a second thought. After all, it's a given that the power is always there when we need it—except, of course, for those times when a power line is knocked out during a storm or other natural disaster. Electricity isn't something we should take for granted, however, since we rely so heavily upon it. And not just in our homes, but in our vehicles as well.

It's never any fun to discover your vehicle has an electrical problem. Of course, diagnosing that problem is not always easy. Since vehicles run on DC, or direct current, dealing with their electrical problems is different from when you've got an electrical problem in your home (which runs on AC, or alternating current).

To diagnose your vehicle's electrical issues, you can use any one of the following tools:

• A circuit tester, used primarily to check whether a circuit is "hot" in automotive wiring. This probe with a see-through handle has a light inside it and a lead attached to the other side, usually with an alligator clip. To check for the presence of a live circuit, you attach the clip end to a suitable ground on the vehicle and touch the probe tip to the point you think is hot. If it is indeed hot, the light in the handle glows.

Another invaluable diagnostic tool for electrical work is a good autoranging multimeter with a digital readout. A multimeter can measure AC and DC voltage, resistance, capacitance, continuity, and many other functions to diagnose and help you correct electrical problems. Courtesy: The Eastwood Company

One of the most valuable tools you can have for troubleshooting vehicle electrical problems is a circuit tester. When using it, you attach the lead with the alligator clip to a known ground of the circuit to be tested, and then touch the tester's probe tip to a positive contact point. If the bulb inside the tester doesn't light up, there's a short or break somewhere in the circuit. Courtesy: NAPA

• Continuity tester, checks if a circuit is unbroken or "continuous," hence its name. Usually equipped with an LED or an audible buzzer, the tip of the tester is touched to one point of the circuit while the attached probe lead is touched to the opposite end. If the circuit is continuous, the LED lights up or the buzzer sounds. If nothing happens, that indicates that there is a break in the circuit. Continuity testers usually have an internal battery to power them.

• Multimeters, electronic instruments that measure DC voltage, AC voltage, RMS, DC and AC current, resistance, capacitance, inductance, frequency/periods, and diode measurements. Powered by an internal battery, multimeters are supplied with at least one set of leads. Many multimeters can also indicate continuity and perform other functions. Specialty automotive multimeters can also provide tachometer, dwell, and other functions, too. Available in either analog (needle and dial) styles or digital readouts, a good multimeter is a must-have tool in any well-equipped garage.

• Fault finder, a handy tool to have when working on automotive electrical circuits. Fault finders locate shorts, opens, broken wires, or current leaks inside wire bundles, under carpet, or behind panels. Designed to read 6- through 42-VDC circuits, fault finders do not require you to pierce wire. You simply connect the unit's transmitter in series with the wire and scan the current path with the tracer's probe.

• Battery load tester, not an absolute necessity, but inexpensive enough to have a place in your garage. This instrument will accurately report the condition of a battery in a minute or two, and this is good information to have, since recharging a bad battery only gives it temporary or "surface power." A freshly charged battery may accept and hold a surface charge, yet still not crank an engine over. The load tester will let you know if it's time to replace the battery or not.

• Spark checker, a handy device that has a spark plug boot on one end, a see-through window in the middle, and a spark plug terminal at the other end. One end of the checker

A specialty multimeter like this Ferret 95 offers additional capabilities for testing automotive functions above and beyond those of a standard multimeter. The Ferret 95, in addition to all the standard multimeter functions, can also measure AC and DC volts from 1 milliVolt to over 200 volts in four different ranges. The ohms function measures from a 10th of an ohm to 40 million ohms. Additionally, the meter can measure up to 10,000 rpm on two- or four-cycle engines and measure from 10 milliamps to 20 amps. Courtesy: GXT, Inc.

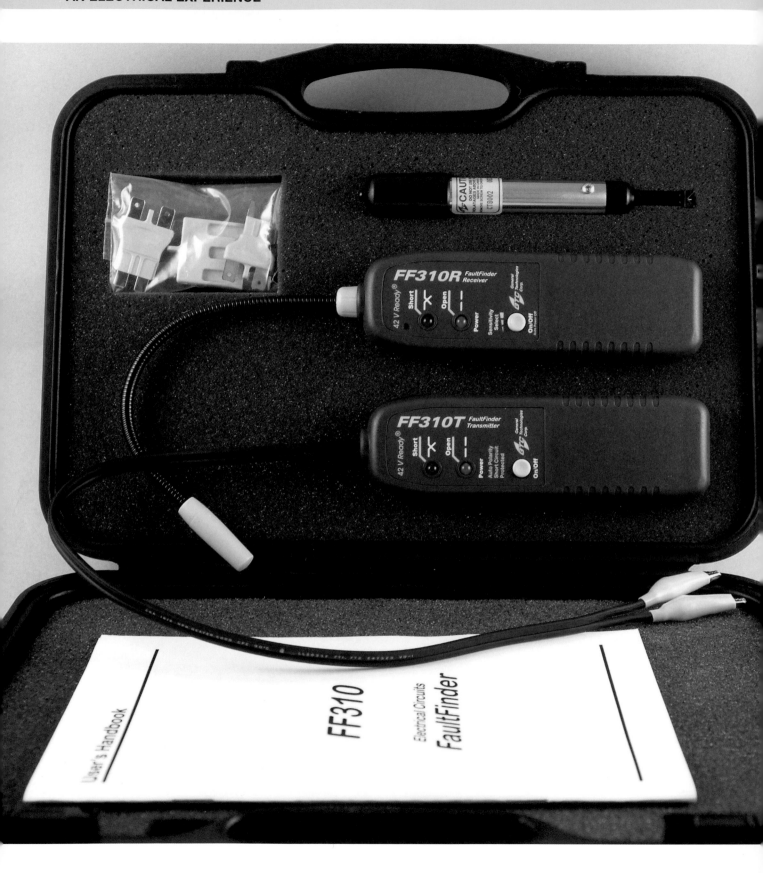

A digital electric circuit fault finder is an invaluable tool for locating shorts and broken circuits, as well as tracing circuits and locating faults in automotive wiring. If you do a lot of this kind of work, it is definitely worth the investment. Courtesy: The Eastwood Company

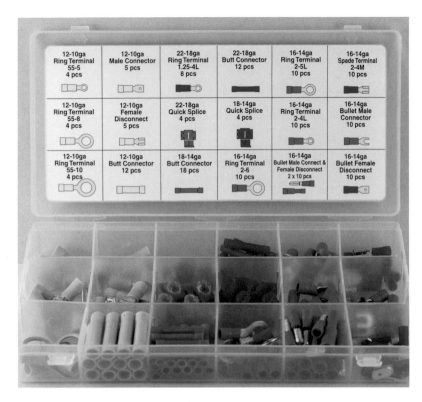

12-10ga Ring Terminal 55-5 4 pcs	12-10ga Male Connector 5 pcs	22-18ga Ring Terminal 1.25-4L 8 pcs	22-18ga Butt Connector 12 pcs	16-14ga Ring Terminal 2-5L 10 pcs	16-14ga Spade Terminal 2-4M 10 pcs
12-10ga Ring Terminal 55-8 4 pcs	12-10ga Female Disconnect 5 pcs	22-18ga Quick Splice 4 pcs	18-14ga Quick Splice 4 pcs	16-14ga Ring Terminal 2-4L 10 pcs	16-14ga Bullet Male Connector 10 pcs
12-10ga Ring Terminal 55-10 4 pcs	12-10ga Butt Connector 12 pcs	18-14ga Butt Connector 18 pcs	16-14ga Ring Terminal 2-6 10 pcs	16-14ga Bullet Male Connect & Female Disconnect 2 x 10 pcs	16-14ga Bullet Female Disconnect 10 pcs

If you've ever done any electrical work on a vehicle and needed a terminal connector, but didn't have the right one on hand, you can appreciate how having an assortment of the most popular connectors is a good thing to keep in your garage. Courtesy: The Eastwood Company

attaches to the spark plug that you're testing and the plug wire from the engine attaches to the opposite end of the checker. When the engine is started, the spark is visible in the window of the checker if all is operating as it should be. If no spark is visible, there is a problem in the circuit, which may be with the plug wire, the distributor, the distributor cap, the coil, or another ignition component.

• Benchtop power supply, a useful piece of gear for checking the functionality of such components as windshield wiper motors, power window motors, horns, and more, especially if you don't have a jump box or fully-charged battery available for such testing purposes.

An extremely handy device to make sure electrical current is reaching a spark plug, this spark checker attaches between the plug wire and the spark plug. A spark is visible in its viewing window if everything is functioning as it should. Courtesy: The Eastwood Company

A battery load tester will accurately report the condition of a battery in a minute or two and let you know if it's time to replace it. Courtesy: The Eastwood Company

JUST NEED ONE MORE JOLT

So you battery is dead, at least that's what your battery load tester says (that, and the fact you can't even turn your car over). If you call yourself a gearhead, you should have no worries, though. You've got the essentials to get some volts back into your powerless car, right?

Well, if you don't, here's what you need to get your vehicle running again:

• Battery charger, which can keep power level up on seldom-used vehicles or charge dead batteries. The power, size, and price of battery chargers vary from about $30 to several hundred. Most users can get by with a modest charger in the under $100 price range, but if you have several vehicles, you may find it to be a better investment to go with a heavy-duty charger that has a fast-charge cycle on it. It's important not to skimp on a charger, however. You definitely want to get one that has built-in overload protection, since this will protect both the charger and the battery.

• Trickle charger, a particularly useful piece of gear for vehicles that are stored over the winter or used infrequently. A trickle charger maintains a full charge on the vehicle's battery without overcharging it and draws very little household current while in use.

• Booster cables. Again, the best advice I can give you here is not to be penny-wise and dollar-foolish. Spend a few dollars extra to get a good set of cables with multistranded conductors, preferably shielded, of at least 15-feet in length. The spring clamps on both ends should also be insulated and have good mating on the "teeth" of the clamp, so they will grip the battery terminals securely. A cheap set of cables won't conduct sufficient electricity to successfully jump the battery,

A trickle charger like this Battery Tender will keep your battery fully charged without overcharging it. This is a very useful piece of equipment for vehicles that are infrequently used or stored for long periods of time. Courtesy: The Eastwood Company

and the cables will become hot, indicating that they are not good conductors. By purchasing a good set of booster cables, you'll be getting a piece of gear that should last you for many years and give you trouble-free service. Think about it for a minute: what good is a set of booster cables that don't do what they're supposed to do when you need them?

• Terminal kits. Many different types of electrical terminals and connectors are used in automotive electrical work, and these various items can be expensive if you purchase them individually. For the sake of both economy and convenience, it makes more sense to purchase a kit that contains all of the most commonly used terminals and connectors, so you'll always have what you need on hand in your garage.

• Jump boxes, also called "hot boxes." These are self-contained batteries with terminal clamps attached that are designed for jump-starting vehicles with weak or dead batteries. Again, as with other tool and gear purchases, don't go with the bargain basement jump box. Some of the better jump boxes also have built-in lights and charge gauges. Some even have air compressors to pump up a slow leak on the roadside.

A jump box, also called a hot box, can be a real lifesaver when you have a dead or weak battery. Essentially, it is a sealed, rechargeable 12-volt battery enclosed in an easy-to-carry case. It has cables and terminal clamps already attached. A built-in voltage meter gives you an accurate reading of the cranking power available and the charge state of the jump box. Courtesy: Husky Tools

Tool Tip

MAKE YOUR OWN TEST LIGHT

Electrical problems can be particularly vexing to diagnose and fix on just about any vehicle. For that reason, a test light is an essential tool that should be in every toolbox. You can purchase a test light at a local auto parts store or catalog supplier, or you can save yourself the $20 and make one yourself from components that you probably have in your spare parts box. If you don't have any of these components, you can get what you need for a couple of bucks at the local Radio Shack.

But before you build one, you should know what to use it for. A test light, also known as a line tester or circuit tester, determines whether electrical power is being supplied to a given circuit and/or whether the circuit is grounded. Test lights usually have an alligator clip on their ground terminal and a probe on the positive terminal. To check for current, the alligator clip is attached to a ground and the probe is used to check the circuit; live current will cause the tester to light up. You can also use it in reverse by simply attaching the alligator clip to a known positive current source and using the probe to test and identify a proper ground. Now, let's make one.

Here are the components you'll need to make a test light:

- 2 to 3 feet of dual-conductor speaker wire.
- An empty translucent 35-millimeter film canister (you can also use an old translucent prescription container).
- A 12-volt bulb (this is a dash-gauge lightbulb—they last the longest).
- An alligator clip, a pop rivet, and a crimp connector.

Step 1: Start by splitting the ends of the speaker wire about 2 inches and stripping about a half-inch of insulation off each of the four ends.

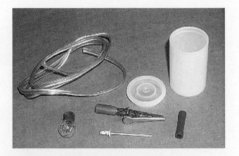

Step 2: Use rosin-core electronics solder and a pencil soldering iron to tin each of the stripped ends of the speaker wire.

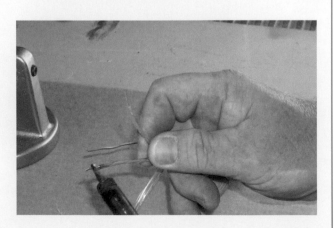

Tool Tip

Step 3: Wrap the bulb in a couple of layers of quilted paper towels and use a mini-vise to _gently_ hold it in place. Solder one of the tinned ends of the speaker wire to the base contact of the bulb, and then solder the other lead of this pair to the brass side contact of the bulb.

Step 4: Here's what you'll have with both leads soldered onto the bulb. My speaker wire was copper and silver, so I soldered the copper side to the base contact and the silver to the side contact. The base will be "positive" and the side "negative" under this scheme.

Step 5: Bore a quarter-inch hole in the bottom of the translucent film canister or empty prescription container for the speaker wire to pass through.

Step 6: Tie a knot in the speaker wire about an inch away from the bulb to act as a cable stop, and insert the opposite end into the canister, pulling the wire through the bottom until the stop prevents it from going further. You can snap the top on the canister or container at this point, with the bulb safely inside it.

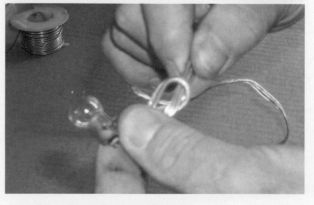

Tool Tip

Step 7: Slide the sleeve of the alligator clip over the remaining silver side of the speaker wire and solder the wire to the alligator clip. Then slide the sleeve back over the alligator clip. The negative side of the test light is now complete.

Step 8: "Pop" the rivet using your pop rivet tool and discard the rivet, but retain the shaft—this will be our probe. Use a bench grinder or Dremel to sharpen the point of it.

Step 9: Tap the pointed end of the rivet shaft into a piece of scrap wood, and then tap the crimp connector onto the shaft until it is in about a quarter of an inch down.

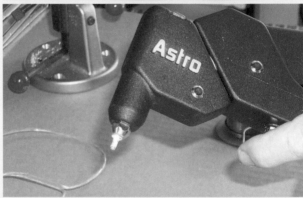

Step 10: Crimp the connector securely onto the rivet shaft after extracting it from the wood.

Tool Tip

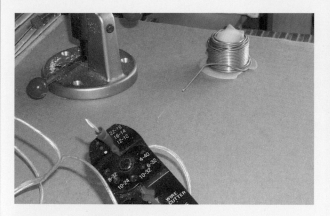

Step 11: Insert the remaining copper side of the speaker wire into the connector and crimp tightly to secure it.

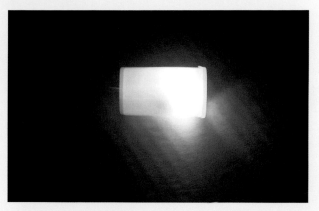

Step 12: Clamp the alligator clip to the negative terminal of a 12-volt battery and touch the probe to the positive terminal to test your new tool. Let there be light and—*voilà*—there it is.

ALL JUICED UP

Take a good look around your garage, and you'll see how important electricity is—not only for the lights, but also to power all of your electrical tools, battery chargers, stereo system, refrigerator, fan, and other items you'll probably find there. To gain a better understanding of all that juice running through your vehicle oasis, this sidebar will further help fill you in.

Since AC is the power we depend upon most in the garage, exploring the gear that uses alternating current is a must. So here are some of the absolute AC-powered necessities you should have available in your garage:

• Extension cords. A 12-foot and a 25-foot extension cord will serve you well for just about any requirement you may have. When purchasing an extension cord, it's always wise to go with a heavier-gauge cord capable of 15-amp capacity and you should always use grounded (three-prong) cords, since they are your best insurance against getting a nasty shock from an ungrounded connection.

• Surge suppressors. Some extension cords have built-in surge suppressors and circuit breakers that automatically protect your equipment from sudden surges or spikes in the electrical current and disconnect it in the event such a surge occurs. These are fairly inexpensive, and they are well worth the money for the extra protection they provide.

• Multi-outlet strips. These make several electrical power outlets available in one convenient strip that can be mounted on or above your workbench. The best ones have built-in circuit breakers and/or surge protectors, and they are always grounded for added safety.

• Cord winders. Like air hoses, extension cords can be a real pain to wind and store, but not if you get a cord winder for your garage. Equipped with a net basket and a convertible crank handle that can be switched for left- or right-handed operation, one of these winders will keep your extension cord neatly coiled and ready for use all the time.

• Generators. What do you do if and when the power does go out as the result of a storm or someone plowing into an electrical pole that supplies your neighborhood with juice? I originally purchased my generator as a backup power supply for such emergencies, but I've put it to additional use on several occasions. For instance, when I use my MIG welder, it really pulls a lot of house current, as does my large vertical air compressor. This is particularly problematic during the summer months when brownouts are common, so I just crank up the trusty old generator, plug in my gear, and do my work without making the utility bill look like the national debt of a small country. For a couple of bucks worth of gas, I have power to spare, I don't blow any of the house circuit breakers so the air conditioners stay on, and there is peace throughout the land (or at least in my home). The price of portable generators has come down so that a decent 5,000-watt generator on wheels is genuinely affordable, and something you should seriously consider for your garage.

CHAPTER 14
HOT STUFF

There's an inseparable relationship between fire and metal that goes back to the days when the first metal tools were made. After all, the heat of a fire converts ore into malleable metals and alloys that then can be made into useful implements. The way we generate and apply this intense heat has evolved, though, as we learned to harness and use fire to our advantage.

In your garage, harnessing this heat occurs whenever you're soldering, brazing, welding, heating, and cutting.

Soldering

Soldering joins two pieces of metal, such as electrical wires, by melding them together with another metal to form a strong, chemical bond. In this process, a special material, called solder, flows over two pre-heated pieces and attaches them through a process similar to brazing (which will be covered shortly).

Soldering involves the use of three basic ingredients: an electric soldering iron or gas torch; solder, which is usually an alloy that needs a lower melting point than the metal you're joining; and a cleaning resin called flux that ensures the joining pieces are incredibly clean. Flux removes all the oxides on the surface of the metal that would interfere with the molecular bonding, allowing the solder to flow into the

The advantage of a butane-powered soldering iron like this one from Solder-It is that there's no cumbersome electrical cord to get in your way or limit your mobility. The iron is well-balanced, lightweight, portable, and features an automatic ignition system.

Courtesy: Solder-It Corporation

Shaded safety goggles like these are an absolute must when brazing or welding. When using a torch, they will prevent eye damage from the intensely-bright light.

Courtesy: Bernzomatic Corporation

Solder-It's PT-500 professional butane torches are a top-of-the-line product. They feature a large fuel tank for up to 200 minutes of use. They also feature a state-of-the-art waterproof piezo electronic ignition system, a high-output wind-resistant flame, and a comfortable ergonomic grip. The company also manufactures a varied line of flux-less solders for all sorts of applications. Courtesy: Solder-It Corporation

Plastic body filler has largely replaced using lead solder as a filler and molding material in autobody work. However, if you're a purist who wants to dabble with body solder, Eastwood makes this complete kit with tinning butter, solder bars, shaping files, wooden paddles, and even a training video to show you how it's done. *Courtesy: The Eastwood Company*

joint smoothly. And oh, yeah—you also need two things to solder together.

The first step in soldering is to clean the surfaces, initially with sandpaper or steel wool and then by melting flux onto the parts. Sometimes, flux is part of the alloy of the soldering wire, in an easy-to-use mixture. Then, the pieces are both heated above the melting point of the solder (but below their own melting point) with the soldering iron or torch. When touched to the joint, this precise heating causes the solder to "flow" to the place of highest temperature and makes a chemical bond. The solder shouldn't drip or blob, but spread smoothly, to coat the entire joint. When it cools, you have a sturdy, even connection.

Brazing

Brazing joins two pieces of base metal when a melted, metallic filler flows across the joint and cools to form a solid bond. Similar to soldering, brazing creates an extremely strong joint, usually stronger than the base metal pieces themselves, without melting or deforming the components. Two different metals, or base metals such as silver and bronze, can be joined by brazing.

You can braze pipes, rods, flat metals, or any other shape as long as the pieces fit neatly against each other without large gaps.

Prior to brazing, the entire surface area to be joined must be cleaned so the braze will flow evenly without clumping. You can clean the area by washing, wire brushing, or buffing with steel wool. Then apply the melted flux to the surfaces. The flux removes oxides, prevents more

MAPP gas has replaced propane for most torch applications, and Bernzomatic has a number of MAPP-capable torches available to suit just about every need—including this handy 360-degree, trigger-start swivel head torch kit. *Courtesy: Bernzomatic Corporation*

This compact and lightweight Oxygen/MAPP gas torch kit is economical and ideal for those garage projects that involve brazing, welding, or cutting. Courtesy: Bernzomatic Corporation

oxidation during brazing, and smoothes the surface so that braze "flows" evenly across the joint.

A torch is used for brazing due to the high temperatures the process generates (often between 800 and 2,000 degrees Fahrenheit, or 430–1,100 degrees Celsius). The torch can be fueled by oxygen and another gas, such as acetylene, hydrogen, or MAPP. The temperature must be low enough so that the base metals don't melt, yet high enough to melt the braze. Torches have sensitivity controls to reach the proper temperature by adjusting the gas mixture depending on the associated melting points.

Braze, like solder, comes in a stick, disc, or wire, depending on your preference or the shape of the joint. After the base metals near the joint have been heated with the torch, the braze is applied to the hot pieces. The braze then melts, flowing around the joint. "Flow" means that the braze penetrates the joint and works into every cavern. If the brazing is performed correctly, the bond is nearly unbreakable when it cools and solidifies.

There are significant advantages to brazing over soldering or welding. For example, a brazed joint can be plated so the seam disappears and the braze conducts electricity like the

This compact butane micro torch features piezo ignition. It's wind-proof, and it puts out an incredible 2,400-degree flame. It uses either an included refillable fuel cell or a disposable butane lighter. Courtesy: Solder-It Corporation

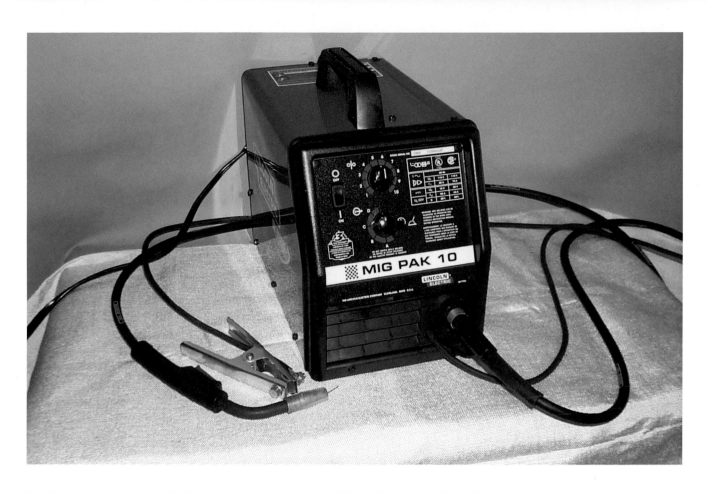

This MIG welder manufactured by Lincoln Electric is small, lightweight, and runs on household 120-volt AC current. It's capable of welding steel stocks up to 1/4-inch thick. It is resting on a fiberglass welding blanket, which is very useful for keeping spatter off adjacent areas and also for shielding. Courtesy: The Eastwood Company

These magnetic holders are available in a couple of different sizes and styles. They're great for holding steel panels together while you're tack or seam welding them, especially if the work is to be done at right-angles. Courtesy: The Eastwood Company

This magnetic grounding disc makes sure you have a solid contact point for the grounding clamp of your MIG or TIG welder or plasma cutter. A solid electrical ground is essential to the proper and safe operation of these devices. Courtesy: The Eastwood Company

base alloys. Probably the biggest advantage of brazing is that it can join dissimilar metals, such as bronze, steel, aluminum, wrought iron, and copper, with different melting points.

Welding

I've always been fascinated with welding, since it literally joins two or more individual pieces of steel together with a controlled fusion. How cool (or should I say, hot) is that?

Welding is the most economical and efficient way to join metals permanently. It is also the only way of joining two or more pieces of metal to combine them into a single piece.

Welding can trace its historic development back to ancient times. The earliest examples come from the Bronze Age. During the Iron Age, the Egyptians and people in the eastern Mediterranean area learned to weld pieces of iron together. Many welding tools have been excavated in those areas and are estimated to date from about 1,000 B.C. The art of blacksmithing came about during the Middle Ages, and it was not until the nineteenth century that welding as we know it today was invented.

Nowadays, there are many ways to make a weld, including the methods described in the paragraphs below.

Oxy Fuel Gas Welding (OFW)

There are four distinct processes within this classification, and in the case of two of them, oxyacetylene welding and oxyhydrogen welding, the distinction is based on the fuel used in the process. In the third process, air acetylene welding, air is used instead of oxygen, and in the fourth category, pressure gas welding, pressure is applied in addition to the heat from the burning of the gases. This welding process normally utilizes acetylene as the fuel gas. The oxygen thermal-cutting processes have much in common with this welding processes.

MAPP gas is liquefied petroleum gas mixed with methylacetylene-propadiene. MAPP is a trade name, and it has become increasingly popular over the last decade as a replacement for oxyacetylene and oxyhydrogen welding.

The gas is used for welding due to its high combustion temperature of 2,927 degrees Celsius (5,301 degrees Fahrenheit) in oxygen. Although acetylene has a higher welding temperature (3,160 degrees Celsius), MAPP has the advantage in that it requires neither dilution nor special container fillers during transport, allowing a greater volume of welding gas to be transported at the same given weight.

MAPP is colorless in both the liquid and the gas forms. The gas has a pronounced garlic odor at concentrations above 100 ppm (parts per million), and it is toxic if inhaled at high concentrations.

Another big advantage of MAPP welding is that its tanks and torches are smaller, lighter in weight, and, consequently,

An auto-dimming welding helmet is absolutely essential for eye protection when doing any type of work with electric arcs, such as MIG, TIG, or plasma work. This helmet is solar-powered, so no batteries are needed, and it features variable darkness adjustments. Thanks to the flame motif, everyone will know you're hot stuff when you're wearing it.
Courtesy: The Eastwood Company

much less expensive than either oxyacetylene or oxyhydrogen gas welding alternatives. Generally speaking, the cost of a MAPP welding setup (filled tanks, regulator/torch) is about one-third the cost of the equivalent oxyacetylene setup.

MIG Welding (GMAW or Gas Metal Arc Welding)

MIG (metal inert gas) is an arc welding process that fuses metals by heating them with an arc. The arc is between a continuously fed filler metal (consumable) electrode and the work piece. Externally supplied gas or gas mixtures provide shielding. Common MIG welding is also referred to as short-circuit transfer.

Metal is deposited only when the wire actually touches the work, since no metal is transferred across the arc. MIG welders are small, simple, and affordable. Many can be powered by normal 120-volt AC house current, making them a favorite piece of garage gear for many hobbyists. They're also widely used in autobody repair shops. A small MIG setup can be had for well under $500, and it should be more than adequate for any project you're likely to undertake in your garage workshop.

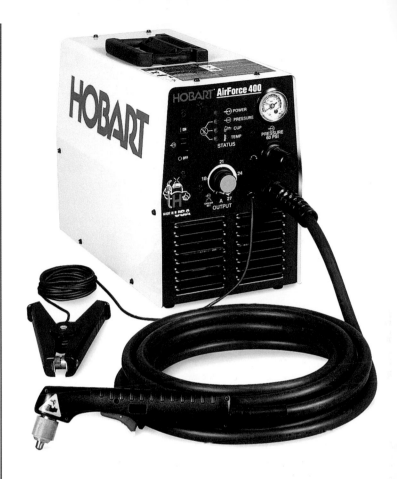

A plasma cutter like this Hobart unit uses a high-intensity electrical arc rather than a blade to cut through sheet metal easily, quickly, and smoothly. Courtesy: The Eastwood Company

TIG Welding (GTAW or Gas Tungsten Arc)

Often called TIG (tungsten inert gas) welding, this welding process fuses metals by heating them with a tungsten electrode, which does not become part of the completed weld. Filler metal is sometimes used and argon inert gas or inert gas mixtures are used for shielding.

Cut to the Chase

Since this chapter is about hot stuff, I'd be remiss if I didn't include plasma cutters here. In addition to using intense heat to join metals, the heat can also be used separate metal, which is exactly what plasma cutters do.

Plasma arc cutting is an arc-cutting process that severs metal by using a constricted arc to melt a small area of the work. This process can cut all metals that conduct electricity, and plasma cutters are available that will work with a house's current for light metal-cutting jobs. Like MIG welders, plasma cutters are small, easy to use, and affordable, which makes them desirable if you intend to be doing a lot of metal cutting.

Carrying the Torch a Bit Further

Please don't get the impression that MIG and TIG welders are the be-all and end-all when it comes to garage gear. While they are indeed wonderful for what they can do, you'll still need a good old torch that puts out heat for several tasks, such as heating up stubborn nuts and bolts that refuse to budge otherwise.

In fact, a colleague and friend of mine refers to his oxyacetylene torch setup as his "heat wrench."

There will be times when you'll want to solder or braze, and these are jobs an arc welder can't handle, so the trusty old torch will be the ticket here. If you already have an oxyacetylene setup, great—use it whenever you need to. However, if you don't currently have a torch setup, I recommend going with a MAPP torch outfit. They're economical, small, easy to use, and much more stable than oxyacetylene. They do a terrific job.

Another handy device you'll most definitely want to have in your garage is a small butane-powered torch. These diminutive fire sticks are compact, lightweight, and generate a very hot flame. In addition to using them for heat-shrink tubing; stretching and bending vinyl, plastic, and PVC; and thawing frozen locks, they're also tremendously useful for soldering and for heating and drying applications. Butane torches are available in a variety of sizes, heat strengths, and price ranges. They're well worth the investment.

135

CHAPTER 15
COME TOGETHER

All devices and equipment with multiple parts are held together by fasteners. The only other assembly alternatives are welding or using special adhesives, both of which are generally more expensive methods that render the component difficult to disassemble. Manufacturers can choose from hundreds of thousands of standard fasteners, not to mention millions of specialized types. Materials for fasteners range from metal to plastics, ceramics to special alloys, all of which can be made in an endless array of shapes and sizes.

The most common fastener for gearheads is the threaded type, which include bolts, screws, and studs. Bolts are technically described as externally threaded fasteners designed for insertion through holes in assembled parts. Specifically, a bolt is normally tightened and released by turning a mating nut.

These plastic hole and thread gauges are available in metric (yellow) and fractional (white) from BoltDepot.com, and they are extremely handy to have in your garage. You can also download paper gauges free of charge at the company's website: www.boltdepot.com. Courtesy: BoltDepot.com

Fastener assortments like this one are a great way to have the right hardware on hand for any occasion that may arise. These assortments are available in all the popular fastener sizes and styles and in a variety of materials, including chrome. Courtesy: BoltDepot.com

Any garage workshop worth its salt will have a good assortment of nuts, bolts, washers, screws, and other various fasteners on hand. You have several options to store these, including everything from customized storage boxes to household containers rescued from your recycling bin.

Generally speaking, it's a good idea to choose plastic or metal containers for fastener storage rather than glass, since a glass jar will shatter and break if you should drop it or accidentally knock it off your workbench. Of course, see-through containers let you identify the contents immediately, but opaque containers that are labeled work well, too.

BoltDepot.com sells many fastener storage options, including empty compartmented tray boxes and larger lockable storage cases. These larger cases are also usually equipped with positive-locking latches and carry handles to make moving them around a bit easier. The company also offers carry indexes that will hold a number of smaller cases, such as screw assortments, and they keep things nicely organized within a minimal amount of space. Many of these carry indexes can be stacked and bolted together to create larger assemblies, too.

You can also check your local dollar store for inexpensive plastic compartmented boxes. They're great for holding small items that you don't want to lose track of, especially while disassembling something during a project.

Of course, nothing beats the price of what you might find in your recycling bin. Bolts, nuts, and screws can easily be stored in any of the containers you might have around the house.

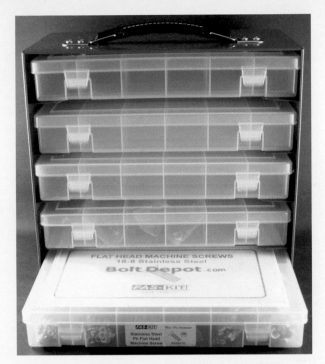

Stackable carry indexes like this one make storing and moving compartmented tray boxes easy. These indexes can be bolted together to form larger units as well. BoltDepot.com sells the indexes, empty compartmented tray boxes, and assortments of fasteners, so you can get your indexes empty or filled. Courtesy: BoltDepot.com

Containers like these, rescued from the recycle bin in the kitchen, make great containers for storing fasteners, small parts, and other odds and ends in the garage. The see-through containers let you know at a glance what's inside, while the opaque ones need only a simple label to tell what's inside. Author's Collection

Left: *Clear plastic compartmented boxes like this one are inexpensive and can be found at the local dollar store or in the housewares aisle of the supermarket. They're great for holding small items that you don't want to lose track of.* Author's Collection

Bolts

The nomenclature of bolts can be confusing until you under-stand what is what. The most common types you're likely to come upon in your garage work are as follows:

• Stove bolts, named for their original purpose, which was the assembly of cast-iron stoves. They are available in diameters from 5/32 inch to 1/2 inch and in lengths from 3/8 inch to 6 inches. They have slotted heads for screwdrivers (some more modern versions can have Phillips heads), and the heads themselves are available in round (half a sphere), flat (flat on top, tapered to threads), or pan (wide, rounded head).

• Carriage bolts, a class of bolts that generally have round heads with small square sections underneath. They usually fit into square holes, thereby "locking" themselves in

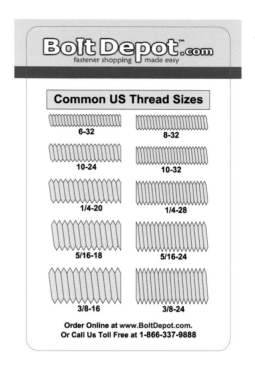

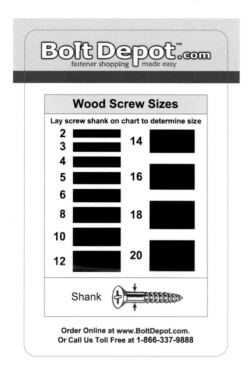

place so that a nut can be turned tight without spinning the bolt itself. Sometimes carriage bolts have ribbed necks rather than square ones.

• Step bolts, carriage bolts that have enlarged heads that "step down" to the square neck. The flanged heads spread loads over a very large area. Bumper bolts are typically step bolts, so that the chromed, round head gives a better appearance.

• Joint bolts, tapered at the tip to act as a "self-aligning" device to center the bolt in a captive nut and start threading straight. Joint bolts are found in many areas on automobiles and other vehicles, as well as some machinery.

• T-head bolts, specially made with a T-shaped head instead of the usual hex or square heads. They are used in situations where there is no easy way to put a wrench on the head. Engine blocks and transmission cases frequently utilize these bolts.

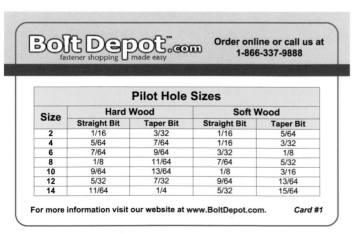

• Countersunk bolts have heads that are flat on top and tapered to the shaft. They usually have hex sockets (Allen), but sometimes have large Phillips sockets. They are used in applications where there is no space for the head to protrude.

Screws

What's the difference between a screw and a bolt, you ask? Well, a screw differs from a bolt in that it mates with an internal thread, into which it is tightened or released by turning its head with the appropriate driver.

Lots of folks call any threaded fastener larger than about 1/4-inch in diameter a "bolt." While that's not technically correct, I won't split hairs here about the absolute technical definition. Instead, from this point on, let's just assume bolts can sometimes be inserted directly into threaded holes and screws can be used with nuts. Even though that's not the usual scheme of things, I think you get the idea here, right?

Screws vary widely in design, size, and purpose. Hex cap screws are frequently found throughout automobile construction and are frequently considered the same as bolts (in actuality, cylinder head bolts are really hex cap screws). Screws are found with hex socket caps, Torx socket caps, and even slotted and Phillips heads. There are wood screws, sheetmetal screws, self-tapping screws, and many, many others. Other than those screws that hold engines, transmissions, and drive gear together, self-tapping and trim screws are the most common on automobiles.

Machine screws are used for the assembly of metal parts, so virtually every one of these on a car and most other metal machinery is a machine screw.

Studs are rods that are threaded on either one or both ends, and the thread type is often different on opposing ends. The most common studs found on automobile and other engines are on the intake and exhaust manifolds.

Washers

What would you call a bolt or screw without a washer? Loose, for starters! Most fasteners are installed where vibration and temperature changes occur. Mechanical motion, over time, causes fasteners to back off and loosen, hence the need for something to help prevent that effect. The primary function of a washer is to provide a surface against which the head of the fastener or surface of a nut can bear. Flat washers do this

If you have larger nuts and bolts that require storage, BoltDepot.com has you covered with these large compartmented storage cases. They feature steel lids with positive-locking latches and carry handles for convenient transport. Courtesy: BoltDepot.com

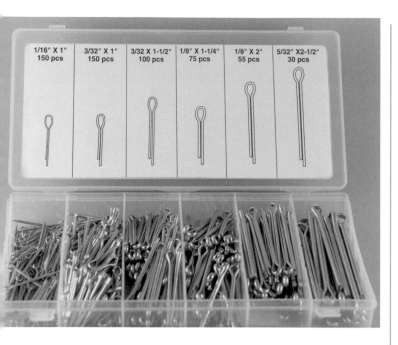

Cotter pins are available in a variety of sizes, but it always seems like you never have the size you need on hand when you need it. That is, of course, unless you have an assortment like this one in your well-stocked garage! Courtesy: The Eastwood Company

being the split (helical) ring washer and the toothed washer.

Split washers function in much the same way that helical springs do. When the bolt is tightened sufficiently, the ends of the washer come together under compression and resist movements of the bolt by creating a certain degree of friction against which the bolt would have to overcome. Toothed washers work very well because their many teeth bite into the surface against which the head or nut bears, creating large amounts of friction. They come in external, internal, and internal-external tooth forms.

It's interesting to note that the softer the surface under the teeth, the better the locking washer works.

Nuts

I'd have to be nuts not to cover these little buggers in this chapter, wouldn't I? When you come right down to it, a bolt can't really do its job if it doesn't have a nut holding it on. With that thought in mind, any threaded fastener that doesn't screw into a mating surface needs a nut to hold it in place. There are as many different nuts as there are washers and other hardware items because they are designed to accommodate different methods of tightening and applications. Some also have provisions for locking. Most nuts are hexagonal in shape to accommodate wrenches, but some square nuts are to be found as well. If there's one cardinal rule when it comes to nuts, it is this: the nut used must be the same grade of metal as the bolt or failure will surely and eventually occur!

very well and spread loads, but normally don't help to keep the fastener tight. Lock washers are designed to keep fasteners from loosening. They come in many forms, the two most common

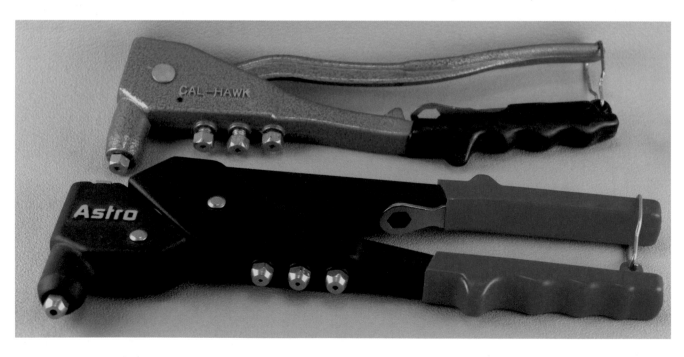

The only way to apply a pop rivet is with a pop rivet tool. The blue one at the top is the basic variety, which is inexpensive and functional. The red-handled one below it is a deluxe model with a rotating head and better leverage, so less hand pressure is required to set the rivet. Courtesy: The Eastwood Company

Pop rivets come in numerous sizes, lengths, and depths, so there's something available for just about any fastening chore you might have. Author's Collection

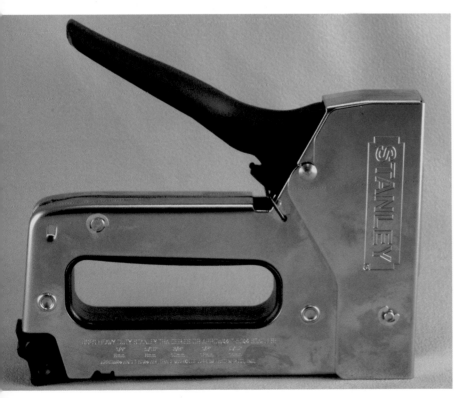

A good staple gun deserves a spot in every garage. This unit from Stanley takes a wide variety of staple sizes and styles, and it gives you plenty of leverage. Courtesy: Stanley Tools

Some of the more common nuts you'll probably be dealing with in your garage are listed below:

• Machine screw nuts, fine-threaded and frequently used to hold brackets and other assemblies.

• Track bolt nuts, frequently found holding fixtures in place (usually square). These are often held "captive" in some sort of housing that allows some degree of movement and adjustment, such as door-latch mechanisms.

• Jam nuts, typically thin and used for applications where space is critical. You'll frequently find them used for automotive dash trim and radio assemblies.

• Thick nuts, typically used for coarse-threaded bolts and in applications where great holding strength is necessary—for instance, securing bumpers to their mounting brackets.

• Slotted nuts cut in several places to accommodate the use of cotter pins or other devices that act as safety systems to prevent loosening. Axle nuts are typically slotted.

• Castle nuts, also known as castellated nuts. They are slotted, taller nuts used for high-hold situations. Castle nuts are frequently available with plastic or metal inserts that exert high friction while turning as added insurance to keep them tight.

• Flange nuts, made with a wide-bottom flange to spread loads over a large surface. They are frequently found securing fenders to car and truck bodies.

• Cap nuts, typically with solid tops that are acorn-shaped. Cap nuts are used in situations where they will be seen in the finished product and are often chrome-plated. These nuts require the use of a specific-length bolt.

How Fine is Coarse?

Essentially, a thread is an inclined plane cut along the surface of a fastener. Varying the angle of the plane determines the cut or thread: increasing the angle produces a coarse thread, while decreasing it results in a fine thread.

Fasteners are graded according to how many threads there are to the inch for SAE (Society of Automotive Engineers) fasteners, or centimeters for metric ones. Most threaded fasteners are available with either coarse threads conforming to Unified National Coarse (UNC) standards, or Unified National Fine (UNF) threads. Fine threads have more threads per inch than coarse.

Coarse threads are easier and faster to use. They provide an easier "start" of the fastener, with less likelihood of cross-threading. Nicks and burrs from handling are less likely to affect assembly; they are less likely to seize

TYPICAL TORQUE VALUES FOR GRADED STEEL BOLTS

Grade		SAE 1 or 2	SAE 5	SAE 6	SAE 8
Grade Mark (Raised Lines)		None	3	4	5
Bolt Diameter		Threads/Inch	Foot	Pounds	Torque
1/4 Inch	20	5	7	10	10
5/16 Inch	18	9	14	19	22
3/8 Inch	16	15	25	34	37
7/16 Inch	14	24	40	55	60
1/2 Inch	13	37	60	85	92
9/16 Inch	12	53	88	120	132
5/8 Inch	11	74	120	169	180
3/4 Inch	10	120	200	280	296
7/8 Inch	9	190	302	440	473
1 Inch	8	282	466	660	714

TYPICAL TORQUE (FT-LBS) FOR COMMON TYPES OF STEEL

Diameter	Threads/in	Mild Steel	Stainless Steel	Alloy Steel
1/4	20	4	6	8
5/16	18	8	11	16
3/8	16	12	18	24
7/16	14	20	32	40
1/2	13	30	43	60
5/8	11	60	92	120
3/4	10	100	128	200
7/8	9	160	180	320
1	8	245	285	490

in temperature applications and in joints where corrosion is likely. Additionally, coarse threads are less likely to "strip" and are more easily tapped into brittle materials.

On the other hand, fine threads provide superior fastening (typically 10 percent stronger holding power than coarse) in hard materials and they can be adjusted more precisely due to their shallower helix angle. They are also better in situations where length of engagement (depth) is limited and where wall thickness is limited, again because of their smaller thread cross-section (coarse threads are cut deeper into the shaft of the fastener than fine).

None of this is worth a hill of beans, though, if the fastener isn't properly installed, and that leads us to a different twist on the subject.

How Tight is Tight?

All fasteners have to be correctly tightened in order to perform the job for which they are intended, and that degree of tightness is referred to as the torque specification. Let's say, for instance, that two steel plates need to be tightened together with a force of 100 pounds. Let's also say that a single 3/4-inch diameter bolt is used to create the binding force. Once tightened, the two plates are held together just as if a 100-pound weight were sitting on top of them.

However, if the bolt was loose, external loading, vibration, and temperature change would eventually cause the plates to come apart because they would fatigue. (The simplest form of fatigue is that of metal being bent back and forth, but in this

SAE BOLT DESIGNATIONS

SAE Grade No.	Size range	Tensile strength, ksi	Material	Head marking
1	1/4 thru 1 1/2	60	Low or medium carbon steel	
2	1/4 thru 3/4	74		
	7/8 thru 1 1/2	60		
5	1/4 thru 1	120	Medium carbon steel, quenched & tempered	
	1 1/8 thru 1 1/2	105		
5.2	1/4 thru 1	120	Low carbon martensite steel, quenched & tempered	
7	1/4 thru 1 1/2	133	Medium carbon alloy steel, quenched & tempered	
8	1/4 thru 1 1/2	150	Medium carbon alloy steel, quenched & tempered	
8.2	1/4 thru 1	150	Low carbon martensite steel, quenched & tempered	

ASTM BOLT DESIGNATIONS

ASTM standard	Size range	Tensile strength, ksi	Material	Head marking
A307	1/4 thru 4	60	Low carbon steel	
A325 Type 1	1/2 thru 1	120	Medium carbon steel, quenched & tempered	A325
	1 1/8 thru 1 1/2	105		
A325 Type 2	1/2 thru 1	120	Low carbon martensite steel, quenched & tempered	A325
	1 1/8 thru 1 1/2	105		
A325 Type 3	1/2 thru 1	120	Weathering steel, quenched & tempered	A325
	1 1/8 thru 1 1/2	105		
A449	1/4 thru 1	120	Medium carbon steel, quenched & tempered	
	1 1/8 thru 1 1/2	105		
	1 3/4 thru 3	90		
A490 Type 1	1/4 thru 1 1/2	150	Alloy steel, quenched & tempered	A490
A490 Type 3	1/4 thru 1 1/2	150	Weathering steel, quenched & tempered	A490

BWS (BRITISH WHITWORTH STANDARD) THREAD DATA

Angle of thread (inclusive) = 55 degrees
Sizes range from 1/16 inch to 2 1/2 inches.

Diameter (inches)	TPI	Pitch (inches)	Core Diameter (inches)	Tapping Drill Size
1/16	60	0.0167	0.0411	Number Drill 56 (1.20 mm)
3/32	48	0.0208	0.0672	Number Drill 49 (1.85 mm)
1/8	40	0.0250	0.0930	Number Drill 39 (2.55 mm)
5/32	32	0.0313	0.1162	Number Drill 30 (3.20 mm)
3/16	24	0.0417	0.1341	Number Drill 26 (3.70 mm)
7/32	24	0.0417	0.1654	Number Drill 16 (4.50 mm)
1/4	20	0.0500	0.1860	Number Drill 9 (4.50 mm)
5/16	18	0.0556	0.2413	Letter Drill F (6.50 mm)
3/8	16	0.0625	0.2950	5/16 inch (7.94 mm)
7/16	14	0.0714	0.3461	Letter Drill U (9.30 mm)
1/2	12	0.0833	0.3932	Letter Drill Z (10.50 mm)
9/16	12	0.0833	0.4557	12.1 mm (0.4764 in)
5/8	11	0.0909	0.5086	13.5 mm (0.5315 in)
11/16	11	0.0909	0.5711	15 mm (0.5906 in)
3/4	10	0.100	0.6220	16.27 mm (41/64 in)
13/16	10	0.100	0.6845	18 mm (0.7087 in)
7/8	9	0.1111	0.7328	19.25 mm (0.7579 in)
15/16	9	0.1111	0.7953	20.75 mm (0.8169 in)
1	8	0.125	0.8400	22 mm (0.8661 in)

The Whitworth information provided above in this table is courtesy of British Tool Company.

case the bolt would be elongated enough for the joint to loosen.) The strength of any joint is dependent upon two factors: 1) the strength of the fastener itself; and 2) the degree to which it is tightened. Tightness can be accurately controlled by the measurement of the torque (twisting force, measured in foot pounds). Torque applied to a fastener creates inner tension (stretching) that, in turn, creates the holding power desired.

Special tools called torque wrenches (see Chapter 7) perform this task. The strength of the fastener is determined by the raised markings (called Grade Markings, covered later in this chapter) on the head of the bolt or screw. These head markings were developed by the SAE for automotive applications and the ASTM (American Society of Tests and Measurements) for structural applications.

A Couple of Asides, FYI

Foot pound is the measurement that calculates a one-pound weight, or force applied to a lever arm one foot long, is equal to one foot-pound, or 12-inch pounds, of torque. Technically, the expression is known as a pound foot, but conventional usage favors "foot-pound."

Head markings can be read by adding two to the number of marks. No marks on the head indicate a Grade 1 or 2, three marks indicate a Grade 5, four marks is a Grade 6, and six marks is a Grade 8.

The first thing to know about grade markings is that no markings is considered to mean the fastener is made of mild steel. Conversely, the more marks on the head, the higher the quality and strength. Therefore, bolts of the same diameter will vary in strength depending upon the material they are made of and the number of threads per inch.

Torque According to the Tables

The table on page 142 shows typical torque values for the most common bolts you are likely to encounter on automobiles and heavy machinery. While other factors can affect the torque (which will be discussed a little later on), these general levels indicate a safe "starting point" or level of torque to be applied.

Grades 3 and 7

The reason grades 3 and 7 were skipped is that you don't see these grades very often (if ever) in the real world. Grade 3 bolts are only slightly different from grades 1 and 2 in that all these bolts are generally made from cold-worked steel with either a low or medium carbon content. It isn't until you get to grade 5 that bolts are made of medium carbon steel that is quenched and tempered (to make them harder and stronger).

Grade 7 bolts are specialized too, in that they are medium carbon alloy steel, quenched and tempered, with "rolled" threads rather than cut threads. Rolled threads are relatively expensive to produce and such bolts are mostly used in aircraft and military applications. They are very hard to find at local auto parts suppliers and hardware stores and, if encountered, can be easily replaced by a grade 8 bolt, which is even stronger.

Mitigating Torque Factors

There are several factors that affect overall torque on a fastener: the type of lubricant used, the material from which the fastener is made; the type of plating on the fastener; the type of washer used; and the finish of the thread surfaces, as well as other factors.

Because there are so many variables involved, it isn't possible to create a one-size-fits-all torque chart that indicates the exact tightness for every bolt and screw for every situation.

Hex Head Bolt Markings

The strength and type of steel used in a bolt is supposed to be indicated by a raised mark on the head of the bolt. The type of mark depends on the standard to which the bolt was manufactured. Most often, bolts used in machinery are made to SAE standard J429, and bolts used in structures are made to various ASTM standards. The tables on page 143 give the head markings and some of the most commonly needed information concerning the bolts. For further information, see the appropriate standard.

There are often "extra" marks on a bolt head—marks in addition to those shown in the charts, and these marks usually indicate the bolt's manufacturer.

ASTM A325 Type 2 bolts have been discontinued, but are included because they can be found in existing structures. Their properties can be important in failure investigations.

While the bolts shown are among the most common in the United States, this list is far from exhaustive. In addition to the other bolts covered by the SAE and ASTM standards, there are a host of international standards, of which ISO is perhaps the most well known.

And Now, a Few Words from the Other Side of the Pond

Though it is all but obsolete nowadays, if you happen to have an old Morris Minor, Austin, or vintage MG hanging around in your garage (or some other really old British machinery), knowing something about British Whitworth standards may come in handy. If not, you can skip the chart on the adjacent page.

Other Fasteners

While threaded fasteners are the ones you'll deal with most of the time while working in your garage, there are indeed other fasteners that you'll undoubtedly use from time to time, and some of the more common are covered below:

• Cotter pins are used for lots of fastening chores, and they're usually inserted into holes to keep things like wheels, levers, and bushings from coming off shafts.

• Hog rings are sharply pointed metal staples used predominantly in upholstery work, applied with hog ring pliers that squeeze the pointed tangs together.

• Pop rivets, handy little gadgets that are inserted into pre-drilled holes to hold two panels together. They are applied using a pop rivet tool, which employs mechanical force to compress the aluminum rivet around both sides of the hole and causes the pilot shaft of the pop rivet to snap off and disengage.

• Staples. A good staple gun and an assortment of staples will come in handy for all kinds of jobs.

• Duct tape, the stuff that keeps the universe together, as legend has it. While that's really a big exaggeration, it is indeed handy for taping and binding all kinds of things together.

• Adhesives. We're talking about all kinds of glues here, including epoxy, super glue, rubber cement, spray adhesives, rear-view mirror adhesives, hot-melt glue, and just about anything else that will bond two surfaces together.

• Thread lockers. Loctite makes a variety of thread lockers in both removable and permanent formulations that are excellent for keeping nuts securely fastened to their bolts.

• Cable ties. Available in different lengths, colors, and thicknesses, these locking plastic straps are useful for a plethora of other jobs besides keeping bundles of cables securely wrapped.

Well, that wraps up the chapter on fasteners. It's time for me to bolt out of here and get into Chapter 16!

THREAD DATA CHART: METRIC THREAD—COARSE PITCH

Nominal Size ISO M	Thread Form Type	Majr Diameter mm d=D	Pitch mm p	Root Radius mm r	Pitch Diameter mm d2=D2	Minor Diameter Male Thd. d3	Minor Diameter Female Thd. D1	Thread Height Male Thd. h3	Thread Height Female Thd. H1	Tap Drill Diameter mm
1.0	M	1.0	0.25	0.036	0.838	0.693	0.729	0.153	0.135	0.75
1.1	M	1.1	0.25	0.036	0.938	0.793	0.829	0.153	0.135	0.85
1.2	M	1.2	0.25	0.036	1.038	0.893	0.929	0.153	0.135	0.95
1.4	M	1.4	0.30	0.043	1.205	1.032	1.075	0.184	0.162	1.10
1.6	M	1.6	0.35	0.051	1.373	1.171	1.221	0.215	0.189	1.25
1.8	M	1.8	0.35	0.051	1.573	1.371	1.421	0.215	0.189	1.45
2.0	M	2.0	0.40	0.058	1.740	1.509	1.567	0.245	0.217	1.60
2.2	M	2.2	0.45	0.065	1.908	1.648	1.713	0.276	0.244	1.75
2.5	M	2.5	0.45	0.065	2.208	1.948	2.013	0.276	0.244	2.05
3.0	M	3.0	0.50	0.072	2.675	2.387	2.459	0.307	0.271	2.50
3.5	M	3.5	0.60	0.087	3.110	2.764	2.850	0.368	0.325	2.90
4.0	M	4.0	0.70	0.101	3.545	3.141	3.242	0.429	0.379	3.30
4.5	M	4.5	0.75	0.108	4.013	3.580	3.688	0.460	0.406	3.80
5.0	M	5.0	0.80	0.115	4.480	4.019	4.134	0.491	0.433	4.20
6.0	M	6.0	1.00	0.144	5.350	4.773	4.917	0.613	0.541	5.00
7.0	M	7.0	1.00	0.144	6.350	5.773	5.917	0.613	0.541	6.00
8.0	M	8.0	1.25	0.180	7.188	6.466	6.647	0.767	0.677	6.80
9.0	M	9.0	1.25	0.180	8.188	7.466	7.647	0.767	0.677	7.80
10.0	M	10.0	1.50	0.217	9.026	8.160	8.376	0.920	0.812	8.50
11.0	M	11.0	1.50	0.217	10.026	9.160	9.376	0.920	0.812	9.50
12.0	M	12.0	1.75	0.253	10.863	9.853	10.106	1.074	0.947	10.20
14.0	M	14.0	2.00	0.289	12.701	11.546	11.835	1.227	1.083	12.00
16.0	M	16.0	2.00	0.289	14.701	13.546	13.835	1.227	1.083	14.00
18.0	M	18.0	2.50	0.361	16.376	14.933	15.394	1.534	1.353	15.50
20.0	M	20.0	2.50	0.361	18.376	16.933	17.294	1.534	1.353	17.50
22.0	M	22.0	2.50	0.361	20.376	18.933	19.294	1.534	1.353	19.50
24.0	M	24.0	3.00	0.433	22.051	20.319	20.752	1.840	1.624	21.00
27.0	M	27.0	3.00	0.433	25.051	23.319	23.752	1.840	1.624	24.00
30.0	M	30.0	3.50	0.505	27.727	25.706	26.211	2.147	1.894	26.50
33.0	M	33.0	3.50	0.505	30.727	28.706	29.211	2.147	1.894	29.50
36.0	M	36.0	4.00	0.577	33.402	31.093	31.670	2.454	2.165	32.00
39.0	M	39.0	4.00	0.577	36.402	34.093	34.670	2.454	2.165	35.00
42.0	M	42.0	4.50	0.650	39.077	36.479	37.129	2.760	2.436	37.50
45.0	M	45.0	4.50	0.650	42.077	39.479	40.129	2.760	2.436	40.50
48.0	M	48.0	5.00	0.722	44.752	41.866	42.857	3.067	2.706	43.00
52.0	M	52.0	5.00	0.722	48.752	45.866	46.587	3.067	2.706	47.00
56.0	M	56.0	5.50	0.794	52.428	49.252	50.046	3.374	2.977	50.50
60.0	M	60.0	5.50	0.794	56.428	53.252	54.046	3.374	2.977	54.50
64.0	M	64.0	6.00	0.866	60.103	56.639	57.505	3.681	3.248	58.00
68.0	M	68.0	6.00	0.866	64.103	60.639	61.505	3.681	3.248	62.00

THREAD DATA CHART: METRIC THREAD—FINE PITCH

Nominal Size ISO M	Thread Form Type	Majr Diameter mm d=D	Pitch mm p	Root Radius mm r	Pitch Diameter mm d2=D2	Minor Diameter Male Thd. d3	Minor Diameter Female Thd. D1	Thread Height Male Thd. h3	Thread Height Female Thd. H1	Tap Drill Diameter mm
1.0x0.2	M	1.0	0.20	0.029	0.870	0.755	0.783	0.123	0.108	0.80
1.1x0.2	M	1.1	0.20	0.029	0.970	0.855	0.883	0.123	0.108	0.90
1.2x0.2	M	1.2	0.20	0.029	1.070	0.955	0.983	0.123	0.108	1.00
1.4x0.2	M	1.4	0.20	0.029	1.270	1.155	1.183	0.123	0.108	1.20
1.6x0.2	M	1.6	0.20	0.029	1.470	1.355	1.383	0.123	0.108	1.40
1.8x0.2	M	1.8	0.20	0.029	1.670	1.555	1.583	0.123	0.108	1.60
2x0.25	M	2.0	0.25	0.036	1.838	1.693	1.729	0.153	0.135	1.75
2.2x0.25	M	2.2	0.25	0.036	2.038	1.893	1.929	0.153	0.135	1.95
2.5x0.35	M	2.5	0.35	0.051	2.273	2.071	2.121	0.215	0.189	2.10
3x0.35	M	3.0	0.35	0.051	2.773	2.571	2.621	0.215	0.189	2.60
3.5x0.35	M	3.5	0.35	0.051	3.273	3.071	3.121	0.215	0.189	3.10
4x0.5	M	4.0	0.50	0.072	3.675	3.387	3.459	0.307	0.271	3.50
4.5x0.5	M	4.5	0.50	0.072	4.175	3.887	3.959	0.307	0.271	4.00
5x0.5	M	5.0	0.50	0.072	4.675	4.387	4.459	0.307	0.271	4.50
5.5x0.5	M	5.5	0.50	0.072	5.175	4.887	4.959	0.307	0.271	5.00
6x0.75	M	6.0	0.75	0.108	5.513	5.080	5.188	0.460	0.406	5.20
7x0.75	M	7.0	0.75	0.108	6.513	6.080	6.188	0.460	0.406	6.20
8x0.75	M	8.0	0.75	0.108	7.513	7.080	7.188	0.460	0.406	7.20
8x1.0	M	8.0	1.00	0.144	7.350	6.773	6.917	0.613	0.541	7.00
9x0.75	M	9.0	0.75	0.108	8.513	8.080	8.188	0.460	0.406	8.20
9x 1	M	9.0	1.00	0.144	8.350	7.773	7.917	0.613	0.541	8.00
10x0.75	M	10.0	0.75	0.108	9.513	9.080	9.188	0.460	0.406	9.20
10x1	M	10.0	1.00	0.144	9.350	8.773	8.917	0.613	0.541	9.00
10x1.25	M	10.0	1.25	0.180	9.188	8.466	8.647	0.767	0.677	8.80
11x0.75	M	11.0	0.75	0.108	10.513	10.080	10.188	0.460	0.406	10.20
11x1	M	11.0	1.00	0.144	10.350	9.773	9.917	0.613	0.541	10.00
12x1	M	12.0	1.00	0.144	11.350	10.773	10.917	0.613	0.541	11.00
12x1.25	M	12.0	1.25	0.180	11.188	10.466	10.647	0.767	0.677	10.80
12x1.5	M	12.0	1.50	0.217	11.026	10.160	10.376	0.920	0.812	10.50
14x1.0	M	14.0	1.00	0.144	13.350	12.773	12.917	0.613	0.541	13.00
14x1.25	M	14.0	1.25	0.180	13.188	12.466	12.647	0.767	0.677	12.80
14x1.5	M	14.0	1.50	0.217	13.026	12.160	12.376	0.920	0.812	12.50
15x1	M	15.0	1.00	0.144	14.350	13.773	13.917	0.613	0.541	14.00
15x1.5	M	15.0	1.50	0.217	14.026	13.160	13.376	0.920	0.812	13.50
16x1	M	16.0	1.00	0.144	15.350	14.773	14.917	0.613	0.541	15.00
16x1.5	M	16.0	1.50	0.217	15.026	14.160	14.376	0.920	0.812	14.50
17x1.0	M	17.0	1.00	0.144	16.350	15.773	15.917	0.613	0.541	16.00
17x1.5	M	17.0	1.50	0.217	16.026	15.160	15.376	0.920	0.812	15.50
18x1.0	M	18.0	1.00	0.144	17.350	16.773	16.917	0.613	0.541	17.00
18x1.5	M	18.0	1.50	0.217	17.026	16.160	16.376	0.920	0.812	16.50
18x2.0	M	18.0	2.00	0.289	16.701	15.546	15.835	1.227	1.083	16.00
20x1.0	M	20.0	1.00	0.144	19.350	18.773	18.917	0.613	0.541	19.00
20x1.5	M	20.0	1.50	0.217	19.026	18.160	18.376	0.920	0.812	18.50
20x2.0	M	20.0	2.00	0.289	18.701	17.546	17.835	1.227	1.083	18.00
22x1.0	M	22.0	1.00	0.144	21.350	20.773	20.917	0.613	0.541	21.00
22x1.5	M	22.0	1.50	0.217	21.026	20.160	20.376	0.920	0.812	20.50
22x2.0	M	22.0	2.00	0.289	20.701	19.546	19.835	1.227	1.083	20.00
24x1.0	M	24.0	1.00	0.144	23.350	22.773	22.917	0.613	0.541	23.00
24x1.5	M	24.0	1.50	0.217	23.026	22.160	22.376	0.920	0.812	22.50
24x2.0	M	24.0	2.00	0.289	22.701	21.546	21.835	1.227	1.083	22.00
25x1.0	M	25.0	1.00	0.144	24.350	23.773	23.917	0.613	0.541	24.00
25x1.5	M	25.0	1.50	0.217	24.026	23.160	23.376	0.920	0.812	23.50
25x2.0	M	25.0	2.00	0.289	23.701	22.546	22.835	1.227	1.083	23.00
27x1.0	M	27.0	1.00	0.144	26.350	25.773	25.917	0.613	0.541	26.00
27x1.5	M	27.0	1.50	0.217	26.026	25.160	25.376	0.920	0.812	25.50
27x2.0	M	27.0	2.00	0.289	25.701	24.546	24.835	1.227	1.083	25.00
28x1.0	M	28.0	1.00	0.144	27.350	26.773	26.917	0.613	0.541	27.00
28x1.5	M	28.0	1.50	0.217	27.026	26.160	26.376	0.920	0.812	26.50
28x2.0	M	28.0	2.00	0.289	26.701	25.546	25.835	1.227	1.083	26.00

CHAPTER 16
FINISHING TOUCHES

Putting the finishing touches on your projects is something you will undoubtedly do many times in the confines of your garage. Whether this means giving something a coat of primer, rust-preventative paint, clear coat, blackening solution, powder coating, or whatever, the job isn't finished until the finish is applied. Yet how do you apply these finishes? Well, application methods vary as much as—and depend upon—the finishes being applied. So let's get a look at both, OK?

Rust Never Sleeps

Any time you're dealing with ferrous metal—iron, tin, steel—rust is bound to be a problem if the metal isn't covered with some sort of protective coating to keep air and moisture from reaching it and causing oxidation (rust). Treating and preventing rust is, therefore, a major concern that has to be addressed on a more-or-less continuing basis. There are several great products available to help you successfully wage war on rust, including the following:

• Rust-Oleum paints, available in a wide range of colors and in aerosol or brush-on forms. Rust-Oleum is readily available at the local hardware store or home improvement center, and it comes in flat, satin, and glossy formulations. For best results, remove any surface rust with a wire brush and/or steel wool before applying it.

• Rust Encapsulator, a proprietary product from The Eastwood Company. Available in red, black, silver, and clear,

A POR-15 starter kit gives you everything you need for those small projects, including latex gloves, while applying the rust-preventative paint. The gloves are necessary since if you get the POR-15 on your skin, nothing will get it off except for time and wear. Courtesy: POR-15/RestoMotive

POR-15 is available in black, silver, and clear and in half pints, pints, and quarts, so there's a size that will be appropriate for your project. Courtesy: POR-15/RestoMotive

it can be applied directly over rust and it is available in both aerosol and brush-on versions. The clear can also be tinted using the Eastwood tints (black, white, red, yellow, blue). You simply remove any loose rust, degrease the surface and apply it.

• POR-15, another product that can be applied directly over rust without pre-cleaning. It dries to an almost ceramic-like hardness. Available in flat, satin, and high-gloss formulations, POR-15 is best applied with a brush, and it provides an extremely durable surface.

Turning the Heat Up

Surfaces that get hot—really hot—such as exhaust manifolds, brake calipers, engine blocks, and other such surfaces need finishes that can withstand such high temperatures. There are paints and other finish products specially formulated for these purposes.

Exhaust manifold dressing, available in both liquid and paste formulations, is gray in color and, when applied, gives the appearance of fresh cast iron. The heat of the manifold helps to set and cure the dressing, and it can be applied using a brush or a coarse rag.

High-temp paints, available in aerosols and cans, come in a variety of colors that approximate or duplicate OEM factory finishes for parts such as engines, carburetors, valve covers, radiators, brake drums, and such. These are best applied while the recipient surface is cold to the touch.

Eastwood stocks an assortment of specialty coatings that are especially made for automotive restorations, among other projects. You'd be hard pressed to find carburetor-colored paint or zinc paint at the local hardware store, for sure. Courtesy: The Eastwood Company

The Diamond Clear paints are available in satin and high-gloss for both bare metal and painted surfaces. The brake caliper paint looks like freshly cast iron, while the trunk paint produces a speckled black/gray spatter. It's very unique. Courtesy: The Eastwood Company

As you can see from this assortment of Eastwood aerosol finishes, all shades of black are not equal, nor are they intended for the same purposes. Choosing the right paint for the job is the first step toward achieving a successful result. Courtesy: The Eastwood Company

Silver is another one of those colors that has myriad variations, and there's a special formulation for every project, from bland to bling. Courtesy: The Eastwood Company

Specialty Finishes

This is kind of a catch-all category, since there are lots of specialty finishes. Here are just a few of them:

• Wrinkle finish paint, available in aerosol form only, dries with a textured, durable finish. It's suitable for interior or exterior use. When dry, it has a satin black "crinkle" finish like that found on microscopes or other high-end laboratory equipment. This stuff is excellent for creating accents on parts to contrast against high-gloss surfaces.

• Trunk paint, an amazing aerosol paint, that produces a black/gray spatter finish that looks just like the OEM finish that car manufacturers use to cover the interior of car trunks. Easy to apply, it dries to a hard, durable finish.

• Carb renew bronze, an aerosol paint approximates the bronze color found on vintage caburetors when they were new.

• Faux Cad, a three-paint aerosol kit that starts with a gold base coat, to which mists of red and green tint are applied to give the appearance of cadmium plating.

The Grays Are Here

No, not the little gray beings that crashed in Roswell. I'm talking about the myriad shades of gray (and silver) that abound in both aerosol and brush-on forms. There certainly seems to be a shade of gray or silver for any application you can think of. For starters, these include:

• Silver high-temp coating
• Aluminized exhaust paint
• Factory gray high-temp coating
• Stainless-steel high-temp coating
• Zinc tank tone

Eastwood's paints are also available in quarts and other sizes for brushing on or for filling your spray gun. For large projects, this is the more economical way to go rather than using aerosol cans.
Courtesy: The Eastwood Company

- Detail gray
- Silver Cad
- Carb renew silver
- Aluma Blast aluminum finish
- TiCoat titanium silver
- Charcoal gray
- Argent silver
- Detail silver
- Almost chrome
- Cast caliper coating
- Spay gray

I Can See Clearly Now

Clear finishes are great for protecting bare metal or painted surfaces. They provide a transparent coating that seals the surface they're protecting while letting the underlying finish show through. In addition to the numerous brands of polyurethane finishes available at the local hardware store and home improvement centers, there are clear finishes specifically designed and formulated for automotive and other uses on metal surfaces. These include the following:

This blackening kit will give any unpainted ferrous metal a uniform black color just like it came from an OEM. The sealant helps to keep the nice finish looking that way for a long, long time. Courtesy: The Eastwood Company

- Diamond Clear gloss provides a high-gloss transparent finish. It is available in aerosol form for both bare metal and painted surfaces.
- Diamond Clear satin, a less glossy transparent finish, is also available in aerosol cans for both painted and bare metal surfaces.

Black Is Black—Or Is It?

One would think that black is black, but there are more shades of black than you could shake a stick at. Just to name a few, these shades include the following:

- Satin chassis black
- Satin radiator black
- Brake drum coating black
- Chassis black primer
- Black self-etching primer
- Gloss radiator black
- Satin under-hood black
- Satin black for wheels
- Satin black high-temp
- Gloss chassis black

Black 202

There's also a blackening chemical agent kit available from Eastwood that consists of two liquids; the first is a blackening solution and the other is a sealant. The bare metal (ferrous) part to be blackened is immersed in the blackening solution for the prescribed amount of time, then it is immersed in the sealant to preserve the newly-blackened finish. No electricity is required and replacement chemicals are also available from Eastwood to replenish as needed.

Takin' It All Off

While there are lots of finishes that permit you to apply them over pre-existing paint, most of the time you'll want to start with a clean surface completely devoid of paints or other surface coatings. So, with that in mind, here is some information about how to strip off the old stuff.

Basically, you have two choices here. The first is to use abrasives to remove the old finish. That means using sandpaper, media blasting, stripping/cleaning discs, or other abrasive means of rubbing/wearing the old finish off to expose the bare structural material underneath it. The downside to this method is that it generates a lot of dust and, if you're using air tools, it's noisy. The other method uses chemical means to remove the old finish material, and this can be a brush-on liquid or gel chemical that dissolves the original paint.

Let's Get It On

Applying a finish also gives you a few options as to how you're going to get it onto your target surface, which include contact

This HVLP spray gun features its own regulator for dialing in the precise pressure you want. It's a feature that's especially useful for doing special paint effects like flames, ghosting, and fogging. Courtesy: The Eastwood Company

and non-contact means. The contact method involves actually making contact with the surface, as in using a brush, roller, or some other type of contact applicator. The non-contact method includes spraying the finish on or dipping the item to be finished in a solution.

For contact finishing, your choices are bristle brushes and foam applicators, with the latter being preferable for the majority of metal-finishing tasks since they are less likely to leave stroke marks. Bristle brushes also have the downside of leaving bristles behind. Either way, contact finishing isn't an ideal solution for applying paint.

For non-contact finishing, you have two choices: aerosol cans or a compressor/spray gun setup. It's a popular misconception that you can't get a decent finish using aerosol-based paints. And that's exactly what it is—a misconception! The reason most folks don't get a decent finish using aerosols is that they don't apply them correctly. Everyone always seems to be in a rush when using spray paints. The secret to getting a good

paint job with a spray can is to apply several light coats with sufficient drying time between coats, whereas most folks try to cover it all in one heavy coat that usually results in runs and spotting. Patience is a virtue, especially when using aerosol-based paints.

The Case Against Spraying

If you're thinking about painting your entire vehicle or even just a part of it, you should consider some important things before you fill up your paint cup and turn the old compressor on.

Without a professional facility and right equipment, the chances for a really great paint job are significantly diminished. A professional body shop is equipped with a paint booth, which is essentially a sealed room with circulating fans and filters to remove and trap dust to keep it from settling on the new paint being sprayed onto the vehicle. In addition to yielding a superior finish and protecting the environment, paint booths are mandatory in some states and it is illegal to use automotive finishes outside of an EPA-approved paint booth. In other words, you can get a hefty fine for painting in your garage.

A paint booth also keeps the resulting paint particles' overspray from circulating freely in the atmosphere. I have a friend who decided to paint his Corvette in his garage, and he made a makeshift paint booth using overspray sheeting to form a tent around the car while he did his work. Even with this tenting, the neighborhood was treated to generous clouds of orange dust and the noxious vapors of automotive base coat and clear coat. Because he has considerable skill with a spray gun, the paint job came out surprisingly nice considering the circumstances it was applied under. Suffice it to say that he was not voted "good neighbor of the year" on his block, however. That was a few years ago, and he still finds traces of the custom orange base coat around the garage even after all this time.

Paint vapors and the airborne particulates that are a byproduct of overspray are decidedly not good for your lungs or respiratory tract, and this is something you should take into consideration very seriously. If you are absolutely hellbent on doing any paint spraying in your garage, a professional-grade respirator is absolutely essential, and a painter's coverall suit and good eye protection should also be on the must-have list. You can also add to the bill of goods a pro-caliber spray gun, paint mixing and filtering equipment, and a compressor capable of putting out a sustained volume of air.

You also have to realize that there is always a fire hazard present when using flammable liquids like paints, thinners, and solvents. And it's not just the liquids themselves, but their vapors as well. Would your homeowner's insurance policy cover you for a fire resulting from you painting in your garage? It probably wouldn't it, especially if it violated your local fire codes, which is highly likely.

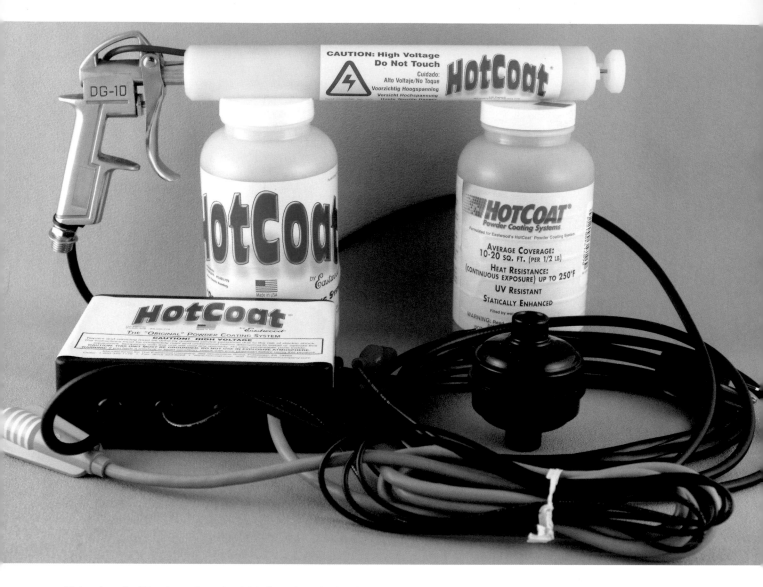

A hot powder-coating kit is an inexpensive way to get started in powder coating. Aside from the kit, all you need is an air compressor, an electric outlet, an old electric oven, and some appropriate eye and respiratory protection. Gas ovens are not recommended, and you should never prepare food again in an oven that has been used for powder coating. Courtesy: The Eastwood Company

So, after you weigh the expense involved in acquiring all the equipment you'll need, plus the fuss and bother of getting everything set up properly, plus the expense of the paint, thinner, and other requisite supplies, you have to ask yourself seriously if you want to tackle a paint job yourself or farm it out.

The Case for Painting Your Project Yourself

There may be an occasion where you just have a small spot that needs a touch-up or a small part that requires painting. For these very small jobs, you may elect to do it yourself to save some bucks, especially if you already own a decent compressor. You may decide to build a small spray booth if you have the room in your garage (Richard Newton provides plans for building a great small spray booth in his *Ultimate Garage Handbook*, published by MBI Publishing Company).

When using a compressor/spray gun setup, you have two choices. You can use a siphon spray gun that requires a decent amount of air pressure to suck the paint up from the cup and atomize it (which also produces copious amounts of overspray), or you can use a gravity-fed HVLP (high-velocity low-pressure) gun that has the paint supply above the air stream. The advantage of the HVLP setup is that you don't need an overly powerful compressor. More paint is delivered with less pressure, and that results in less overspray.

Even when using a compressor/spray gun setup, the same rule of several light coats as opposed to a single, heavy coat

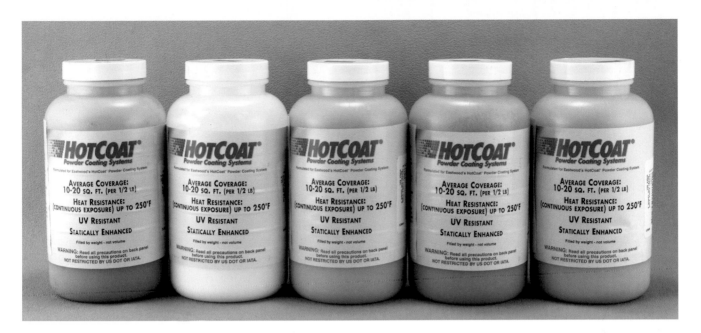

Hot powder-coating powder is available in dozens of colors, some even metallic. The powder is also available in various sized containers, so if you have a big project you can save some money by purchasing the large economy-size jars. Courtesy: The Eastwood Company

applies. A great finish is the result of proper prep and plenty of time and patience during the application.

Powder Power

There's another finishing option that has grown increasingly popular over the past few years, and that's powder coating.

Unlike spray painting liquid paint, powder coating uses high-voltage electricity, compressed air, and heat to achieve its objective.

Powder coating can't be applied to any painted surfaces or any surface that has plastic body filler on it (this stuff explodes when heated). So the first step is to strip the metal down until it is bare, and the best way to do it is with media blasting so there is no residue from chemical paint removers left on the metal.

Then the power unit (which produces high voltage with low amperage) is connected to the powder coating gun that already has its cup filled with the desired color powder.

The compressed air supply is then connected to the gun, which creates turbulence in the cup (only 8–10 psi is required).

The powder in the cup is fluidized and forced up into the gun nozzle, where it is electrostatically charged to give it a positive charge.

The object to be coated has a ground electrode attached to it to give it a negative charge. This negative charge strongly attracts the positively-charged powder coming from the gun.

When the part is fully coated, it is baked in an electric oven (or with ultraviolet lights if ultraviolet curing is being used), which causes the powder to flow into the nooks, crannies, and crevices and cure to give the part a uniform smooth, glossy finish.

The advantages of powder coating are that the resultant finish is durable, chip resistant, and good looking. A starter system can be had for just a little more than $100, so powder coating is something you may want to seriously consider.

CHAPTER 17
I'VE GOT THE POWER

Let me start this chapter by saying that I have nothing at all against hand tools. Indeed, hand tools are wonderful in that they make my life easier in one way or another literally every day. But as great as they are, hand tools require your hand (and arm) muscles to make them do anything useful. Power tools, on the other hand, just require you to guide them, and their motors supply the muscle for them to be productive. What's not to love, then?

OK, so now that we agree power tools are time and work savers, let's get into their nuances. First, you have a choice when it comes to most power tools, and that choice is whether to go corded or cordless. There are pros and cons for both, however.

Corded power tools require an AC outlet for their power, but—barring a power failure—as long as the juice is flowing the tool will keep on working, which is a good thing for those long stints. The downside of corded power tools is that you're tied (literally) by that umbilical cable to an AC outlet. If you need to use the tool in a remote location where there's no AC power available, you're up the proverbial creek without a paddle. There's also the very real hazard of electrical shocks when working near water or in the rain with these tools.

Cordless power tools have come a long, long way since they were introduced. The early tools were semi-anemic with their power output, and they were real battery suckers with a

This palm-sized cordless screwdriver is really a mighty-mite. Its internal battery will give you about an hour of driving power between charges, and it packs a surprising amount of torque for its diminutive size. Courtesy: Black & Decker

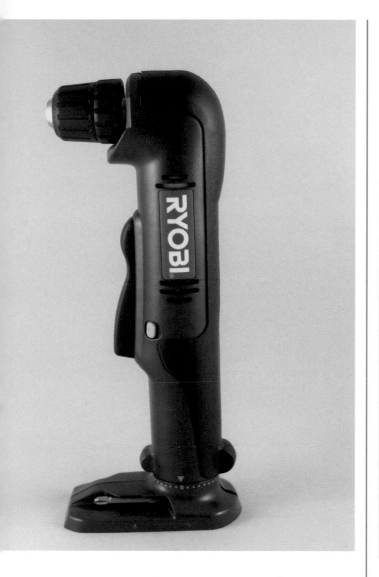

For getting into tight places, this cordless 18-volt close-quarters right-angle drill is just the ticket. It's part of Ryobi's One+ 18-volt cordless tool assortment. Courtesy: Ryobi

A cordless impact driver is great for jobs that require a lot of torque, and it makes an attractive (and practically silent) alternative to using an air tool. This one uses an 18-volt battery pack for lots of power and working time. Courtesy: Ryobi

short useful charge time. This disadvantage limited the kind of jobs you could do with them and how long they could be used between charge cycles. Now, however, they rival the power of their corded counterparts, and they also have the advantage of being able to operate literally anywhere.

For years, manufacturers have been on a quest to perfect their cordless tools, and the heart of this quest was in designing batteries that could deliver the power needed to operate them for usable periods of time.

It's no wonder, then, that when you approach the subject of cordless tools, the attention quickly moves from the tools to the batteries that power them. The type of battery is of utmost importance. There are two major types of batteries for powering cordless tools: NiCad cells and NiMH batteries.

NiCad cells were, until recently, the battery of choice for cordless tools. Rated at 1.2 volts per cell, these batteries can be recharged quickly and have a constant discharge rate. The consistent discharge rate results in a steadier use of the tool. NiCad cells are connected together in a series to provide power for cordless tools: 10 cells produce 12 volts, and 11 cells produce 14.4 volts. This progression continues with 18-, 19.2-, and 24-volt tools.

The downside is that after about 1,000 individual charges they have run their course. Another bad point is that NiCad cells contain heavy, toxic metals that can't be thrown out in the trash. The batteries must be recycled or disposed of in a hazardous waste landfill.

NiMH batteries are nickel-metal-hydride batteries that manufacturers are still developing to improve their perform-

The heart of Ryobi's One+ cordless tool system is this 18-volt battery pack that can be used to power the entire line of One+ cordless tools. Courtesy: Ryobi

This cordless drill/driver is another one of the One+ cordless tools. It features a 3/8-inch keyless chuck for fast bit changing. Courtesy: Ryobi

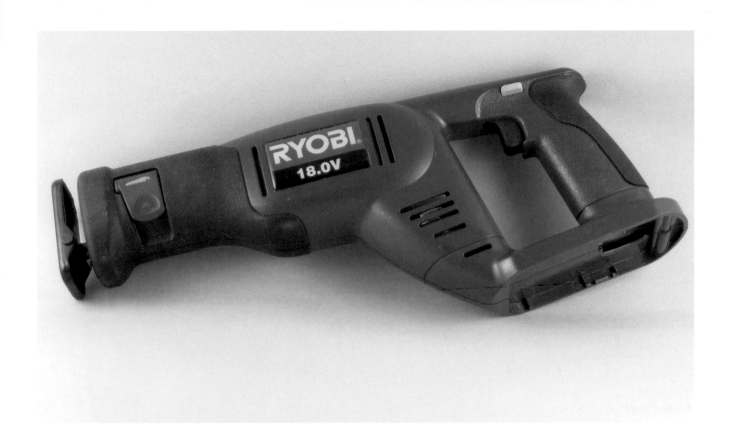

Depending on the projects you have in mind, you may or may not feel you'll need a reciprocating saw like this one. If you think you will have a need (and most folks will sooner or later), you may want to check out Ryobi's "The Works" pack. It contains this saw and other "homeowner" cordless tools at a substantial savings over purchasing them individually. Courtesy: Ryobi

This cordless 18-volt variable-speed orbital jigsaw, also called a saber saw, is very handy for cutting sheet metal, fiberglass, and other materials. The absence of a power cord eliminates the possibility of cutting through one and giving yourself a nasty shock. Courtesy: Ryobi

A very useful piece of garage gear is this wet/dry cordless vacuum, which is great for fast cleanup chores that inevitably result from working on various projects. Courtesy: Ryobi

Skil's iXo palm-sized cordless screwdriver comes with an assortment of bits and a handy charger/stand. Equipped with an internal, rechargeable lithium ion battery, this powerful little tool can hold its charge for up to 18 months. Courtesy: Skil Tools

ance. Since NiMH batteries don't contain cadmium, they are more environmentally friendly than NiCads.

Power by the Hour

Another consideration is the battery's AH (ampere-hour) rating, which is a measure of how long a charge will last. NiCads seem to be limited to a top end of 2 AH, where NiMH are at 2 AH now and will be hitting 3 AH soon. Since a 3 AH battery will last one and a half times as long as a 2 AH battery, and higher AH batteries don't generally weigh more than those with a lower rating, you should choose the higher AH of the same voltage. At the moment, and for the foreseeable future, the NiMH batteries cost more than NiCads.

Heavy-Weight Voltage

Battery packs are composed of a number of individual 1.2-volt cells, which must be strung together to produce the voltage required. Eight batteries will produce 9.6 volts, 15 batteries will produce 18 volts, etc. More cells produce greater voltage, but they also increase the total weight. Consider the power-versus-weight tradeoff carefully to get a tool that can do the job and still be comfortable to use. The average home handyman who only uses a cordless power tool occasionally will probably be very happy choosing 9.6 to 14.4 volts. Heavier users will prefer 18-volt tools and, if you're into weightlifting and body building, the 24-volt monsters will help you work-out while working on your projects at the same time.

Charge!

Don't assume when you purchase a cordless power tool that the battery and charger will be included in the package. Otherwise you may be in for a disappointment. While most manufacturers do include these items, not all do, so be sure to check it out before you get to the checkout counter.

This 12-volt FireStorm drill/driver packs plenty of punch and it's lighter in weight than comparable 14.4-volt and 18-volt tools. It also comes with a nice assortment of bits, a battery, and a charger.

Courtesy: Black & Decker

If you have to purchase a charger separately, be sure to get one that has a built-in overload protector to prevent overcharging the battery. Most chargers on the market do this as well as letting you know if the battery is charging or is fully charged, and some "diagnostic" chargers go beyond that with other features, such as sensing the battery's temperature. This latter feature is a nice "bells and whistles" option that you don't absolutely need, however.

The industry standard charging time is one hour. There are also 15-minute chargers and other "speed" chargers available, as well as in-vehicle chargers if you need to recharge while on the go. Then there are the less expensive chargers that require from three to five hours to fully recharge your batteries. These are good for overnight charging, especially if you only use the tool(s) occasionally.

This RTX high-speed rotary tool is great for a number of jobs, including grinding, cutting, engraving, drilling, and more. It comes with an assortment of accessories and a flexible shaft extension for even more versatility. Courtesy: Black & Decker

This Dremel high-speed rotary tool kit comes with a flexible shaft attachment and a plethora of useful accessories. While this is a corded model, Dremel also makes an excellent cordless rotary tool, and the bits and other accessories are interchangeable between models. Courtesy: Dremel/Robert Bosch

This MBX electric blaster system is a corded tool that is unbeatable for removing paint, plating, rust, or other surface coatings. This particular piece of garage gear is also available in a pneumatic version as well, if you prefer air power. Courtesy: Monti Tool Company

An excellent choice for a corded buffer/polisher, this DeWalt unit is well balanced, powerful, and built to last a lifetime. Courtesy: The Eastwood Company

This AC-powered FireStorm buffer/polisher from Black & Decker features a side-brace handle that can be mounted for use by right- or left-handed users. Courtesy: Black & Decker

Pick a Pack of Power

It has become vogue among major manufacturers to bundle their most popular tools together into economy packs. While you will see some corded tool packs offered, the vast majority will be cordless tool packs. Companies like Ryobi, Skil, and Black & Decker, to name but a few, are all offering economy cordless tool packs. Typically, these packs will consist of a cordless drill/screwdriver, saber saw, reciprocating saw, circular saw, a flashlight, a charger, and one or (usually) two batteries.

While you may well think that you don't need the reciprocating saw and the circular saw, when you add up the total for purchasing the other tools individually, you'll find that you're getting the two saws for free. But don't buy one of these economy packs just to save money. If the pack doesn't contain the tools you'll need and rely on often, then it really isn't a bargain after all.

One last bit of advice: as with all your other tool purchases, stick with the name brands because the well-known, reputable manufacturers will stand behind their products if you have a problem or need service or replacement parts.

And now it's time to charge on to Chapter 18.

CHAPTER 18
EVERYTHING BUT THE KITCHEN SINK

In the overall scheme of things, lots of items belong in your garage and don't neatly fit into any of the predefined categories I've covered in the preceding chapters. That is the reason they are in this chapter—covering every miscellaneous thing you might want in your vehicle oasis.

Magnetic Attraction

Magnets are great—I like to think of them as nature's Velcro when it comes to ferrous metals. They most certainly have their uses in the garage. If you've ever dropped a nut, bolt, washer, or other small metal item into an inaccessible place, then you can readily appreciate how handy a magnet on a telescoping wand or a sweep magnet can be. It is really an essential piece of garage gear.

A magnetic holder on your air hose will keep it stuck to the compressor, so it's there whenever you need it. Magnetic welding jigs are also a great help. Buy a few magnets for your garage and you'll be surprised at how many uses you can find for them without even trying.

Where's the Leak?

Leaking automotive fluids are more than just a nuisance; they can indicate a serious mechanical problem. A leak finder will help you to locate the source, which is the first step in correcting the problem. A good multipurpose leak finder kit will help you to trace A/C, oil, coolant, power steering, ATF, fuel, hydraulic, and autobody leaks. If you're finding wet spots on your garage floor, a leak finder will be a worthwhile investment.

Suck It Up

Here's a piece of garage gear you can find at the local supermarket or perhaps even commandeer from the kitchen. It's a turkey baster, and it's absolutely great for adding water to your vehicle battery and other chores that require sucking a liquid up or squirting it out. The tapered tip makes it ideal for getting into small places, too.

A bulb-activated siphon hose is another handy thing to have in your garage. Useful for transferring gasoline or just about any other kind of fluid, the bulb gets the siphoning action started so you don't have to wind up with a mouthful

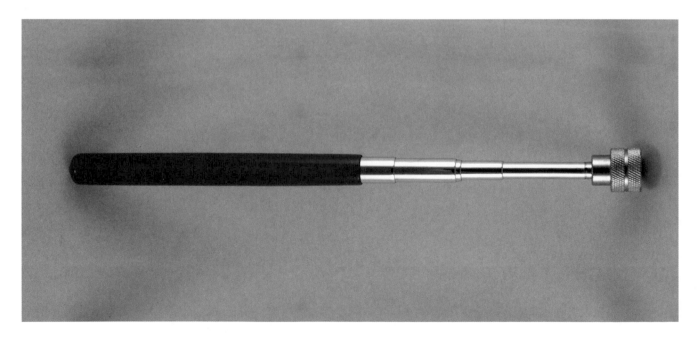

A wand magnet like this one is extremely handy for retrieving dropped items that fall in inaccessible places. This one telescopes to 30 inches and has interchangeable magnetic tips.

Courtesy: The Eastwood Company

This Tracerline LeakFinder Kit includes everything you need to trace A/C, oil, coolant, power steering, ATF, fuel, hydraulic, and autobody leaks. Courtesy: The Eastwood Company

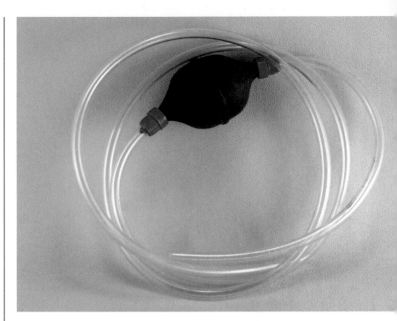

You never know when you might have to siphon something, so having a bulb-siphon hose around the garage is a good thing. They only cost a couple of dollars and they don't take up much space, so why not have one on hand? Author's Collection

of liquid from sucking on the hose yourself—progress is a wonderful thing!

Bleeding brake lines is all but impossible to do unless you have a vacuum line bleeder. With one of these units, you simply connect the hose to the bleeder valve and pump the handle to evacuate the line of fluid and/or air. The best part is that you don't have to persuade a friend or family member to keep pumping the brake pedal for you.

What's the Buzz?

Ever have to work on a vehicle with the driver or passenger door open? Doesn't the sound of the buzzer or chime drive you nuts? I'll bet you've tried everything from wedging a screwdriver in the door to using duct tape to depress the buzzer button to shut it up—all to no avail, right? What you need is a set of door-buzzer sanity tools. These spring-loaded gadgets snap in the door jamb to keep the buzzer button depressed. Silence is golden, and these babies will deliver it, for sure.

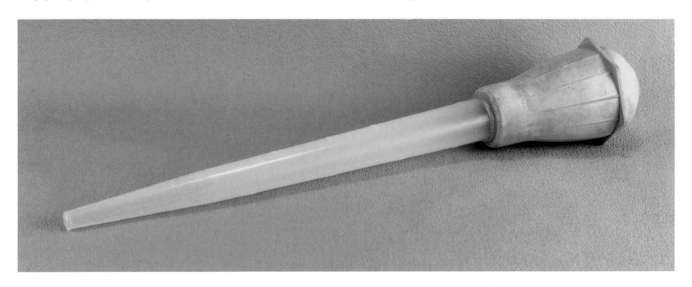

Rescued (or should I say requisitioned?) from the kitchen, this turkey baster is ideal for replenishing water in batteries and siphoning and transferring other fluids in the garage. Author's Collection

A Mighty-Vac brake system evacuation kit makes bleeding your brakes a simple, one-person job. Courtesy: The Eastwood Company

Cradle It, Baby!

Anyone who's ever had to drill a piece of pipe or tubing with a drill press will know how difficult it is to keep the pipe steady so you get a completely perpendicular hole. Life doesn't have to be this difficult if you use a drill press cradle, also known as a v-block centering fixture. You simply put the pipe or tube in the cradle and the angled sides keep it from moving about. Sometimes the most elegant solutions are the simplest.

In the Rubber Room

Grommets and O-rings are items that you may only need once in a blue moon, but usually when the need does arise,

the local auto parts store is closed or you can't get the size you need from the hometown hardware store. So, if you believe an ounce of prevention is worth a ton of aggravation, you'll probably opt to have an assortment of each on hand as part of your supply, as I do. Hey, it's cheap insurance, and you never know when you're going to need one or a couple, right?

Lend a Helping Hand

There are times when you can't get a good grip on something you're trying to move, and you don't have a helper around to assist you. That's when a helping hand can really come to the rescue. Basically, it's a suction cup with a handle attached that

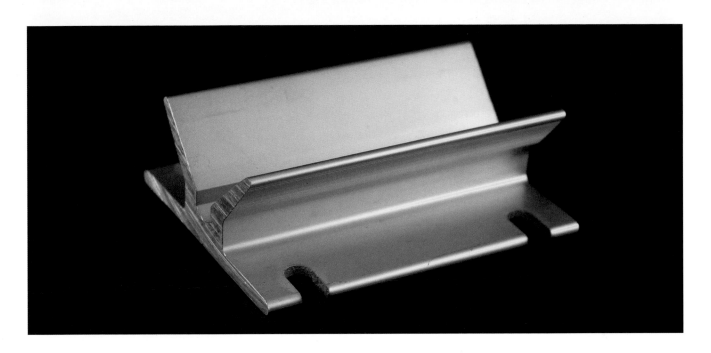

This V-block centering fixture virtually guarantees that you'll be able to bore straight, perpendicular holes with your drill press in round stock, such as pipes or tubing. Courtesy: The Eastwood Company

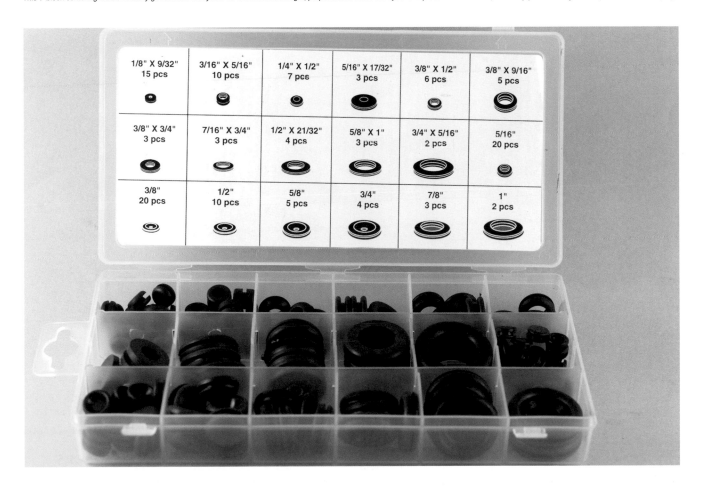

1/8" X 9/32" 15 pcs	3/16" X 5/16" 10 pcs	1/4" X 1/2" 7 pcs	5/16" X 17/32" 3 pcs	3/8" X 1/2" 6 pcs	3/8" X 9/16" 5 pcs
3/8" X 3/4" 3 pcs	7/16" X 3/4" 3 pcs	1/2" X 21/32" 4 pcs	5/8" X 1" 3 pcs	3/4" X 5/16" 2 pcs	5/16" 20 pcs
3/8" 20 pcs	1/2" 10 pcs	5/8" 5 pcs	3/4" 4 pcs	7/8" 3 pcs	1" 2 pcs

Rubber grommets are used for lots of jobs, including providing smooth runways for wiring, tubing, and other tasks. This assortment contains several grommets of the most used sizes and comes with this handy see-through storage case. Courtesy: The Eastwood Company

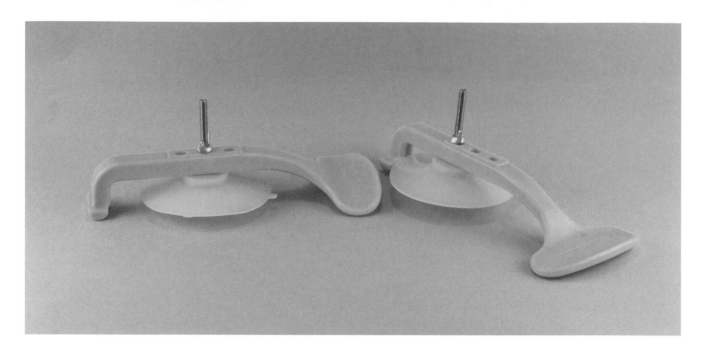

These are called helping hands and that's exactly their function. The adjustable-height suction cup affixes to any smooth surface, instantly giving you a secure gripping handle.
Courtesy: The Eastwood Company

These suction dent-pullers are surprisingly effective and easy to use. Simply moisten the suction cup, attach it to the center of the dent, and give it a yank to pop the dent out without paint damage. Courtesy: The Eastwood Company

you can stick onto any smooth surface for a more positive grip. The suction cup height is adjustable via a screw that attaches it to the handle, and that makes it more versatile. It really is a good tool to have on hand, pardon the pun.

The Dent-ist

One of the oldest methods of removing dents from autobody panels and sheet metal is using suction, and that's what autobody suction cups are all about. You simply moisten the

cup surface, position it in the center of the dent you want to pull, and give it a yank. You may have to move the cup and repeat the application if it's a big ding, but in many cases, you should be able to pull the dent without damaging the paint or requiring body filler to finish the job.

Go to Your Corners

When cleaning the inside of your windshield, isn't it a pain in the butt to get into the corners? I know I've tried

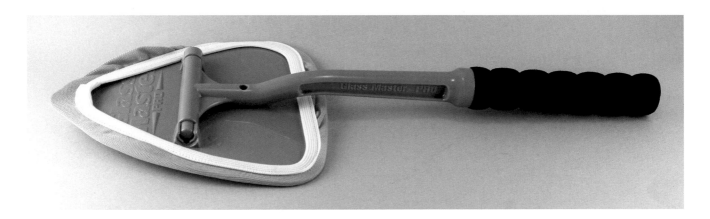

Reaching the corners when cleaning the inside of your windshield is no longer a problem with this Glass Master Pro tool. Courtesy: The Eastwood Company

This master rethreading set will bail you out when you come across a cross-threaded fastener, regardless of whether it's SAE or metric. Courtesy: The Eastwood Company

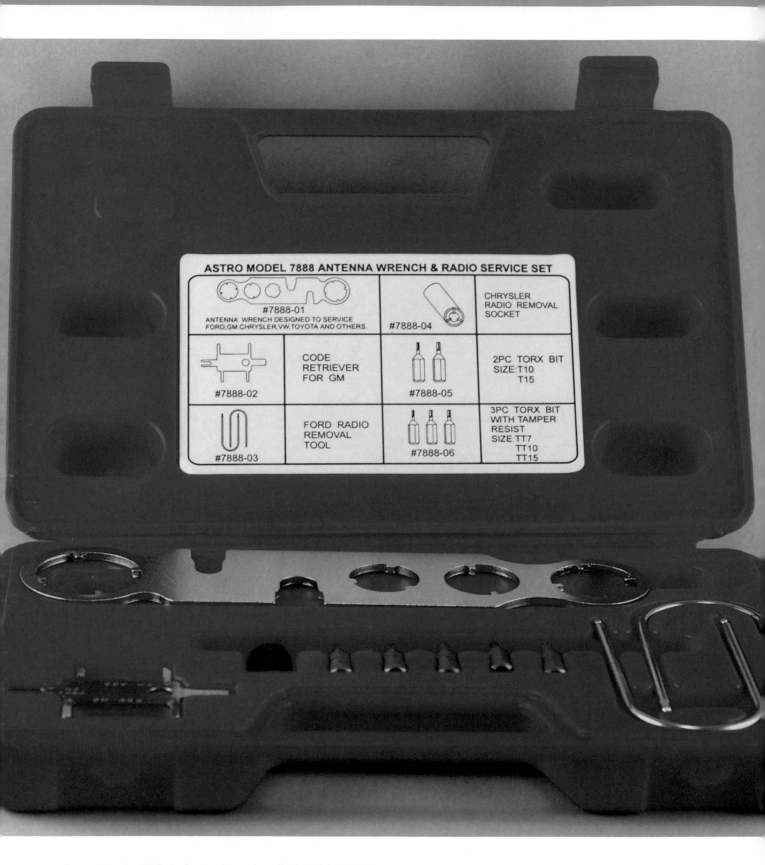

If you need to work on GM, Ford, or Chrysler radios or antennae, this tool set is just the ticket. Courtesy: The Eastwood Company

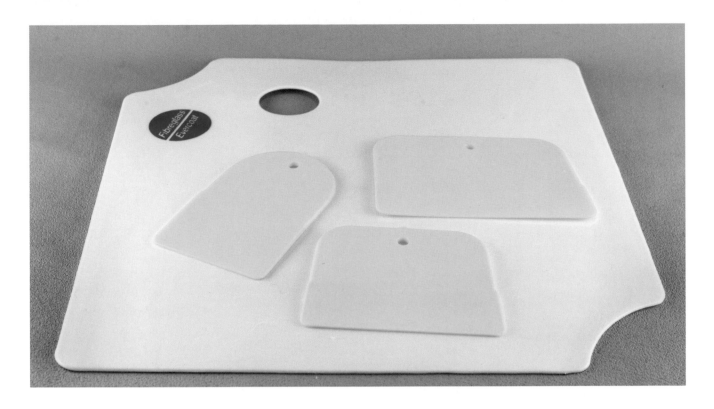

A non-stick palette like this one sure beats using a piece of cardboard for mixing body filler, and the non-stick spatulas are the way to go as well. Courtesy: The Eastwood Company

everything, including wrapping a folded rag around a wooden ruler to reach into the corners, but these attempts were only mildly successful at best. Then along comes this nifty gadget designed for getting into the corners (the Glass Master Pro), and what was previously a frustrating task has now become a breeze. Every car care bucket should have one of these in it.

A New Set of Threads

Sooner or later, you'll come across (or be the cause of) a stripped nut or bolt and, as fate would have it, it's not one that can be easily replaced (if at all). So, what to do here? You reach for the trusty old master rethreader kit, that's what. Regardless of whether it's a nut, bolt, or stud in SAE or metric thread, this kit will save the day. A rethreader kit is another worthwhile addition to your gear arsenal.

Radio Daze

Anytime you have to work on the radio or antenna of a fairly late-model vehicle, you'll be glad you have one of these wrench and service sets at your disposal. The set has everything you need to work on GM, Ford, or Chrysler radios and their antennae. If you do a lot of work on car/truck stereos, this is an indispensable piece of equipment.

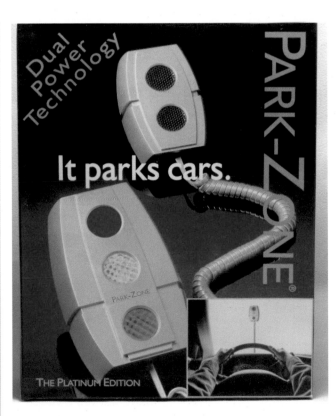

You'll be in the zone when you park in the garage if you have one of these Park-Zone units.

The distance can be adjusted to custom-program when the warning lights will flash.

Courtesy: Genuine Hot Rod Hardware

173

Keeping your tools and other gear secure is not only a way to prevent things from "growing legs," but it's also a good safety precaution if you have small children who access the garage.

Courtesy: Winner International

Lookin' Good

An inspection mirror comes in handy in the garage more times than you would think. There will be numerous times when you'll need to get a look at a fastener, connection, or other item that isn't readily visible, and that's where an inspection mirror is worth its weight in gold. Add a light to the mirror and you'll have even more versatile viewing!

Something Palletable

Sure, you can mix body filler using an old piece of cardboard box, but you don't always have a box around when you need one and, besides that, you're likely to pick up contaminants that are on the cardboard. It's better and more professional to use a fiberglass mixing palette. It has a smooth, sturdy surface and cleanup is a snap, since the dried filler doesn't stick to the palette. While you're at it, get yourself a few non-stick spatulas for applying the filler, too.

Safe and Secure

There are items in your garage that you'll want to secure for one reason or another. Perhaps you have kids and you don't want them touching your tools, or even friends and neighbors that like to borrow stuff without telling you. At any rate, having a couple of good padlocks available will serve you well for keeping your gear safe and secure. The choice of combination or keyed locks is yours, but no matter which style you choose, it will only protect your stuff if you use the locks religiously.

Keep Your Distance

Regardless of your driving skill level, it never hurts to have a little assistance when parking in the garage, and this gadget is just the ticket. The Park Zone has a series of green, amber, and red lights that light up as your vehicle gets closer to the wall. When the red light comes on, you're as close as you want to get, and the distances that trigger each light are adjustable.

Tool Tip

BODY FILLER SQUEEGEE

You can make a great disposable squeegee for body filler and glazing putty applications from an empty plastic milk or spring water container. Use a marker to outline the shape on the side of the container and cut it out using a pair of scissors.

You can get at least four squeegees from a carton and the best thing is that they don't cost a cent! Fiberglass/SMC body fillers and glazing putty won't stick to this plastic, so you can reuse them again and again.

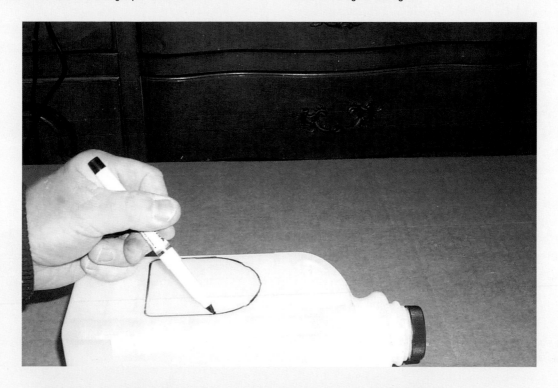

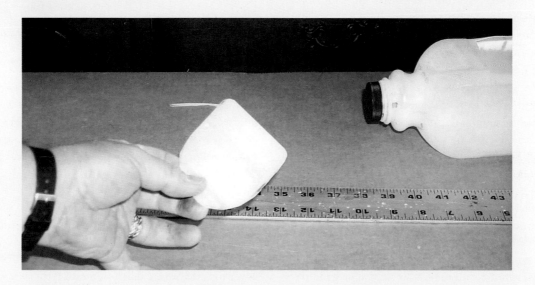

CHAPTER 19
TAKE A LOAD OFF YOUR FEET

While some folks just like to hang out in their garages, others put in a full day's worth of work out there. Needless to say, spending several hours standing on a cement floor can really be hard on your feet and back, which is why you should consider putting some ergonomic comforts out in your garage.

Rubber floor mats can help cushion your feet and leg muscles. They are an inexpensive solution and can be found in the housewares section of your local department store, home improvement center, or even at the supermarket.

It's No La-Z-Boy, But . . . .

You also might want to sit for a spell when you're out working. Now, the classic empty milk crate turned on its side or a stack of tires won't really leave you feeling better by the end of the day. Neither will sitting on the corner of a portable toolbox that was never intended to provide support to your derriere. Even if it's only a folding chair, you deserve to have a proper seat in your garage, don't you?

A roll-about stool is good for working at low levels, and it can be a comfortable seat for just kicking back a bit, too. These are inexpensive, and the better ones have a height adjustment that lets you raise or lower the seat several inches. They also usually have a tray for holding tools, nuts, bolts, and other small things for whatever you're working on.

A plastic step stool will also serve as a perch in a pinch. And while it's a welcome seat for short periods, you probably won't want to while away the hours sitting on it.

You're also going to need a creeper in the garage, so if you get yourself a combination creeper/seat you're killing two birds with one stone. These units convert from comfortable seats into full-fledged creepers so you can lie down in comfort while working under a vehicle; in seat mode it provides a comfortable, padded cush for your tush.

A dual-foam mechanic's mat is also a good thing to have if you need to get under the vehicle for short periods, you have to kneel for a little while, or you need to sit on the floor while working on something. The foam not only cushions, it also insulates you from the cold cement floor, so it's a good thing to have around—especially if you don't have knee protectors!

It's also nice to have a comfortable seat while working at your workbench in the garage, and a bar stool fits the bill just

An adjustable-height roll-about stool like this one permits you to change the seat height to suit the elevation you need, and the tray underneath will hold tools, nuts, bolts, or small parts. The ball-bearing casters enable it to glide around the garage floor effortlessly.
Courtesy: Mid America Motorworks

dandy for this purpose. I'm partial to stools with back rests, but this is just my preference. Bar stools without backs are perfectly satisfactory seats, too, and they invariably have lower bars that make dandy footrests.

Folding canvas chairs that stow away in pouches are also really good seating solutions for the garage since they don't take up much space when they're not being used. These

This roll-about stool has a swing-out shelf that holds parts and tools, along with a lower shelf that provides extra carrying space. Courtesy: Mid America Motorworks

This step-on stool will also do double duty as a seat, and it has a removable storage tray that's great for carrying small tools, parts, etc. Courtesy: StoreHorse/The Lehigh Group

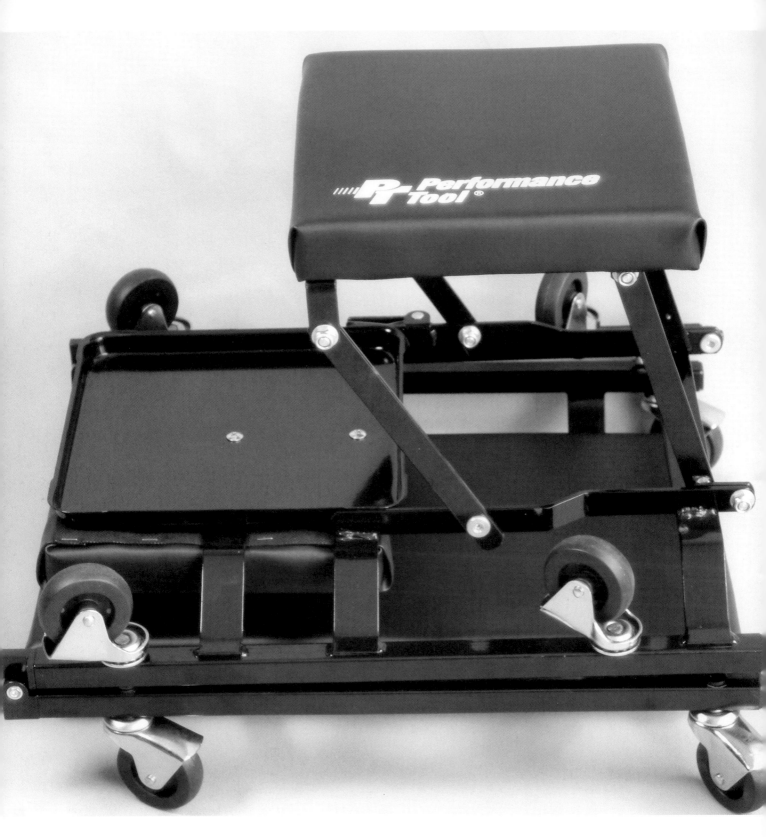

This full-size ball-bearing creeper converts to a handy roll-about stool in just seconds. The creeper and seat are comfortably padded, too. Courtesy: Mid America Motorworks

These folding canvas chairs are great seats for the garage and, when not in use, they stow away in their carry pouches and don't take up much room at all. Lightweight, sturdy, inexpensive, comfortable—who could ask for anything more? Courtesy: Mid America Motorworks

Creature Comforts

While some would argue that having a computer and a refrigerator in the garage is ludicrous, I don't agree with that train of thought. I am of the belief that you should be comfortable in your work environment, and that means having all the creature comforts you want—provided they don't cause distractions. That means that it's OK to have a stereo or radio playing while you're working. Yet, a TV, VCR, or DVD player may cause you to look away from your work to see what's happening on the screen and it may be an invitation to an accident and injury. Of course, if you want to watch a step-by-step instruction video, maybe you should watch it a few times before you actually try to do the project yourself.

Your garage can not only become your project haven, but it also can be a hangout for your friends. I know a fellow who has a bean bag chair and an old couch in his garage, and both are lined up for viewing the wide-screen plasma TV he recently installed for watching the NASCAR action on the weekends with his buddies. The TV is never on when he's out there wrenching or welding, however, and the remote control is kept locked in the toolbox to avoid temptation while he's working. Self-imposed discipline is a good thing because it produces good work habits.

A comfortable bar stool, with or without a back on it, is a great seat for working at the workbench in the garage. Most will have a foot rail, too. Courtesy: Mid America Motorworks

chairs are big hits at car shows, picnics, the beach, and lots of sporting events. They're very inexpensive, sturdy, and durable. You can get them in a variety of colors and styles, and some have built-in cup-holders, too.

This dual-foam mechanic's mat is great for saving the knees from the hard garage floor, and it can also be used as a creeper or even a seat. Courtesy: The Eastwood Company

If you have a toilet in the garage, that's great and you're probably the envy of all your gearhead friends. If you have any way of running plumbing and drain lines into the garage, I recommend installing a "slop sink" first, though. It's a deep fiberglass basin on legs that's great for washing up before you go back into the house. Keep a roll of paper towels nearby, along with your hand cleaner, and you'll be a real hero for not messing up the terry cloth towels in the bathroom.

A cell phone and/or a cordless phone will help you to stay in touch with those trying to reach you while you're in your sanctuary. An intercom between the house and the garage is also a handy thing, as is a bug-zapping light for when you're working out there in the warmer months with the door open.

Making Your Place Your Place

The whole point of this book is that your garage should have everything you need and want for it so that it becomes an environment you like to work in. The suggestions I've made in this book are exactly that—suggestions. Don't be afraid to think outside the box. Make the garage what you want it—a place you just can't help but want to spend time in—and you'll have many happy gearhead years ahead of you.

Tool Tip

MAKING A CHEAPER CREEPER

If you don't want to shell out the bucks for a mechanic's creeper for under-car work, especially if you only have to go under your vehicle once in a blue moon, then you're going to like this item. Take a trip to your nearest Home Depot, Lowe's, or your local building supply/home remodeling center and get yourself a 4x8-foot sheet of Owens-Corning Energy Shield Outside Insulation; it shouldn't set you back more than $10 for a sheet.

The stuff is described as "a rigid polyisocyanurate foil-faced foam board," according to the manufacturer. I describe it as a 3/4-inch thick expanded-foam board with foil facing on both sides. The stuff is light, cuts easily with a utility knife, and is very comfortable to use as a shield between you and the driveway when working on your vehicle.

You can cut four 4x2-foot cheaper-creepers from a single sheet. You can reuse the same piece several times and, when it's finally reached the end of its useful life, toss it into the trash can. Even though I have a professional-quality mechanic's creeper, I find that I use the lighter (and more comfortable) cheaper-creeper for most of my projects.

CHAPTER 20
CHEMICAL KARMA

If you're a real gearhead, your garage always has more than its share of oil and grease. But when it's time to finally unveil that sweet ride you've been rebuilding, or move on to the next significant part of your project, you're going to have to clean up the mess your work has left behind.

For these tasks, you'll want to have an arsenal of solvents available because some work better than others for certain degreasing jobs.

In the old days (I'm talking decades ago, now), one of the most popular grease-cutting solvents was regular pump gasoline. It was readily available and cheap, but it was also highly flammable. Its fumes were extremely combustible, too. I guess after several garages burned down to the ground, folks who could put two and two together figured that maybe gasoline wasn't such a good idea after all. It wasn't . . . and it still isn't.

Denatured wood alcohol, which is also flammable, is nowhere near as volatile as gasoline, so if you need a free-running liquid solvent, this is a good choice. Take the same precautions you would around exposed gasoline, however. That means no smoking or sparks around the alcohol. Also make sure there is plenty of ventilation for the fumes to escape. Keep the wood alcohol tightly capped in a flame-proof (metal) container when not in use, and keep it out of the reach of kids or anyone else you don't want to touch it.

Aerosol carburetor and fuel injector cleaner is also a strong solvent, as is aerosol engine starting fluid. Both are also highly flammable, in addition to giving off some offensive vapors. For these reasons, they're not to use in the garage. In fact, I really don't condone using any flammable solvents in the garage, since there are so many good degreasing solvents available that aren't flammable.

Here are some of the better choices:

• Spray Nine Cleaner, a strong, general purpose cleaner that does an excellent job of degreasing.

Even though this starting fluid contains no ether, it is still highly flammable and shouldn't be used as a solvent. Courtesy: WD-40 Company

Grez-Off is an industrial-strength degreaser that removes even the most packed, caked-on grease and oily dirt. The trigger sprayer directs the degreaser right where you want it to go. Courtesy: Spray Nine Corporation

Citrus Blaster is a heavy-duty grease, tar, and asphalt remover in an aerosol can that works fast on even the most stubborn patches of grime. Courtesy: WD-40 Company

This 3-in-One High-Performance Penetrant Spray comes in aerosol and "oiler" cans. It does a great job of freeing rusted nuts, bolts, and other frozen parts. Courtesy: WD-40 Company

• Spray Nine Grez-Off, an industrial-strength degreaser that rivals any of the flammable solvents for dissolving crusty, caked-on grease.

• Spray Nine Citrus Blaster, an aerosol-based solvent for dissolving grease, tar, and asphalt.

There are lots of other non-flammable solvents/degreasers available from other manufacturers, too, but I've used these Spray Nine products for years and I can personally vouch for their effectiveness.

Rub-A-Dub-Dub in a Parts Cleaning Tub

An inexpensive and worthwhile investment you may want to consider for your garage workshop is a parts cleaning tub. These are available in a wide variety of sizes and price ranges, and you can get them from just about any automotive supply outlet. In addition to containing the mess, these tubs permit the solvent(s) to be recycled, thus increasing their economy of use and containing the spent liquid until it can be disposed of in an ecologically-responsible manner.

Slick Stuff

Lubrication is the life-blood of all things mechanical, since it reduces friction and promotes smooth operation. Using the right lubricant for a given job is very important, since there are many different types of lubricants that were devel-

Silicon spray lubricant is an aerosol that dries quickly and is safe on rubber, wood, metal, and vinyl. Courtesy: WD-40 Company

183

WD-40 is the great granddaddy of spray lubricants and its moisture displacement properties are legendary. This essential garage chemical comes in several sizes, and it even has its own website: www.wd40.com. Courtesy: WD-40 Company

oped for specific applications. Regardless of their uses, they all fall into these basic categories:

• Oils, liquid lubricants that can be organic, petroleum-based, mineral-based, synthetics, or blends.

• Greases, thicker than oils, sometimes extremely so. These, too, can be made from petroleum, minerals, chemicals, or even organic substances (animal byproducts).

• Penetrants, specially-formulated lubricants that are designed to penetrate through rust. They're used predominantly for freeing rusted nuts and bolts.

• Silicone lubricants, great for most general lubricating purposes.

• Moisture repellers, specially-formulated lubricants available in aerosol form that displace and repel moisture. These are great for general lubrication and rust prevention. These are also great for coating tools and bare metal tool surfaces in unheated garages, where moisture from condensation can promote rusting. WD-40 and Boeshield are two of the more popular brands, and both work great.

Let's Have a Show of (Clean) Hands

Sure, you probably love to work in your garage, but your hands don't have to announce it to the world. Even if you wear gloves while working, it's almost an absolute given that you're going to get your hands dirty. And that dirt will most likely be grease in one form or another.

GoJo Fast Wipes are disposable hand-cleaning towels that are great for wiping dirt, grease, and grime off your hands while working on projects. They come in a variety of packaging, allowing gearheads to choose larger quantities and save some money in the process. Courtesy: GoJo Industries

Lava Soap has been around for as long as I can remember, and it has always been a favorite hand cleaner for mechanics. Now in addition to the familiar bar soap, Lava is also available in citrus-based liquid and cream formulations. Courtesy: WD-40 Company

Total Look Tire & Vinyl Dressing is a great product for making your tires, vinyl top, and other rubber and vinyl parts look real spiffy. Courtesy: Spray Nine Corporation

The Chrome and Aluminum Wash products from Busch can't be beat when it comes to cleaning these metals, and the company's aluminum polish, wax, and sealant products are equally good. Courtesy: Busch Industries

Ibiz car care products are the best I've ever used, and I say that with no reservation. The products cost a bit more than competitive products, but the results they deliver are head and shoulders above the others. A little Ibiz goes a long way, so you will save money in the long run. Courtesy: Ibiz

Grease Grabber is Spray Nine's liquid hand cleaner with pumice for getting the greasy grime out of your pores and lanolin to soften your skin. Courtesy: Spray Nine Corporation

While regular hand soap will get them clean with enough rubbing and scrubbing, there are other ways of cleaning up your act so you don't have "grease monkey" paws. Here are some ways to get those meat-hooks clean:

• Hand wipes, pre-moistened disposable towelettes with grease-cutting cleanser. These are great for wiping away light dirt and grease on your hands while working.

• Hand cleaners, waterless hand cleaners that dissolve grease and oil from the skin. These are usually fortified with lanolin and/or moisturizers to help soften the skin.

• Pumice soap, available in bar, liquid, and cream formulations. Pumice soap contains actual volcanic pumice to help remove stubborn, ground-in dirt, and grease. This stuff has been around forever because it works so well.

Looking Good

The other chemicals you're most likely to have in your garage are dedicated to appearance—making your vehicle(s) look good. These include car washes, shampoos, upholstery cleaners, leather conditioners, aluminum/chrome polishes, tire dressings, and a host of other products to make your ride shine.

APPENDIX
TOOL SUPPLIER LIST

Aearo Technologies (Aearo Safety)
5457 West 79th Street
Indianapolis, IN 46268
800-327-3431
www.aearo.com

American Saw & Mfg. Co. (Lenox Saw)
301 Chestnut Street
East Longmeadow, MA 01028
413-525-3961
www.lenoxsaw.com

Arrow Group Industries
1101 North 4th Street
Breese, IL 62230
1-800-851-1085
www.arrowsheds.com

Auto Chic, Inc.
6-B Hamilton Business Park
85 Franklin Road
Dover, NJ 07801
(800) 351-0605
www.autochic.com

BernzOmatic
92 Grant Street
Wilmington, OH 45177
1-800-654-9011
www.bernzomatic.com

Black & Decker
TW150
701 East Joppa Road
Towson, MD 21286
800-544-6986
www.bdk.com

Brother International
100 Somerset Corporate Boulevard
Bridgewater, NJ 08807-0911
908-704-1700
www.brother-usa.com

Brute Industries, Inc.
8506 M.5 Road
Gladstone, MI 49837
866-464-2788
www.raceramps.com

Busch Enterprises, Inc.
908 Cochran Street
Statesville, NC 28677
704-878-2067

Craftsman Tools
All Sears Stores Nationwide
www.craftsman.com

Dell, Inc.
One Dell Way
Round Rock, TX 78682
800-www-dell
www.dell.com

Dremel
4915 21st Street
Racine, WI 53405
800-437-3635
www.dremel.com

The Eastwood Company
263 Shoemaker Road
Pottstown, PA 19464
800-345-1178
www.eastwoodcompany.com

Garden of Speedin'
4645 Ruffner Street
Suite Q
San Diego, CA 92111
800-668-6743
www.gardenofspeedin.com

Genuine Hot Rod Hardware
29313 Clemens Road
Westwood Centre 2G
Westlake, OH 44145
800-575-1932
www.genuinehotrod.com

GoJo Industries
P.O. Box 991
Akron, OH 44309-0991
800-321-9647
www.gojo.com

Griot's Garage
800-345-5789
www.griotsgarage.com

GxT, Inc.
(formerly Ferret Instruments)
1310 Higgins Drive
Cheboygan, MI 49721-1061
800-627-5655
www.ferretinstruments.com

Henkel Consumer Adhesives, Inc. (Loctite)
32150 Just Imagine Drive
Avon, OH 44011
800-321-0253
www.loctiteproducts.com

Ibiz, Inc.
750 E. Sample Road, Building 7, B7
Pompano Beach, FL 33064
800-FOR-R-WAX
www.ibiz-inc.com

Irwin Industrial Tools
92 Grant Street
Wilmington, OH 45177
800-464-7946
www.irwin.com

Johnson & Johnson Consumer Products Company
Attn: Information Center
199 Grandview Road
Skillman, NJ 08558-9418
866-JNJ-2873
www.bandaid.com

Lehigh Group, The (Storehorse/Crawford)
2834 Schoeneck Road
Macungie, PA 18062
610-966-9702
www.lehighgroup.com

Lenmar Enterprises, Inc.
4035 Via Pescador
Camarillo, CA 93012
800-424-2703
www.lenmar.com

Martel Electronics Corporation
P.O. Box 770
Londonderry NH, 03053
800-821-0023
www.marteltesttools.com

Mechanixwear
24950 Anza Drive
Valencia, CA 91355
800-222-4296
www.mechanix.com

Microflex Corporation
2301 Robb Drive
Reno, NV 89523
800-876-6866
www.microflex.com

Mid America Motorworks
#1 Mid America Place
P.O. Box 1368
Effingham, IL 62401
800-500-1500
www.mamotorworks.com

Monti Tools, Inc.
80 Oak Street
Norwood, NJ 07648
201-784-7940
www.montitools.inc.

O'Sullivan Industries, Inc.
10 Mansell Court East
Roswell, GA 30076-4823
678-939-0800
www.osullivan.com

Pactiv Corporation (Hefty bags)
1900 West Field Court
Lake Forest, IL 60045
888-828-2850
www.heftybrand.com

Panther Vision
213 W. Main Street
West Dundee, IL 60118
847-783-5900
www.panthervision.com

POR-15, Inc.
P.O. Box 1235
Morristown, NJ 07962
800-726-0459
www.por15.com

Powermate Corporation (Coleman Powermate)
4970 Airport Rd
P.O. Box 6001
Kearney, NE 68848
800-445-1805
www.powermate.com

Rust-Oleum Corporation
11 Hawthorn Parkway
Vernon Hills, IL 60061
800-553-8444
www.rustoleum.com

Ryobi Technologies, Inc.
1428 Pearman Dairy Road
Anderson, SC 29625
800-323-4615
www.ryobitools.com

Skil Tools/Robert Bosch Tool Corporation
1800 W. Central Road
Mount Prospect, IL   60056
800-301-8255
www.skiltools.com

Solder-It Co.
404 Irvington Street
Pleasantville, NY 10570
800-353-7941
www.solder-it.com

Spray Nine Corporation
251 North Comrie Avenue
Johnstown, NY 12095
800-477-7299
www.knightmkt.com

Stanley Tools Product Group
480 Myrtle Street
New Britain, CT 06053
860-225-5111
www.stanleytools.com

SuperLifts, Inc.
P.O. Box 606
909 Industrial Drive
Aurora, Missouri 65605
800-218-7036
www.superlifts.com

T & L Industries Co. (GoJaks)
300 Quaker Lane Suite 7
Warwick, RI 02886-6682
800-524-1504
www.gojaks.com

WD-40 Company
P.O. Box 80607
San Diego, CA 92138-0607
888-324-7596
www.wd40.com

WINNER INTERNATIONAL LLC (Juice batteries)
32 West State Street
Sharon, PA 16146
800-258-2321
www.theclub.com

INDEX

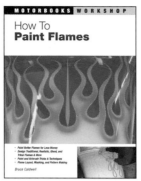

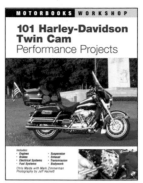